Australia, you little* beauty

Australia
you little* beauty

Inside Test cricket's dream team

JUSTIN LANGER
and Robert Wainwright

ALLEN&UNWIN

First published in 2010

Allen & Unwin
83 Alexander Street
Crows Nest NSW 2065
Australia
Phone: (61 2) 8425 0100
Fax: (61 2) 9906 2218
Email: info@allenandunwin.com
Web: www.allenandunwin.com

Cataloguing-in-Publication details are available
from the National Library of Australia
www.librariesaustralia.nla.gov.au

ISBN 978 1 74237 351 5

Set in 12/18 pt Goudy Old Style by Post Pre-press Group, Brisbane, Australia
Printed and bound in Australia by Griffin Press

10 9 8 7 6 5 4 3 2

Mixed Sources
Product group from well-managed
forests, and other controlled sources
www.fsc.org Cert no. SGS-COC-005088
© 1996 Forest Stewardship Council
FSC

The paper in this book is FSC certified.
FSC promotes environmentally responsible,
socially beneficial and economically viable
management of the world's forests.

Dedicated to all of my mates that I have sung the Australian team song with. And absent friends.

Contents

'Australianism means single-minded determination to win—to win within the laws but, if necessary, to the last limit within them. It means where the "impossible" is within the realm of what the human body can do, there are Australians who believe that they can do it—and who have succeeded often enough to make us wonder if anything is impossible to them. It means they have never lost a match—particularly a Test match—until the last run is scored or their last wicket down.'

John Arlott (1914–91), legendary English broadcaster and
journalist, writing at the completion of the
1948 Invincibles tour of England

Introduction

I am convinced the addiction of sport lies in winning. That feeling of victory is the drug that makes us go back for more, regardless of the fact that in chasing the glory of triumph we must also risk the pain of defeat. Winning takes many forms—it can be the moment the ball leaves your bat to bring up a century or, more importantly, the moment the last wicket is taken or the final run scored. Either way, the addiction is in the triumph of success.

For me, the emotion of victory—when you stand arm in arm with your mates, caps donned, drinking beer and singing the team song—is what Test cricket is all about. The shared experience of working hard towards a goal and then swimming in the euphoria of success is more satisfying than any individual glory.

People often ask me to nominate my greatest moment in Test cricket. The expectation is that I'll choose an innings I played, probably one of my 23 Test centuries. But they would be wrong. While individual achievement is important and gratifying, if you focus on it you miss the whole point of team sport and, frankly, the main reason most successful cricketers play the game.

Without doubt, the highlight of my Test career was playing in every one of Australia's first world-record sequence of sixteen Test victories between 1999 and 2001. It was hard enough to win one or two in a row, let alone sixteen, and the lessons I learned, the memories I have and the friendships I formed with those blokes are indelible. The most powerful memory of that time is of singing the team song sixteen times in sixteen Tests. Winning on the field was fun, but nowhere near as fun as the celebrations afterwards.

1. Songmaster

I t seems the unlikeliest of places but one of the greatest moments in my career happened in March 2004 on a hot, dusty afternoon in Galle, Sri Lanka. Australia had just won a hard-fought victory over the home side and we sat enjoying the moment in the sparse cement surroundings of the change rooms above the ground.

The match was memorable for several reasons, not on a personal level—having scored 12 and 32—but as a team embarking on a new era. It was Ricky Ponting's first Test as captain, having taken over from Steve Waugh, and he had been feeling the pressure. The Sri Lankans had taken a big first innings lead and really had us under the pump until several heroes emerged. Matty Hayden, Damien Martyn and Darren Lehmann had all scored centuries in our second innings fightback before Shane Warne grabbed five wickets, among them his 500th, and Stuart MacGill four, to lead us to an unforgettable First Test victory. The team had responded.

Victory secured, the mood in those concrete Galle Cricket Club changing rooms was buoyant. As was our tradition, we sat there for hours, savouring the moment over a few beers and watching as the crowds outside wandered off back home. The change room, regardless of where we were playing around the world, was always our sanctuary and only the core group of players and coaching staff shared its meaning. For five days it had been hot and the cricket intense, the contest perhaps magnified by the tiny ground which resembled a small club ground rather than a Test match arena like the MCG or Lord's.

There are three Test grounds in Sri Lanka: one in the royal city of Kandy, high in the mountain in the middle of the tiny island; another in the humid, noisy big-city jumble of Colombo, where your shirt is wringing wet before you get to the middle of the ground; and one in Galle on the south coast, where the air is salty, you can hear the sounds of the beach behind the row of palm trees on one side of the ground, and spectators mostly collect on grassy knolls or sit atop the walls of an old Dutch fort nearby to watch the action.

It was there in Galle, on that afternoon, that one of my dreams was realised. Having scored few runs in the game, I could have been down in the dumps, but we'd won—and that is the beauty of play-ing team sport. Regardless of my personal efforts, the beer was cold, the music was loud and all faces were smiling as we celebrated our win. As usual, I was sitting in a corner talking about cricket with Tim Nielsen, our assistant coach—a pair of 'nuffies' (cricket tragics) enjoying each other's fanaticism for the game, sharing our opinions and debating in a loud and animated way.

Such was the passion of our conversation, I didn't really notice that Punter had slid in next to me and was politely making an attempt to join in, or so it seemed. For some reason I ignored him, forgetting he was the new captain, and kept on nattering with Tim.

Punter tried again, this time nudging me to indicate that he wanted—no, needed—my full attention. Again I fobbed him off, which I'm embarrassed about every time I think about it, and carried on talking to Tim.

But Punter didn't give up and go away. Instead, he shoved his mobile phone into my hand: 'Here, read this,' he insisted.

Expecting a congratulatory message about our win, I was shocked and had to quickly reread the words on the screen in front of me. They went something like this:

JL, I want you to be the new team songmaster until the end of your career.

It took a few seconds for the message to sink in. When it did, I realised that Punter wanted me to become the new custodian of the team song—the person who leads the triumphant celebrations after a victory. He, as the new captain, had to relinquish the role, which he'd held since Ian Healy retired, and now he wanted *me* to take over. There had been some speculation before and during the game about who Punter might choose; I hadn't dared to think I was a candidate.

In a state of blissful panic, I grabbed Punter and dragged him into the shower room and shut the door. I couldn't quite believe what had just happened and wanted to make sure it was real. Next to captaining the team, being songmaster was regarded within our group as one of the biggest honours. The tradition had started with Rod Marsh in the 1970s who handed it to Allan Border. Border handed it to David Boon, then it went to Ian Healy and then to Punter. And now he was picking me.

I'd been pessimistic because of the constant discomfort I'd always felt about my place in the team. I can't explain why, but I'd always felt I was on trial and had to prove myself to senior players like Mark Taylor and Mark Waugh. There was no reason I picked those players—it was just how I felt for many years. And I couldn't help but be affected by the media's almost constant warning that I was an innings away from being dumped. Border once said that I seemed to be the player who was last picked and first dropped, and while I never wanted to believe this, my insecurity always lingered just below the surface.

This was why Punter's offer was so important to me. The moment he asked me to become our songmaster was the moment I finally felt I was a bona fide part of the Australian Test side. He wanted me to lead the victory song 'until the end of my career'. That meant I had a career, not just a handful of opportunities in which I was always a few innings away from oblivion.

In the Galle shower room, he told me, 'I think you're the right man to take the song. You believe in it, and I reckon you're going to be around for a while.'

Imagine that! Not only was I given the responsibility of upholding a magnificent tradition within the Australian cricket team, but the new skipper was also giving me a tick of approval as one of his right-hand men. I'm certain that I hugged Punter then, and pretty certain I shed a tear or two before we rejoined the others.

No one had noticed we were missing. As the evening continued, I just sat smiling like a Cheshire cat every time Punter winked at me across the room as if saying: 'You and I have a secret. We're the only ones who know what is about to happen.'

Traditionally, the song is sung at the end of the celebrations. It signifies the conclusion of a triumph and the moment we move on to the next challenge—an acknowledgement of our achievement, but also a reminder that tomorrow we start again.

It's probably more of a chant, actually:

Underneath the Southern Cross I stand,
A sprig of wattle in my hand,
A native of our native land,
Australia, you fucking beauty!

The words have been published many times and often the word 'little' or 'bloody' appears as the second-last word. It would be silly of me to suggest that's what we really sing. It simply doesn't have the same oomph as the other word, which is hardly out of place in a locker room.

Anyway, for the rest of the night I sat quietly in the corner wondering what I should do when I led my first team song. I wanted to make an impact from the very start. How could I be different?

An idea came to me.

When Punter finally announced me to the team as his successor, I told the guys to grab their baggy green caps and follow me. We stocked up an esky with cold beers, filled the music box with batteries and then piled onto the team bus. We drove out the gates and through the village at the rear of the ground, heading for the beach. I stopped the driver at the Galle lighthouse, which sat on a peninsula overlooking the spectacular and tranquil waters that, within a year, would turn into the deadly wash of the Boxing Day tsunami.

I jumped onto a wall at the base of the majestic structure. I was as nervous as I had been in my first Test match. Leading the team song was something to be proud of, and I certainly didn't want to mess it up. I led loud renditions of 'True Blue' and 'Khe Sahn' before telling my team-mates, one by one, how they had made an impact on the game. Then, pulling my baggy green firmly on my scone, we roared into those famous words: 'Underneath the Southern Cross I stand . . .'

This victory was a pinnacle for several reasons. We had taken a big step towards a series win, we'd installed a new captain, and I had cemented a place in one of the game's finest-ever teams. That was sweeter than any Test century—and guess what? It was definitely the best rendition ever . . . it always is.

● ● ●

Rod Marsh was the first songmaster, back in 1975, but it was probably Ian Chappell who was responsible for bringing it into the team. I wrote to Chappelli as I was compiling this book, asking if he could remember where it all began. His recollection was that it probably emerged for the first time in the rooms after Australia won the first Test of the 1974–75 Ashes series. The match was played in Brisbane and was the Test in which the gun-slinging Jeff Thompson emerged as a match-winner, taking 6 for 46 to rout England in their second innings. But the song's beginnings were far more humble, as he wrote:

I learned it from a mate, Ray Hogan, while playing in the Lancashire League in 1963. I think Ray had learned it from John McMahon, another Australian from Adelaide who played for Surrey, among other teams, in the UK. Macca was an avid reader, and I suspect the verse had been written by either Henry Lawson or Banjo Paterson, although I've never been able to confirm it.

I used to sing the song a bit in Australia, usually when having a beer, and Bacchus would have heard my rendition a few times. When we won the First Test at the Gabba in 1974–75 Bacchus let loose with the song a couple of times in the dressing room and then to a larger, mixed audience in the Wally Grout Lounge in the cricketers club. This caused the Queensland Cricket Club secretary Lew Cooper, who had invited us to the lounge, to send us back to the dressing room with a cartoon of beer, which seemed like a good deal to us! From then on it was sung on a more regular basis, but I'm not sure it was after every victory. And it wasn't always in the dressing room. Bacchus tended to be the one to start the singing. As a responsible captain, I stayed in the background, especially when it was a crowded restaurant such as in Sydney when we won that Ashes series. I think we sang 'Underneath the Southern Cross' that night, although I'm not one hundred per cent sure.

Regards,
Chappelli

2. Sue

Hi, it's Sue Langer here—Justin's wife and the mother of his four daughters, Jessica, Sophie, Ali-Rose and Grace. I thought this book could do with a woman's perspective, in amongst all the great stories of the Australian cricket team on and off the field. Although Justin's accomplishments are his—and I'm obviously very proud of them—he is always the first to acknowledge that he had a great support base behind him every step of the way. We lived every moment with him, high and low. It's been a long road, and at times a bumpy one, but I am pleased to say we have lived through it to tell the tale.

And what a tale it has been! Throughout this book, I'll pop up every now and then with some observations, stories and even the occasional reality check, so that you can get an idea of what really happened. That's what wives do, isn't it? We always like to have the last word, or at least keep an eye on things. That's what Justin tells me, anyway.

Justin and I met at the Perth Royal Show in 1983 when we were in our first year of high school. According to his version, I was smitten at first glance—but I think he's taking some poetic licence there. I've always had a sneaking suspicion that the meeting wasn't pure chance but rather a set-up orchestrated by my best friend, who went to school at Newman College with Justin at the time. The truth is that my first impression was that he was a bit too smooth and a bit cocky. On reflection, I think that was probably his determined personality shining through.

Our relationship was really a friendship at first. We went to different schools but would meet at parties and hang out with a large group of teenagers living in Perth's northern suburbs. It was only a couple of years later that we officially began seeing each other as 'an item', and we have basically been inseparable ever since. In a strange series of coincidences, my mother and Justin's father worked together when they were young, my parents were at his parents' engagement party, and our two families at one stage lived around the corner from one another in Sorrento. But until that day at the Royal Show in 1983, we had never met.

Even as a teenager, Justin was talking about his goals in cricket. At the time, I dismissed them, not because I thought they were pie-in-the-sky, but because we all had big hopes for our futures. The difference between most of us and Justin was his determination to chase his dream relentlessly. It's the reason for his success. These things are never easy, and that's why his achievements were earned and deserved rather than fortuitous.

I have never really known a time when cricket wasn't front-and-centre in our lives. That is still the case, in fact, because I am sure he'll remain associated with the game in one way or another. For Justin, it was always a question of how far and to what level he would go in cricket; he never wanted to do anything else. Never in my wildest dreams, though, did I imagine he would achieve what he did. Cricket was a natural part of our relationship, like having a family or building a house. And just like those aspects of life, there were ups and downs, particularly since he didn't have the security of a 'regular' job.

I left school about the time Justin and I started dating properly and got a job with an advertising company whose offices were near Perth's CBD. I would catch a bus into town each morning; I often met up with Justin, who had transferred to Aquinas College and also had to bus it into the city and then catch a connecting bus to school. We would usually end up in a Hungry Jack's across the road from the central train station, where I'd buy him an orange juice while I had a coffee.

Looking back on it, the situation was pretty funny. I was always dressed in office attire, including high heels and makeup, and he would be dressed in his uniform with a red and black striped blazer and carrying his school satchel. The contrast must have turned a few heads as we walked down the street holding hands. One morning Justin told me the meetings would have to stop because a mother from the school auxiliary had spotted us and told his mum. It was a decade before he sheepishly admitted that he'd made the story up because he was embarrassed. The novelty had obviously worn off, but it was fun while it lasted.

This admission of Justin's, by the way, came under the Langer family's ten-year rule, which allows them to admit past mistakes with a degree of immunity and forgiveness. It's a bit of a joke within the family and the results can be amusing at times, although the day in 1996 they dug up a family time capsule wasn't that funny for me. The family sat around the lounge room, reading the various notes they had penned a decade before. Justin had written about me—his then relatively new girlfriend—in less than flattering terms. Apparently, I had been nagging him all the time and we argued quite a bit. It made me sound like a dragon. I was nearing the end of my first pregnancy when these notes were unearthed and read out; I was hormonal, sick and not in the mood for criticism. I have to chuckle now, but at the time I was definitely a bit offended. I guess that's one of the pitfalls of being teenage sweethearts.

It was always difficult to have to live Justin's career from the other side of Australia or, as it often was, from the other side of the world. Right up until the day he retired, I was sick to my stomach watching him, not because I feared for his safety—although that was tested a few times—but because so much was riding on his performance. I'd say the only one who did it tougher than me was Justin's dad Colin, whose habit was to smoke cigars for as long as Justin batted. Sometimes that meant smoking for six hours.

I was the opposite of Colin. It took me a long time even to listen to Justin play Test cricket, let alone watch him at the ground. At first I wouldn't turn on the TV or the radio, and would always take the phone off the hook—otherwise it was inevitable that someone would call me as soon as he was out, as though I would want to talk about it. I think I'm like a lot of sports fans: somehow we get it into our heads that *we* are responsible for whatever happens to our teams or favourite players. I was convinced I jinxed Justin, which was another reason not to turn on the TV in case he got out—which, of course, would be my fault. I could imagine him glancing up towards the camera as he stalked off, admonishing me for my indiscretion.

If I was at the game and had my sunglasses on top of my head as he began to bat, then I wouldn't put them down again in case it disturbed the flow and aura. It was nuts, I know, but I just wanted him to do well. If he made 30, that was okay, but usually I began to feel comfortable only if he had scored a half-century. But then I'd be willing him towards a century and the nerves would start all over again.

Anyway, I have plenty to share about singing the team song, about the friendships we've made, the family sacrifices, and what it is really like to be married to an Australian cricketer. I hope you enjoy the ride.

3. First steps

I was eleven years old when I knew that I wanted to play Test cricket for Australia. The moment came amid the thunderous climax to the first day's play of the 1981 Boxing Day Test at the MCG against the might of the West Indies. It was a glorious Saturday. The wrapping was barely off the Christmas presents, the leftovers from last night's dinner still edible despite the heat, and my brothers and I had organised a game of cricket with the neighbourhood kids.

This ritual is one of the great joys of an Australian childhood. We played—with a tennis ball to protect the windows—on the broad concrete driveway that ran down the side of my family's home in the northern Perth suburb of Duncraig. When I went back to our old house a few weeks ago I was surprised how small that driveway really is. In my mind it was the size of the MCG. Every few overs we'd have a rest and head for the pool to take 'speccies'. Someone would lob a golf ball towards the centre of the pool so you had to dive and snatch the ball with an outstretched hand, like John Dyson or Rod Marsh, before plunging into the cool water. We'd also watch the Test on a tiny television Dad kept on the bar in the cabana he'd built.

It was one of those unforgettable days of Test cricket, firstly because seven members of the team—including my hero, Kim Hughes—were from Western Australia. Australian captain Greg Chappell, who was in the middle of a horror stretch personally, won the toss and decided to bat first on a diabolical pitch, which was made even worse by the fact that the Australians had to face possibly the greatest fast-bowling attack ever seen—Andy Roberts, Michael Holding, Joel Garner and Colin Croft. The obvious happened and Australia was quickly reduced to 4 for 26, including Chappell for a golden duck. Hughes entered the arena after the third wicket, needing something of a miracle to resurrect the shattered innings.

I couldn't watch and led everyone back to the driveway to resume the game, hoping that Hughes would get a start and be there on 20 or so when I next looked. He was—and he would stay there for the next five hours, playing one of his great flamboyant innings.

While others capitulated around him, Hughes refused simply to hang around and survive. Instead, he jumped down the wicket to Garner and hit him past cover, hooked Roberts to the boundary and hit square drives off Holding. Now I could barely drag myself away from the set to resume the driveway game. Hughes was the last man out as the shadows began to creep across the ground. Australia had been bowled out for 198 but still had 35 minutes to have a crack at the Windies' top order, and that was when Dennis Lillee took over.

Years later, when I faced the same scenario, I would remember the dull light and drama of that day at the MCG, which perfectly demonstrated the great difficulty of batting when you have everything to lose, personally and from a team perspective.

Terry Alderman took the first wicket and then Lillee quickly removed Desmond Haynes and Croft, who had been brought in to protect Viv Richards. The nightwatchman plan had failed, so Viv, chewing gum and rolling his shoulders, sauntered onto the MCG with ten minutes to play. He managed to fend off Lillee and Alderman for the next two overs, even sneaking two singles before he faced the last ball of a remarkable day's play.

Lillee steamed in, the crowd chanting his name, and we kids, glued to the tiny set in the cabana 3000 kilometres away, held our collective breath. The 'Lillee, Lillee' chant was at fever-pitch as he reached the crease—then it exploded when he bowled Richards off an inside edge. The West Indies had been reduced to 4 for 10. Our cabana went wild with delight, matching the delirium of the MCG cauldron. I was transfixed by the image; it still sends shivers down my spine. If this was Test cricket, then I wanted to be a part of it.

As powerful an image as that MCG Test was, most of my early memories of cricket are more fleeting—things that gave me a glimpse of the excitement cricket offered, experiences that could lead to a life that few could experience. I recall some seemingly incongruous things very well, like the anticipation of watching a favoured batsman, or the sight of Trevor Chappell pitching a ball into a change-room wall at the Mt Lawley Cricket Club and catching it countless times to practise his fielding.

My father was probably the biggest single influence on me, not so much for his coaching as for his attitude to life and the game. He was a handy grade player for Scarborough; he played his first first-grade match at the age of just thirteen, but was best known as captain of the club's second-grade team. I remember the day he had his jaw smashed by a fast bowler; he insisted on having it taped up so he could complete a century. Mum, a theatre sister, took him to hospital afterwards and almost fainted when she peeled off the bandage to see his jawbone. That taught me about having guts and confronting problems, and Dad's insistence that his players turn up to our house on a Sunday morning, the day after a game, to have a long run together and play some backyard cricket, beers in hand, taught me about loyalty, camaraderie and being part of a team.

I recently shook the hand of this leathery little bloke named Harry, who looked like he'd stood in the Perth sun for 100 years or more. He turned out to be an old cricket umpire who had known Dad in his playing days.

'I remember your dad,' he laughed. 'In all my years of umpiring, he was the toughest, fieriest little prick I ever met.'

Dad was the second of three brothers. The eldest, Alan, played state baseball, and the youngest, Robbie, played cricket for Western Australia and a couple of seasons for Australia in the early days of World Series Cricket. Some of my strongest memories are of watching Robbie play. I remember the anticipation of waiting to see the colour of the caps in the field. I desperately wanted his side to be batting, so I'd hope to see the opposition caps, otherwise it would be boring, as far as I was concerned.

Space was never a problem in the broad, salty scrub of Perth's northern suburbs. What had been a collection of holiday shacks in the 1950s and 60s was the tip of suburbia by the 1970s, when I was roaming around. We had the traditional quarter-acre block, large enough for the swimming pool (which Mum and Dad dug out by hand) and the cabana. Dad also built us a concrete cricket pitch and net area in the backyard when I was about six or seven, and my brothers, the neighbourhood kids and I would spend hours there. Before I was allowed to use it, though, Dad had made me paint the wooden fence around the pool area. I had reckoned it would take me an hour or so but it ended up taking three weeks, and I've hated painting ever since. That taught me a good lesson about having a work ethic.

Even though it's now more than 30 years ago, I remember a guy named Bryn Martin very well. He would come to our house on a Saturday morning to teach me the basics of the game. It was all about footwork. He'd draw a chalk semicircle across the crease and then show me how to move my feet back and across the area. I had another coach a few years later named Alan Abraham. He was a very happy little bloke who helped me when I played for Warwick Cricket Club. He was a terrific coach, but he also sparked my intense desire to earn caps for the teams I represented. At Warwick, you won a red cap if you scored a half-century, and I was desperate to earn mine, which eventually came.

I've still got my red cap at home, along with my Scarborough cap and my West Australian cap. They are all symbols marking achievements in my career. But the biggest of them all was the day I earned my baggy green.

4. 'Kill him, Bishy!'

It was 10.46 am on 22 January 1993, and already hot outside, the promise of another dry, blue summer day in Western Australia. I was in the kitchen of my family home in Duncraig, chatting with my mum, Joy-Anne, while she boiled a couple of eggs for breakfast. Mum was very traditional like that; she always ran the family kitchen to make sure her brood were properly fed and sent off to whatever their daily activity might be. If you're wondering how I can be so exact about the time, rest assured that I had good reason to note it down in my diary that night. But first, some background.

I was convalescing after being smacked in the head two weeks earlier by a bouncer from Victorian fast bowler Tony Dodemaide during a Sheffield Shield match at the WACA. The ball had gone between my visor and grille and hit my forehead. I'd shaken it off and continued to bat, but it was a nasty blow and the doctors made me take some time off to recover from the mild concussion.

I couldn't even practise, they insisted, even though I was in the best form of my career to that point—if you believed the papers, I was knocking on the door of Test selection in only my second season of Shield cricket. Still, I had also just recovered from glandular fever (probably from overtraining, as usual), and deep down I knew that some rest would do me good. But it was tough staying away from the nets. I used to hit cricket balls every day—hundreds, sometimes—and I loved doing it. By the end of a fortnight I felt like I was having withdrawal symptoms.

So, there I was watching the water bubbling on the stove and thinking about my first practice session for two weeks, which was to be at twelve o'clock with my batting coach, Bob Meuleman, when the phone rang. It was Tony 'Rocket' Mann, the general manager of the Western Australian Cricket Association. We exchanged the usual pleasantries and then he said, 'I've got some good news for you.'

'Yeah? What's that?' I replied, not really thinking.

Rocket was silent for a few seconds while he decided how to tell me the most amazing news of my life. 'Justin, you've been selected to play for Australia in the Test against the West Indies starting tomorrow in Adelaide.'

I don't think I said anything at first. Can you imagine how it feels to be chasing a dream all your life and then, in a flash, it happens? At the age of 22, I'd been selected to play Test cricket for Australia. Thousands of young Australians had dreamt of this and yet only about 400 had achieved it in 130-odd years. The thought still excites me.

Rocket didn't wait for me to ask how my selection had come about. He explained that my West Australian team-mate Damien Martyn had been poked in the eye in a training accident by the coach, Bob Simpson. Damien was in hospital getting treatment and couldn't play.

'But there's one catch,' he announced. 'You have to be at the airport by midday and on a plane at twelve-thirty. It's the only way to get to Adelaide in time.'

So there it was. Not only was I suddenly in the team, but I had just an hour, at best, to come to terms with the idea, to celebrate with my family, and to pack my bags and get to the airport. So much for enjoying the moment. This was how I recorded it in my diary that night:

I got the shakes on the phone; panic, excitement, joy. I went wild. Biggest day of my life. Huge, great, very proud of myself. Tomorrow . . . play straight, look to hit down the ground, singles to the covers, quick feet, play ball by ball.

I put down the phone and turned to my mum, who had realised something fabulous had just happened. She had driven me to every cricket match when I was a junior and, with my father, would politely pat me on the head and encourage me when I declared as a kid that I would play for Australia one day. This is the way with many successful sportspeople. They achieve their goals because of the support around them, and it was just so with me.

My mother, as tiny as she is, picked me up and started shaking me like a baby. My legs were off the ground in her excitement, her hugs, her tears that her little boy was about to play Test cricket for Australia. She finally put me down and I grabbed the phone to call Dad and Sue, who was then my girlfriend. I babbled away for a few minutes, then raced upstairs to my room, grabbed my favourite bat, pulled on a pair of gloves and called out to my younger brother,

Jonathon, to throw me a couple of balls. I hadn't batted in two weeks and I was about to jump on a plane to go and play cricket against the West Indies. I needed to feel the willow in my hands.

Jono, who is four years younger than me, obliged and we headed out into the backyard. It felt like we were kids again, pretending we were off to play Test cricket—but this time it was for real. I hit every ball in the middle of the bat. The sound was solid and sweet. Today I was facing the friendly fire of my younger brother, but tomorrow I would be up against the pace of the West Indies—Curtly Ambrose, Courtney Walsh, Ian Bishop and Kenny Benjamin. I was on top of the world and felt no fear at all.

● ● ●

It was almost five o'clock by the time I arrived at the team hotel in Adelaide. I was dressed in my Western Australia blazer because I had not yet received an Australian team kit. Bobby Simpson had met me at the airport and helped me do a few media interviews, which were very new to me. These days there is a manager, media manager and security guard to meet you at the airport, but then it was just Simmo the coach. My utter confidence of a few hours earlier was beginning to slip a little as reality set in. The media contingent made me realise that this was a big deal.

The team was staying at the Hindley Park Royal. I saw a bar at the left of the hotel's amazing foyer, and standing there in a group were my new team-mates. I was struck again by the moment. Allan Border, David Boon, Merv Hughes, Ian Healy, the Waugh brothers—my boyhood heroes were all waiting for me. I hadn't even met half of them before, and tomorrow I would be walking among them in front of 30,000 people at the Adelaide Oval.

As I look back now, the scene amuses me. Nowadays, the night before a Test match is one of concentrated preparation—meditation, massages, ice baths, hydrating and so on, but then the team was gathered in the hotel bar to have a quiet beer and welcome the new bloke.

Introductions over, I went up to my room, which I discovered I was sharing with Heals. When I walked in I saw a long cardboard box sitting on one bed, with 'JUSTIN LANGER—AUSTRALIAN TEST CRICKETER' written in black on the top. Again I was overwhelmed by what was happening. I dumped my gear, moved the box to the floor and carefully opened it.

It was like Christmas. Inside was all this stuff—jumpers, tracksuits, shirts, sunglasses, cricket gear, everything I could want. I wasn't really interested in the fancy clothes or gadgets. There was only one thing I wanted, and I had to scramble through everything else to find it. It was right at the bottom. Not just *a* baggy green cap, but *my* baggy green cap.

I'm very glad Heals didn't come in during the next twenty minutes, as I was prancing around the room like some sort of knob. My baggy green was on my head, my shirt was slightly open—as if I was Viv Richards—and I was playing every shot in the book with my favourite bat. In those few minutes I'd slogged Ambrose over midwicket for six, cut Walsh for successive fours and reverse-hooked Benjamin. I was back in the backyard with Jono, supreme and untouchable. I'd show them—the Windies couldn't be as tough as they seemed.

Amazingly, Bob Meuleman talked his way onto a flight to Adelaide with Mum, Dad and Sue, arriving later that night with nothing but a few dollars and the clothes he had on his back, just so we could have the batting session I'd missed. He met me at the indoor centre at the Adelaide Oval and put me through my paces for an hour or so in a late-night hit. If nothing else, I was sharp and focused for the challenge ahead.

I slept pretty well that night, considering the excitement. I kept the cap on my head all night—but who wouldn't? It's funny, really, because the cap is a bit strange. It's almost ugly, in a way, and it doesn't quite fit your head properly the first time you put it on. Matthew Hayden, true Queenslander that he is, reckons it's like try-ing on a pair of R.M. Williams boots for the first time—they always feel a bit tight and not quite right. The idea is to wear them until they feel like a second pair of feet.

It's exactly the same with the baggy green. When I first put it on, I was so pumped that it was mine, but it did look bulky and much too new. Over time, though, my cap started to fit me perfectly. It came to represent my place in the side. My baggy green was never quite the same as anyone else's, and maybe it didn't even sit on my head the same way, but it became part of me and my cricketing per-sonality. And that plays a big part in the game.

● ● ●

We arrived at the Adelaide Oval after an excruciatingly nervous—and therefore foodless—breakfast. I needed to have a hit in the nets to calm down. I had been listed to come in at number three, so if we won the toss I could be batting before lunch. I needed to get a feel for the place. As I walked to the nets, I felt a hand on my shoulder. I turned to see this short, stocky guy standing next to me:

'Hey, JL, what do you reckon about playing cricket for Australia today, son?' he said.

I looked at the captain and grinned. 'No worries, AB.'

Imagine that. The great Allan Border was calling me, some kid from Duncraig, by my nickname. And I was calling the great Allan Border by his. I still hadn't faced a ball in Test cricket but I felt like I'd made it.

Practice was good but it wasn't needed, because we bowled first in what would turn out to be one of the greatest Test matches ever played. After a solid opening partnership, the West Indies collapsed to be all out for 252 late on the first day, with Swervin' Mervyn taking five wickets. It was a great start, but it also set up one of the worst scenarios for our batsmen—having to bat for 40 minutes before stumps. There is nothing worse for a top-order batsman. We can't do much other than get out, while the bowlers are fresh and pumped up, knowing they can go all-out for a short time. Batting before stumps is one thing I hated about the game. Having said that, when I did manage to survive through to stumps the feeling was invigorating.

I sat in the change room, thinking about what lay ahead. The moment was getting closer and I needed to relax. David Boon and Mark Taylor walked past me, heading out to open the innings, and I thought, 'What am I worried about? These guys are pros—they'll bat until stumps, I'll get a good night's sleep, then tomorrow I'll go out and have a bat against the West Indies.'

The thought relaxed me and I sat back with my right pad partly strapped. Then everything changed. I heard an almighty appeal— but the Windies boys were shouting 'Hey!' rather than 'Howzat?'. Mark Taylor was out, caught, off the fourth ball of the innings. My moment of destiny had arrived, the time when I would grab my chance and make the most of it, and yet here I was in the change room with one pad half-on. I felt like a schoolkid with his pants around his ankles in the playground.

I got my gear on, grabbed my bat and gloves, thought about the baggy green then decided a helmet was the wiser choice, and went out to start my career as a Test batsman. As I walked down the stairs to the field, people were calling out things like 'Good luck, young fella'. Others—loyal South Australians—were telling me their heroes, Darren Lehmann and Greg Blewett, should have been in the side instead of me. It was a bit of extra stress I didn't need as I walked through the gate to see the Windies boys standing around waiting. They had been waiting so long they must have thought I was scared stiff.

They were right, although I wasn't going to show it.

I took my guard—'Middle stump, please, umpire'—then settled into my routine, telling myself, 'Concentrate, watch the ball, one ball at a time, concentrate.' I looked up and there, in the distance, was the West Indies' fastest bowler, Ian Bishop. The guy was huge, a monster from Trinidad, and the ball, shiny and red and just four deliveries old, looked like a pea in his giant hand. I looked behind me and saw seven figures in the distance—the wicket-keeper, four slips and two gullies. They were standing halfway back to the boundary. I settled over my bat and repeated my mantra silently to myself. 'Concentrate on the ball, watch the ball, watch the ball, concentrate.'

There was a fielder standing so close to me at silly mid-on that he could have reached out and touched me. It was Desmond Haynes, an extroverted, larger-than-life bloke with a big laugh and an even bigger voice. He called out to Bishop in his slow, rolling West Indian drawl. 'Hey, Bishy, he's scared. He's scared, Bishy.'

Here I was, still yet to face a ball in Test cricket, and I was being called a coward. I tried to settle again, but on the other side of the wicket was Keith Arthurton, a middle-order batsman who looked and acted like he was in a nightclub. He was laughing at Haynes, clapping his hands and calling out, 'Kill him, Bishy, kill him, Bishy, kill him, Bishy!' Now I had two of them telling me I didn't belong out there. I settled again. Bishop still hadn't moved.

Then a third guy joined in, this time from behind the wicket. The West Indian players, as I later found out, had a habit of kissing their teeth and making this sucking noise whenever they got emotional or had a strong opinion on something. Brian Lara, the coolest cat to ever play cricket, was kissing his teeth and laughing at Arthurton, who was laughing at Haynes.

'Hey, Bishy, he shouldn't be out here. He should be in high school, man, he should be in high school, not playing Test cricket,' laughed Lara.

High school? I still hadn't faced a ball and now I was being called a scared high-school kid. The pressure was suddenly enormous, and the backyard with Jono seemed a long way away.

The laughter died away as Bishop finally started his run-up. He loomed larger and larger as he approached the wicket. He was like a fire-breathing dragon letting rip with a fireball. It was short and I watched it whistle past my nose—so close I could see the golden Kookaburra emblazoned on the leather—before it thudded into the gloves of the wicket-keeper, Junior Murray.

'Wow,' I thought. 'I've survived my first ball. I reckon I can cope with this. Wasn't too bad, after all that. He's fast, but I watched it, played it well, and I didn't get a golden duck in my first Test.'

I settled over the bat as Bishop started in again and unleashed another thunderbolt. This time I didn't see it, but I certainly felt it. The ball smashed into the back of my helmet, splitting it open and cutting the back of my head. I went down and Dessie Haynes rushed over and had to prop me up.

I sat on the turf by the side of the pitch, my head spinning. David Boon, who'd watched the episode unfold from the non-striker's end, wandered down to check on me. He held me by my arm and leaned down. The smell of stale tobacco was meshed into his moustache and mixed with his minty breath from the P.K gum he always chewed while batting. 'Hey, JL,' he said.

I looked into those Anzac eyes. 'Yes, Mr Boon?' A knock to the head obviously made me extremely polite.

'JL. There are no heroes in Test cricket. Retire hurt, son.'

I couldn't believe it. David Boon, the toughest man in cricket, who never even acknowledged being hit, was telling me to retire at the time that should be my triumph. It would only confirm what the West Indians were saying—that I didn't belong there.

'I can't retire, Mr Boon,' I pleaded. 'My mum and dad are in the stands, my batting coach is up there, and Richie Benaud and Bill Lawry are in the commentary box hoping I'll show some Aussie spirit. Arthurton wants to kill me and Dessie thinks I'm scared. Brian Lara reckons I should be in high school, and a few of the South Australian supporters think I'm rubbish and that Blewy or Boof should be in the team. If it's alright with you, Mr Boon, I'll stay out here a bit longer and see if I can get through this.'

He looked back at me. 'Okay, son. But remember, there are no heroes in Test cricket.'

Mum, of course, was worried about her son, but Dad recalls feeling a bit differently. He was more interested to see if I would get up and keep batting. It was character-building, according to him. If I wanted to play Test cricket, then that was the sort of stuff I'd have to contend with every time I went out to bat.

I dusted myself off and took guard. There was no way I was going off, and after a few more hits to the body we somehow got through to the end of play without losing another wicket. I walked off the ground with David Boon battered and bruised but not out. I'd been hit everywhere from my head to my stomach. The only problem was that I still hadn't scored a run, and Boony had only scored a single. We were 1 for 2 overnight after 40 minutes of batting.

The first over the next day was bowled by Curtly Ambrose, the Windies' other giant fast bowler. The third ball of the morning struck Boony on the point of his left elbow. I winced just watching it, and he was left writhing in pain on the ground. A thought occurred to me—inspired by the brashness of youth, no doubt—and I walked over to him, bent down and said quietly, 'Mr Boon, there are no heroes in Test cricket. You should retire hurt.'

In between grimaces, he looked up at me, nodded and said, 'Son, I think you're right.' And to my great surprise, that's just what he did. The great fighter Mr David Boon put his bat under his arm, and with our legendary physio Errol Alcott by his side he hobbled off the ground to tend to his smashed elbow, which had blown up to the size of a softball.

History shows that I made 20 in that innings and faced 79 hostile deliveries to make them. Boony told me later that if I could survive that, I could survive anything. 'Test cricket never gets harder than this,' he said. Looking back seventeen years later, I realise he was right. It was a baptism of fire, as my diary entry after day two showed:

I've got bruises on both forearms, chest, guts, finger and my head, but it was still really enjoyable. Felt in control, missed a couple of cut shots. Hard work but great. Need to score more in the second dig.

We were bowled out for 213 (Mr Boon came back to score 39 not out), so we were 39 behind on the first innings. Then Tim May and

Craig McDermott knocked the Windies over for just 146, which left us with 186 for a victory that would give us a 2–0 lead in the series.

Naturally, I was pretty excited that night, thinking about what lay ahead and the opportunity to be part of an amazing victory. Not for the first time, I dreamed of being a hero. This is what I wrote in anticipation of what lay ahead:

I'm going to get 60 not out to win it for Australia. Huge chance. Be not out at the end of play.

We lost Mark Taylor and Boony very quickly on the morning of day four, but Mark Waugh and I managed to get through to lunch at 2 for 54. We were feeling pretty comfortable against the hostile attack—like we were on the path to victory. Then Curtly struck and we slumped to 7 for 74.

I had come in at the fall of the first wicket and was still there at tea with Tim May as we inched our way towards an improbable victory. As we headed back onto the ground after the tea break, my father leaned over the fence, grabbed my arm and said, 'Just remember, son—while you're out there, you can still win.' That was something I'll never forget, and it's a story I would often tell younger team-mates to emphasise that you must never give in. When I was a kid, Dad always told me that you can't make any runs from the pavilion; at the Adelaide Oval, however, I was on the biggest stage of all.

After tea we continued to fight against a hostile attack, but with 42 runs still needed I was the ninth man out. I had battled my way to 54, spent more than four hours at the crease and been involved in two great partnerships with tailenders, but it all felt a bit pointless as I walked off the ground. I received my first standing ovation, but I felt shattered when I returned to the change room.

Then, against all odds, Tim and Craig McDermott built a freakish partnership. The atmosphere, which was already tense, became more and more electric as they pushed closer to victory and the Windies' bowlers became more frustrated. The crowd started singing 'Waltzing Matilda', people were rushing from the city to the ground to watch, and on TV the match drew a record viewing audience.

The rest of the Australian team watched nervously from the pavilion as Tim and Craig crept to within two runs of victory. Allan Border was slapping a 'worry ball' from hand to hand as the target got closer. The one thing he had never achieved in his amazing career was a series victory against the West Indies, and this was the moment when his dream could become a reality.

Then Tim slapped a ball off his pads. It should have been four, but Desmond Haynes instinctively stuck out his foot and somehow stopped the ball. We had all gone up with a huge cheer, our arms in the air, but had to sit down again. Still, just one more single would tie the game.

Instead, in the next over, Craig tried to get out of the way of a lifter from Courtney Walsh, got a feather-edge and was caught behind by Junior Murray. We had been beaten by one run. To this day, it remains the closest victory in the history of the game. As the Windies ran around celebrating, AB's worry ball slammed into the wall and ricocheted into the side of my head. What a way to start my Test career. It's a wonder I can remember anything about it, but my diary suggests I did:

What a day. Great crowd, great atmosphere, shit result. I can't believe we got so close. Curtly bowled brilliantly. What a bowler. In hindsight, I should have kept batting safely, stayed with Maysie rather than going for a big pull shot. Must work hard on cut shots and pull shots this week. Great feeling being out there today. It was like being in a dream, waiting for someone to wake me up. Very empty feeling losing for Australia. Somewhat proud but very disappointed.

The Adelaide Oval that day in 1993 was the beginning of a rollercoaster.

5. Swervin' and crashin'

Where do you start with Merv Hughes? The bloke is a walking caricature—a beefy 'Demon' Spofforth with the girth of Warwick Armstrong and the irreverence of Dougie Walters. You wondered sometimes how he could run in and bowl one fiery over, let alone a marathon of overs throughout a day. While he may not have been built like Mitchell Johnson or Craig McDermott, he made up for his less than Olympian frame with a huge heart. Merv came along at the right time for a player with his charisma, slotting into an era where a beer was better than a health shake and a jog was something you did only when you wanted to get off the ground quickly after scoring a duck. (I'm exaggerating a little here, of course!)

Merv was the first bowler I faced in Sheffield Shield cricket, a few days before Christmas in 1991, so he stands at the gateway to my first-class career, which might have lasted a season or so if things had gone wrong but instead lasted a wonderful eighteen years. I can't really recall that first delivery, but I suspect it would have been short and rising, pitched just outside the off stump and jagging in to cramp me up. Merv certainly loved to bowl short and test you out on the back foot, and he backed it up with a Rottweiler stare and a wicked tongue.

He had a presence which could be forbidding but also welcoming and embracing. I would realise just how embracing he could be when I packed my bags for the first time to join the Australian team on a tour to New Zealand in February 1993. I had played in the Fifth Test against the West Indies in Perth, making just 10 and 1, so I had to learn very quickly how to deal with disappointment. Before I had joined the side in Adelaide, Australia was 1–0 up and on the verge of beating the great side. Instead, we lost my first two Tests to lose the series. While the defeats were not really on my shoulders, having depended more on the giant frame of Curtly Ambrose, I still somehow felt personally responsible. I hoped my form would turn the corner in New Zealand.

History shows it didn't, but that tour would be the beginning of a much tougher and, in the end, more satisfying journey of determination and of learning how to deal with adversity than I could ever have expected. And Merv, in his strange way, played a part in two important lessons—about enjoyment and heart.

The first tour match was a three-day game against a New Zealand Board XI in the city of New Plymouth on the south-west coast of the north island. I'd played pretty well in our first innings and made 89—frustratingly close to a century, but enough to make me feel good about what lay ahead. We grabbed a lead of 80-odd runs and had them one wicket down at the end of the second day, with a good chance to press for victory on the final day. Being young and keen, I was still out on the ground after play had finished, running laps around Pukekura Park and stopping occasionally to do push-ups or sit-ups.

As I sweated under the setting sun, Merv wandered out and leaned against the fence, watching me go through my routine. 'Hey, young fella—what are you doing tonight?' he called out.

I stopped, puffing a bit. 'Nothing much. Taking it easy for tomorrow, I suppose.'

'Nah,' he said. 'Let's go out and have a drink.'

I couldn't believe it. 'What do you mean go out? We've got to bowl these guys out tomorrow and win the game.'

Merv flexed his moustache with a big grin. 'Don't worry about that, young fella. You leave that to me.'

I followed him off the ground, pretty amazed that he'd asked me to go with him. I had a shower and we headed out for what I assumed would be a couple of quiet drinks and a heart-to-heart chat. How wrong I was.

After a quick feed, we wandered into a bar called The Saloon, where Merv manoeuvred us not to a quiet corner of the lounge but right into the heart of the dance floor action. I was sipping my way through a soft drink while Merv got stuck into the beer. At one stage I watched in amazement as the bloke who was going to lead our attack the next day was pouring not one but two bottles of Corona down his throat at the same time. There was clearly not going to be any discussion about cricket that night.

I lost track of him for a while, and the next time I saw him he was bending backwards over the bar, his hairy belly exposed as he writhed to some Mexican rumba music and a barman poured tequila into his mouth. He was having a wow of a time and the crowd in the bar was loving it. I didn't know what to do, so I stayed in the background. By the end of the night, around eleven o'clock, my new drinking buddy was having a nightcap of Baileys and ice—not your regular nip of the smooth, milky liquid, however, but a schooner of the stuff, which was dribbling down his moustache. I knew then that it was time to get out of there, so I went up to him to say good-night. He had absolutely no idea who I was.

I headed back to our motel, where I was sharing a room with Steve Waugh, and went to bed. Later that night I heard a light knocking on our door and then someone fiddling with the lock. I must have been in a deep sleep, because I lay there and ignored it for a few minutes. Finally I realised that whoever it was had now got inside and was flicking the lights on and off. I sat up and saw it was Merv. Next he turned on my CD player and put it up full-bore. He did the same with the TV, but thankfully the only thing on in New Plymouth late at night was the test pattern. I flopped back down on the bed, trying to ignore him, and the next thing I know this stinky, hairy bloke is lying on me and kissing my neck. Not only was he hairy and smelly, but he was also stark-naked and laughing his head off, ruffling my hair, poking my ears and looking for a late-night wrestle.

Tugga was awake by then, and as I pushed Merv off me he yelled, 'Get out of here, Merv, you're a bloody disgrace!' Merv staggered off, still laughing.

The next morning I got down to breakfast and sat with Damien Martyn and David Boon, who had his mandatory black coffee and cigarette. I told Marto what had happened.

'He did it to me as well,' he said.

Then Boony started giggling—apparently Merv had been into

his room as well. It turned out he'd gone from room to room and done the same thing to everyone, except for three people: Allan Border, Mark Taylor and Bobby Simpson. Even in his drunkenness, Merv had the nous not to accost the captain, vice captain and coach.

AB eventually got wind of what had happened and collared Merv, who still stank and looked awful. AB gave him a mouthful, calling him a disgrace and saying he'd failed as a role model for the young guys like me, not to mention the fact that he was supposed to be leading the attack that day. He threw Merv the ball as we walked out onto the ground, intent on teaching him a lesson. The first delivery bounced twice before it reached Ian Healy behind the stumps, and we all thought there was going to be trouble.

As he walked back to his mark, Merv asked Tim May, who was fielding at mid-on, how long there was until the first drinks break. While we were all giggling behind our hands, AB was steaming, but it soon became apparent that Merv had got the message.

Digging deep that day, as only Merv could, the score sheet shows that, hungover or not, Merv bowled nineteen overs and took the amazing figures of 4 for 21, as we knocked the New Zealanders over for 150 and won the game in a canter. Perhaps without knowing it, Merv taught me a lesson that day, that at the times we don't feel like being there—whether self-inflicted or not—champions will always find a way to get the job done.

I'm not advocating drunken behaviour by any means—in fact, my record has been the opposite over the years—but sometimes I wonder about the modern game. We used to play the game hard on the field and celebrate hard afterwards. It helped forge team spirit, and the spirit of winning and success. I believe there is a place for that, as it helped set us apart from other cricket sides. Merv Hughes had the spirit of the game in his heart. I guess that's where the tradition of our team song became a point of difference between Australia and our competitors.

The next game—the First Test against New Zealand—also showed me that spirit. It was a special game, in which AB passed Sunil Gavaskar's record for the most runs of any player in the game. This was how Wisden recorded the moment:

Border, fortunate to survive a run-out chance on nine, top-scored with 88 out of 485, although it was his lofted sweep off Patel at 1.52 pm that drew the most attention. As the ball bounced into the fence at mid wicket, Border reached 50 and overtook S. M. Gavaskar's 10,122 to become the leading run-scorer in Tests. Being Border, he painted the achievement as little more than a numerical inevitability for one who had played so many matches—this was his 139th Test. He saluted his team-mates in the stand, acknowledged the applause of the sparse crowd, shook hands with Healy and Parore, the nearest players, and continued his innings.

I took a great lesson from AB's modest attitude to his personal cricketing achievements. He was a man who recognised that we were playing a team game, and that it was the performance of the whole that really mattered. He had a spirit which was magnetic.

After a great win—the first of my Test career—I was on cloud nine. At the age of 22, I was sitting in the change rooms with the great Allan Border and celebrating a huge milestone in the game. It was my first celebration in the change rooms. Boony led the song and we partied afterwards somewhere in Christchurch. Some of the New Zealand players came out with us, including their opening batsman John Wright. At one stage during the night, he came up to me and whispered, 'Jeez, I wish I was an Aussie. You play great cricket but you also know how to celebrate.'

Yes, we did, and while Wrighty, one of the gentlemen of the game, might be the first New Zealander ever to admit to wanting to play for the Australian cricket team, I got his point.

● ● ●

I have to think carefully about whether it was fair to drop me after that tour of New Zealand in 1993. It was devastating to miss out on the Ashes tour, and many people have said I was unlucky and that perhaps the selectors should have stuck with me a little longer, given that I had only just entered the Test arena. But I don't believe in blaming everything on luck. It's very rare to be unlucky. The truth is that I got sidetracked in New Zealand. I was trying too hard and looking to the future and the Ashes tour, rather than taking care of what I was doing in New Zealand. It was a great lesson for me. I also got a bit carried away with the glamour of being part of the Australian cricket team and let a few of my usual disciplines slip.

The Third Test, at Eden Park in Auckland, was what did it. We were 1–0 up in the series but got into trouble on a wicket that was a seamer's paradise. We were rolled cheaply in the first innings but somehow managed to get a lead of 200 after our second innings. As we walked out onto the ground for New Zealand's second dig, Steve Waugh dryly remarked, 'Boys, if we lose this Test then someone's going to pay.'

He was right, and the bloke with his head on the chopping block was me. I'd scored a pair of ducks, being given out LBW in the second innings to spinner Dipak Patel, who'd opened the bowling on the difficult wicket. I felt hard done by, with a stinker of a decision, but the score was in the book. As it turned out, New Zealand got the runs with five wickets to spare, drawing the series and giving the selectors the chance to make a change.

My diary that week reflected my frustration and the sense that I'd muffed my chance to go on the upcoming Ashes tour. The days are all ruled through with a heavy black marker, and the word 'SHOCKER' is scrawled across the pages. My diary entry for 16 March, the last day of the Third Test, reads like my life is over:

Bad Test for me—0 and 0. I'm feeling more down in the dumps than ever before. It's a terrible feeling of rejection and disappointment. I'm not feeling too confident about the England Ashes tour. Simmo assures me it isn't as bad as it looks but it is hard for me to understand that. The tour until this Test has been sensational. I have really enjoyed the company of all the blokes . . . but I do feel I have let myself down in a number of ways. If nothing else, I have learned so much from this experience that hopefully I'll know, and be, better next time I get a chance. Late nights and not total focus and commitment to the job. It's important for me to realise that my job is to consistently score runs and the best way for me to do that is to be prepared properly. To be in this position for the next many years I have to perform consistently.

I had given myself a very stern talking-to, first mentally and then through my diary, and there would be more to come.

Waiting to learn about the selection of the Ashes touring party was awful. There was the usual conjecture in the weeks leading up to the announcement—I was on some lists and not on others. I thought I stood a good chance, given that I'd had a pretty solid start to my Test career with a couple of half centuries and a few long stays at the wicket.

I knew that I'd made a certain impression from my first Test innings. In my first dig I had made 20 off 79 balls in 98 minutes, and in the second I'd scored 54 off 146 deliveries in a little over four hours. That defined me in many ways. It did create some good impressions—that I was gutsy, prepared to take knocks and be there for a long time—but it also posed questions about whether I had enough shots to prosper in international cricket, especially in one-day cricket. This experience showed me the power—both good and bad—of setting an impression.

My diary entry for 23 March is a good example. The rest of the team was still in New Zealand playing the one-day series, but I'd been sent home, a trend that would continue for the rest of my career:

If anyone was to ask me how I'm feeling at present, I really don't know. I guess I'm preparing myself for the worst. People keep telling me I should get selected [for the Ashes tour] but the problem is these people just wouldn't know. I'll be bitterly disappointed if I don't make it. It will hurt a lot, but whatever happens, I'm going to be extra-determined to do better than I've done. Sure, I've played five Tests, but big deal—I haven't done anything yet.

My method of dealing with the wait, the opinions and the conjecture was to train. Looking back, I see that I was punishing my body, but I found it a valuable form of therapy. On the one hand, I was putting myself through a form of retribution for failing in New Zealand, but on the other hand, I was training so that I would be stronger mentally and physically, in order to nail my next opportunity. One day I'd run ten kilometres, then I'd do a day of sprints, followed by swimming and stretching and weights. Some days I'd do aerobics or run ten kilometres and then ride 30 kilometres. These days, it makes me feel tired just thinking about the schedule I set myself, but at the time it seemed like the only way to get through.

The touring party was to be announced on Saturday, 3 April 1993. On the Friday before, Dad got a call from Dennis Lillee, who was having lunch somewhere and had a snippet of information to pass on: I had made it. I was in the squad for my first Ashes tour. What a huge buzz. What an even bigger relief. I was over the moon and had to find a way to release all the tension and excitement that had built up since coming back from New Zealand. I headed to the gym to use the adrenaline for a workout. I still felt charged when I got home, but that was about to change.

While I was sweating away at the gym, Dennis had called Dad back to say he'd got it wrong. I had actually missed out. He apologised but the damage was done. Now it would be doubly disappointing, so Dad didn't phone me straight away. He mulled over what he'd say for hours before coming home to break it to me. I was in the laundry when he appeared at the door and told me there was bad news. There was no good way for Dad to tell me, really, and I probably shed a few tears in the laundry, but my diary that night sums up my reaction:

I feel very, very disappointed. I can't believe I haven't been picked, and the more I think about it the more I can't understand their theory . . . that they didn't want to take three left-handed openers. If that's the case, then why did they pick Matthew Hayden in the first place? Michael Slater, good luck to him, but it's still very disappointing. The worst feeling is that I might get left behind, but when I think about it, opportunities will come up again in the future. My goal now is to work hard to get back into the team. Luck equals preparation and opportunity. No one else is to blame. It's time now to accept the fact that I'm not going to England and get on with the job at hand.

When I look back at this diary, written sixteen years ago, I find the sorts of things I was thinking about incredible. I've still got a three-page letter I wrote to myself in the days after missing selection for the tour. It was basically a plan for how to get back into the Test side, and a list of the things I had to work on, like concentration, playing spin and patience. I summarised:

I am a very good cricketer. I achieved my goals earlier than I might have expected. I love the feeling and the prestige of playing for Australia. By working hard, relaxing and being philosophical, I'll be back. No excuses, no second prizes. Everyone has their different way of getting to the top and being successful. Some can get away with not working so hard, having a beer after every day's play and generally taking it easy. That's not my way. I believe my way is to work on my batting and my fitness. Dennis Lillee always said the hard work begins when you get to the top.

One of the things that went wrong in my first crack at international cricket was that I found myself wanting success so much that the more I chased it, the further away it seemed to be. What I later learned was that if I did the right things and prepared myself properly, without worrying so much, then the opportunities would come. It is clear to me now that there is a fine line between preparing well and trying too hard. My experience is that the harder you try at something the worse you usually do. By this I mean you still have to work hard and prepare meticulously but when you 'try' too hard you tend to tighten up and restrict the natural flow of your body. The key to sporting success is to be loose and relaxed in your body but tight in your mind. When you try too hard the opposite happens— your body becomes tight, your movements slow down and your mind becomes loose and distracted because your body isn't functioning the way you want it to.

Over the years, I have encountered a view—especially within West Australian cricket—that my standards were too high, and therefore that I put too much pressure on the younger players if they didn't act professionally on and off the field. A lot of the younger players probably felt I was very serious about the game, and the truth is I was.

My experience in 1993 was the catalyst for my approach to the game. Knowing how much it hurts to let yourself down, I wanted to help young players avoid some of the pitfalls. One of my favourite sayings is that the pain of discipline is nothing like the pain of disappointment; having lived through the terrible pain of failure, I have learned that the pain of discipline fades away when you gain the rewards of your labours.

6. Back to the drawing board

I'm not sure that 'turning point' is the correct term for the numerous phases of my career, particularly in the early years, when I struggled and almost came to grief many times. But I can identify moments when I came to crossroads in my journey; points at which I had a choice—or a decision was made for me, in some cases—from which stemmed opportunities I would otherwise not have had.

A phone call from Test legend Rod 'Bacchus' Marsh later in April 1993 was one of those times. He was running the Australian Cricket Academy in Adelaide and phoned me in the weeks after I was left out of the Ashes tour to give me an encouraging word. Bacchus suggested that I come and train with him at the Academy, to turn a negative into a positive. Even though I couldn't see past the end of my nose at that point, I agreed to go, if only out of respect for him.

My earliest memories of Rod are from a Test at the WACA

ground in Perth. I was one of the kids playing cricket at lunch-time in front of the fans. While I can't remember much of my first game on the ground, I do remember watching this legend doing his warm-up in shorts and a T-shirt, charging down the track with his tree-trunk legs pumping and his barrel chest thrust out like a pit bull terrier's. He was fierce and powerful, and this made a last-ing impression on me.

Although I wasn't thinking clearly about my future at the time because of the disappointment of being dropped, I knew that Rod's advice would be valuable. In contrast to the pit bull I had seen and idolised as a kid, here was an intelligent, intuitive man who was offering his help. We hadn't had a great deal to do with each other at that stage, but he clearly understood my predicament and, instead of pandering to my woes, offered me a solution, a chance to fight my way back to the top.

In many ways, my association with the Academy epitomised my cricket career in general. In my teen years I had played in sev-eral schoolboy state teams, but I hadn't really shone. In 1989 I was selected in the West Australian under-19 team to play at the national titles in Melbourne. I was desperate to play well. Not only were national selection and international youth Tests up for grabs, but so too was the opportunity to be selected for the (then) newly established Cricket Academy in Adelaide.

But the harder I tried, the worse I got. Sure enough, I missed selection in the national side and any hope of a spot at the Academy was blown out of the water. Rejected and dejected, I used the disap-pointment as motivation to train harder and score heavily in grade cricket. My reasoning was that, regardless of the present circum-stance, which in this case was a shattered ambition, I would just keep scoring runs and hope that fate would take care of me. And, as indeed happened several times through my career, an opportunity opened up under the strangest of circumstances.

The national youth team came to Perth to play a Test against the touring England side. The day before the match, Australia's captain, Jason Gallian—who, ironically, would later play several Tests for England—cut his foot badly while swimming during a trip to Rottnest Island, off the coast of Perth. The selectors were stuck for a last-minute replacement; given that Jason was a top-order batsman, they picked me. I made 30-odd in my first proper game on the WACA, and this, along with my club form, was enough to get me noticed. A few weeks later, and much to my shock, I was selected for the next intake of fourteen young players at the Cricket Academy. It was a salient reminder that life can turn in a moment.

I thrived at the Academy, where all you did was live and breathe cricket. We trained six days a week, twice a day in the winter, and played club cricket on the weekend in the summer. It was like a cricket camp for the whole year, and I dreamed of hitting cricket balls in my sleep. The only thing I didn't really enjoy about the Academy was the day we had to bat for several hours with thermometers up our bums as part of a study by the local university on the hydration levels of athletes.

The head coach was Jack Potter, a quiet and gently mannered man who also ran an ice-cream shop at Glenelg Beach on the weekends. Jack had a great influence on me. Not only did he teach me new aspects of the game, but he also gave me a job in his kiosk—I wandered up and down the beach selling ice-creams. For a nineteen-year-old bloke who regarded himself as a bit of a hoolio, this was a dream job; going up and down the beach wearing nothing but a pair of board shorts and sunnies did a lot for my ego more than anything else.

But Jack helped me in another way, too. I had found myself with a host of schoolboy stars, including Shane Warne, Damien Martyn and Greg Blewett. At times I felt that I was making up the numbers, but this all changed one day in the tiny video room in the indoor centre at the Adelaide Oval. Jack and I were watching a video of my batting technique in the nets. He stopped the tape at one point and turned to me.

'Justin, you'll go just as far, if not further, than anyone else at the Academy,' he said. Jack must have known about my misgivings, because when I started to protest he stopped me. 'Your technique is the best of anyone here. I'm telling you that you have what it takes to play at the top level.'

That was an amazing boost to my confidence, which I still remember clearly two decades later, and it was something I reflected on as I packed my bags to go back to the Academy at the invitation of Rod Marsh. Jack had predicted I could make it to the top, and now that I had played five Test matches I knew I wanted more. I also knew, deep down, that the next time I would need to be more prepared and a better cricketer.

On my return to Adelaide, Bacchus recognised that, although a defensive batting technique was my fundamental armour, my attacking skills needed an overhaul. He told me that I had to change my attitude to batting in the top order.

'It's not about how long you spend out in the middle,' he said, 'but about how many runs you score. You're going to have to learn to play a few more shots.'

He was right. At that stage, I really only had three shots in my locker. I could tickle the ball down to third man or fine leg, and occasionally pull the short ball through square leg. Other than my ability to block stoically all day if necessary, that was about it.

This was a noticeable aspect of my game when I played my first Test match at the Adelaide Oval; I had survived for long periods but found it difficult to score. I was also a product of West Australian cricket. With our fast pitches, we instinctively play mostly from the back foot. If I was going to make it, I was going to have to learn to adapt my game—particularly my front-foot game—to other pitches and conditions around Australia and the rest of the world.

I've often encountered the perception that I only became a more aggressive player after I began to open the batting in 2001, but I'm convinced Rod Marsh was the catalyst for my new approach back in 1993. The late Ken Meuleman and his son Bob, who coached me for many years in Perth, always told me that I would end up a 'slogger' rather than a 'blocker', and I guess they were right in the end. If my Test statistics don't show it, then my performance in domestic cricket after I was first dropped and then worked with Rod would certainly reveal that I became a player looking for runs rather than waiting for them by occupying the crease.

I have two favourite memories of Rod, who was the antithesis of Jack Potter in style. A year after my second visit to the Academy, Rod asked me to come back as an associate coach. I sometimes sat in his office when he had hauled in one of the students to give him a dressing-down, usually about behaviour or attitude. It was never a pretty sight. The player would leave looking pretty shattered, having got the message loud and clear about how he had to improve. When the door closed behind the humbled young cricketer, Rod would be reclining in his chair and sporting a huge grin, revelling in his performance as the grumpy old grandfather who had just taught his grandson a life-changing lesson.

My other treasured memory is of the Friday afternoons when Rod took the coaching staff down to an old colonial pub called the

British Hotel in North Adelaide after a week's work. We'd sit around and have a few freezing-cold schooners of a light beer called Eagle Blue, which Bacchus used to promote. For a couple of hours we would sit with Jack 'Infamous' Clarke, now the chairman of Cricket Australia, Dave Jennings, the owner of the pub, and the coaches, and we'd chew the fat about cricket or red wine. Those Adelaide afternoons were a simple pleasure but so memorable.

I can only imagine what it would have been like in the 1970s to sit around in the change rooms as all the Australian cricket legends shared a beer at the end of a day's play, or as Rodney belted out a rendition of 'Underneath the Southern Cross', with his baggy green cap on his head, his shirt buttoned down to his navel, and holding a can of icy cold beer. For me, such images are the stuff of folklore.

● ● ●

During my stint as an associate coach, two things happened that would be important stages of my cricket journey. Firstly, I was selected for Australia again. While it's strange, I can't really recall the details of my selection to go on the tour to Pakistan in late 1994. I'm sure my selection in the touring party was because of my form for Western Australia. With a renewed sense of urgency in my batting, I had scored three centuries and averaged over 71 for the season, and I was selected as a specialist batsman ahead of my friends Matthew Hayden and Damien Martyn.

I really should remember more about it, given that it was the beginning of a new era in Australian cricket, with the retirement of Allan Border and the appointment of Mark Taylor as captain. Australia had not won a Test in Pakistan since 1959, but there was a generally buoyant feeling about our chances as we flew out. Unfortunately, that bubble burst in the First Test, at Karachi, where Tubby made an inauspicious debut in his first Test as captain, scoring a pair of ducks. Despite this, Tubby was unfazed—a great strength in a captain. Pakistan won an amazing match by a single wicket to take a 1–0 lead. We should have won the Second Test, at Rawalpindi, especially after gaining a 261-run first-innings lead, but Pakistan's captain, Salim Malik, denied us with a double-century that I will never forget. I was twelfth man in both these Test matches.

It all came down to the Third Test, at Lahore—and, due to injury, I was off the bench and back in the baggy green cap. Steve Waugh, who was averaging 57 with the bat in the series, dislocated his right shoulder and had to fly home. Typically of Tugga, he dismissed the idea that his injury was a big loss and praised me as his replacement, even though it was just my sixth Test match and I hadn't played at that level for eighteen months. His comment to the media was also typically succinct: 'Justin's playing well. He'll do a great job anyway, so we're not going to lose much, if anything.' Humility was one of Tugga's greatest strengths.

The thing I remember most clearly about my first comeback Test was my new bat. It was a running joke amongst the younger players that the established Test players are given the better bats by sponsors, but when I arrived in Pakistan there was a box of handmade Kookaburra bats waiting for me. Among them was one magnificent blade, sleek with fifteen dead-straight grains running down its length. It was just about the best bat I'd ever seen—it was a thing of beauty and precision, light (around two pounds eight ounces), as I preferred, with the weight towards the base of the bat.

I always knew the pick-up weight was perfect when I could play a solid stroke with just my top hand. If it was too heavy, I couldn't control the shots; too light, and I tended to try to hit the ball too hard. This was a Goldilocks bat—just right.

I felt as excited as a schoolboy as I nursed this piece of willow; I was even reluctant to bang it on the crease and mark the grain. It made me feel as if I was supposed to be a Test batsman. This was what it was all about—I was getting the best equipment because I was good enough. The quality of the bat made me relax a little, although I was still eager to meet my own expectations. Everything seemed right and I had no reason to doubt my form. I used the bat in the nets during the lead-up to the Test, to knock it in and get a feel for it before the big day. It was an absolute belter and played as good as it looked.

When that big day came, everything was going to plan. We made a solid start in reply to Pakistan's first innings of 373. Michael Slater looked set on 60 and I was batting in the middle order. The pitch was flattish and I had time to relax and prepare mentally.

But everything changed in an instant. On the morning of the third day, when I was likely to bat, I'd gone out onto the ground to have a few throw-downs. One of the team staff was tossing a few balls at me to get my feet moving, and I was hitting the ball back to him without any real power. I simply wanted to get into the day and prepare for my comeback innings.

After a few throws, I chopped down on a full ball that landed near my toes. The moment I hit the ball there was an awful *crack*—the sickening sound of the bat splitting through one of those gloriously straight grains. I could not believe what had just happened. All my preparation had been destroyed in a flash. As ridiculous as it sounds, all these years later, I felt that the sporting gods were denying me my chance of being a successful Test match cricketer.

I spent the rest of the morning stewing on my misfortune, hoping in some mad way that perhaps I wouldn't be called upon to bat. I'd rather a 'did not bat' beside my name than another failure with a less-favoured bat in my hands. For a while, those fickle gods smiled down on me, as Mark Waugh and Michael Bevan put on a century stand. But when Junior was out and we were still over 100 behind, I had to face my demons.

I can't remember a single ball of that innings. The only way of knowing what happened without my favourite new bat is to look at the scorecard, which states that I was 38 not out at the end of the day's play and went on to make my highest Test score at the time— 69. Although I remember little, others thought it was an important innings, helping us to build a first-innings lead and to have a chance to win. In the end Pakistan held on, although not without some drama and another Malik century.

I suppose I was relieved to have done well, but for some reason it left little impact. I had been called into the side as a replacement for the great Steve Waugh and, naturally, would make way for the champion when he returned for the next Test series. I would have to wait a little longer for my real chance.

Rod Marsh, 1st Songmaster, 1975–84

JL: Righto, how did the team song start, mate?

RM: Well, it goes back to Ian Chappell. We were in London one time, having a beer on the Thames. He told me this little ditty and I thought 'that's bloody good', I think we'll use that. So I pulled it out after we won a game and then I decided we would use it when we won a Test match rather than a one-day game.

JL: What year was that?

RM: I reckon it was '75. I then handed it on to AB after me.

JL: Can you remember at the time if it was a big deal when you passed it on to him?

RM: I think it was reasonably . . . the problem was they didn't get to sing it much when AB was in charge of the song.

JL: I spoke to AB and he said the same thing! Can you remember much about the song? Was there a certain routine associated with singing the song?

RM: Yeah, it wasn't long after the end of each win I wouldn't have thought. I used to get up on the table after a beer or two, I would say, and everyone picked up on it pretty quickly.

JL: So you used to get up on the bench and crank it up?

RM: Yeah, absolutely.

JL: Did you give the boys a pep talk first or just get straight into it?

RM: No, pretty well straight into it I reckon. As soon as I got up on the table that was it. Everyone knew what was going on.

JL: Did you always sing it in the change room?

RM: Yes, always in the change room, which made it pretty hard in places like Adelaide when everyone else could hear what was going on, anyway we didn't worry too much about that.

JL: Do you think it is an important thing?

RM: Well, I think it is now and the longer it goes the more important it becomes really because it is one of those things which will carry on forever. It is part of our tradition now.

7. House, wife, tattoo

My adulthood—on and off the field—began in 1995. In that year I purchased my first house and I proposed to Sue, all before setting off on a tour to the West Indies. I was also chosen that year as vice captain of the Young Australians tour of England, when I toured with some future Test team-mates—Ricky Ponting, Matthew Hayden and Adam Gilchrist.

The house purchase was rather drawn-out. Sue and I didn't live together, and I hadn't even popped the question, but I suppose it seemed inevitable to us both that we would get married so we went house-hunting together in January and February. We'd seen a lot of houses and none seemed to fit, until we visited a place in the suburb of Wembley. It was a classic 1940s bungalow with a big rose garden out the front. Sue loved it but the owners wanted $350,000 for it, which was far beyond my financial means, as I was on a small ACB contract and had an uncertain future. Still, Dad insisted that I should put in a bid. 'Offer them $300,000 and see what they say,' he barked. 'Have some guts!' It wasn't the last time I'd hear those words from Dad about real estate.

The offer, as one might expect, was rejected out of hand by the estate agent, who at first said he couldn't even take it to the owners because it was too low. But he did and they, too, dismissed it as a joke. I went away on tour to the West Indies and forgot about it, until about six weeks later I got a call from the agent, who asked if my offer was still on the table. I checked with Dad and reckoned it was still a good deal, so I ended up buying the place while celebrating an amazing Test series victory in the Caribbean.

I'll let Sue tell the engagement story while I duck for cover.

● ● ●

Justin proposed to me in mid-February, as he was preparing to go away on tour. I had an inkling that something was up because there was a lot of cloak-and-dagger stuff going on. Unknown to me, though, he'd gone around to everyone he knew to ask what they thought of the idea.

When he had decided to take the plunge, he rang and asked me out to dinner at a really nice Thai restaurant, but at the last minute he cancelled on me, which left me pretty miffed. He must have taken a deep breath, because then he turned up at my little flat with some takeaway from the same restaurant plus a six-pack of Corona beer to steady his nerves.

After putting on Bon Jovi's ballad 'Always' in the background, he actually got down on one knee, shaking like a leaf, and asked me to marry him. There was no way I could refuse, of course, even though he hadn't got around to getting a ring. Instead, he brought a Russian wedding band he owned. I wore it until he got back from the West Indies and we had time to go out and buy an engagement ring.

• • •

It would surprise most cricket followers that I nominate the 1995 West Indies series as my favourite overseas tour, particularly since I only played a few innings during the whole three months, and they were mostly in games of little significance or atmosphere. While the opening match against the Barbados Second XI—on a ground where sheep roamed the boundaries—was reasonably important to my Test prospects, the others took me as close to a spot in the team as a game of backyard cricket might have. In Guyana I made a painstaking 55, which was followed by a miserable duck against the West Indies Board XI at St Kitts.

I played in just one match of any real significance—the last of the one-day series, which by then the West Indies had already comfortably won. I ran out Mark Waugh and was then run out myself for just six. The only thing more stupid than my innings were the shoes I'd worn, which were rubber-soled rather than studded. I'd never worn rubber-soled shoes in a game before, so why I chose to do it in such a big game is beyond me. Yes, Brian Lara used to wear them, but surely it was a dumb thing to do just because Lara did? Another lesson learned, but at a cost: two runouts and another missed opportunity. It wasn't as if one-day internationals came along every day for me.

I was a fringe player—twelfth man for every Test—but I was young, eager to learn and enjoying being back in the Australian cricket team after missing the previous year's Ashes series. After our series loss in Pakistan, I'd now played in three series and was yet to win one. The Ashes sides of 1993 and 1994–95 had flogged the Poms

4–1 and then 3–1, but I hadn't been a member of either. Having heard David Boon lead the team song just once, in New Zealand, I was craving a chance to sing it again with my mates. We were playing tough Test cricket and yet we just weren't good enough to get over the line.

So, being part of a series win for the first time was a huge thrill, despite my lacklustre form and the small part I played on the field. But there were other reasons that it became such a special tour for me. The first had its roots back in my teenage years.

When I was growing up during the late 1970s and 1980s, the West Indies were the Calypso kings of cricket. They had the most fearsome bowling attack, led by Michael Holding, Joel Garner, Andy Roberts, Malcolm Marshall and Courtney Walsh, and the best and most exciting batting line-up, with Gordon Greenidge, Desmond Haynes, Clive Lloyd and Richie Richardson. They seemed invincible at times, their batsmen plundering the bowlers like marauding pirates, with flashing white teeth and cutlasses for bats, before setting loose their fast bowlers like giant sleek Dobermans with snarling fangs who flung cricket balls like cannon balls. All teams crumbled against the onslaught. And above all the West Indian champions strode the great buccaneer Vivian Isaac Richards.

My uncle Robbie played against Sir Viv in the third of Kerry Packer's World Series Cricket Supertests, in Adelaide in 1977–78. He played another fourteen matches over the next few years, and I remember being riveted by his stories of the game and the legends he'd met. Of them all, my favourite was his description of Richards reclining in a corner of the change room, shirt off and black skin rippling with muscles, his jaw clenched around a cigar.

Robbie's descriptions were perfectly matched by the World Series Cup posters when the West Indians came to Australia in the summer of 1984–85. One was a giant photo of Viv under the lights at the SCG. He was dressed in the pale rose and blue colours they wore at the time, sweat poured off his massive forearms, and his shoulder and chest muscles were clearly visible through the light shirt. He held his head over the ball as he played the perfect forward defensive shot. It didn't matter that he played for the opposition. He was a gladiator and a sporting god.

I was really keen to meet Sir Viv when we got to Antigua for the Second Test. Boldly, I asked one of the senior players—probably Boony—if he could arrange a meeting, and to my great excitement Richards agreed and turned up one afternoon. We stood out the front of the change rooms with Rudy Webster, the West Indian sports psychologist who wrote a brilliant book called *Winning Ways*. I was a bit overawed by it all, but I needn't have been.

Viv may have been a decade older than he was in my memories, but nothing had really changed physically. He was casual as usual—black polo shirt, jeans and a cowboy hat—and reminded me of Clint Eastwood, except that instead of chewing on a piece of straw, Viv had his jaws clenched around a big stogie. His shoulders were still broad and his waist thin, but behind the coolness was a steel glint.

It had been the same with his batting. Viv had always looked as though he were playing in a picnic game. He used to stroll to the middle swinging his bat like a windmill around his shoulder, before settling over it to take his guard, all the while slowly chewing his gum—but his casualness covered a menacing intent.

'Watch the ball like a hawk, you've got to watch the ball like a hawk,' he repeated as we stood there like three mates at a barbecue. 'It's really important that you see the ball out of the bowler's hand so you can pick up the line—not the length, but the line. If you're in the right position, everything else will look after itself.'

Viv also talked about concentration while batting, explaining how he would pick out landmarks outside the ground, like trees above the grandstands or a church steeple in the distance. That way you could have something to look at between deliveries, which would help to take your mind off batting.

This knitted well with the advice coach Bob Simpson had given me when I'd got my break in 1993. The key to batting was concentration, he had told me. The skill was to switch on only when the bowler got to the top of his mark, to watch carefully as he ran in and bowled, then to switch off again between deliveries. 'From the time he runs in to the time you play your shot, it's a matter of seconds,' he said. 'That means you really only have to concentrate for a few minutes, even if you bat all day.'

This might appear to be oversimplifying a complex set of circumstances, but in essence, success as a batsman means being brilliant for ten seconds, over and over and over and over again.

But I digress. Sir Vivian talked for just half an hour or so, but it meant the world to me. Our meeting left such an impression that I've often used his counsel to help others over the years, figuring that if it came from Viv then it must be worth passing on. Since then I've met the great man on half a dozen occasions, and each time he was encouraging and constructive, putting his arm around me, playfully punching me on the shoulder and telling me he had been watching my progress. I even played with him once in a charity match in London; he strolled in, swung the bat to make 20 or so with two big sixes, then retired to the change rooms, where he sat, shirtless, smoking his big-arse cigars and drinking rum and coke. What an experience!

Viv and I both captained Somerset County Cricket Club during our careers. His portrait hangs in the foyer of the main office, and

I used to walk past it every time I went out to play, just to remind me of his impact on the game. One day I hit a triple-century for Somerset; as I came off, someone shouted, 'Hey, you've just gone past Viv Richards' highest score.' Yeah, right, I thought. I took 500 balls and he probably did it in about a quarter of that. I felt the same way about going past Sir Donald Bradman's record as the highest Australian first-class run-scorer. It's nice going past legends, but you've got to keep your achievement in context.

● ● ●

Another reason the tour was my favourite is that the cricket was the toughest and most competitive I had seen, and it signalled the arrival of Australia as a team which could win anywhere and against anyone. For us, though, the tour hadn't started too well. We had arrived, primed to beat the West Indies at home for the first time in decades, but before the first ball had even been bowled, our champion fast bowler Craig McDermott was out of the series. Billy had been running back to the team hotel in Guyana, fell off a wall and twisted his ankle, so he'd had to fly home. His loss was a blow, but somehow it seemed to galvanise the group, and from that point everything clicked into place.

The First Test, in Barbados, was a beauty. Glenn McGrath led the attack as we bowled out the West Indies for 195 on the first day. From there we took a 151-run lead on the first innings before tearing through them again in the second, with Pigeon taking five wickets, to rout them for 189. We knocked off the necessary 39 runs without losing a wicket and suddenly we were one-up—and we had inflicted the first three-day defeat on the West Indies in 30 years.

My diary captures how I felt:

What an unbelievable day and experience. It has been a huge victory by the boys, and the atmosphere in the team is sensational. What a great sight, seeing Boony up on the table singing 'Underneath the Southern Cross I stand . . .' after the fans outside the room sang our national anthem. This has been a great day to remember. I hope there are plenty more like this in my career.

The Second Test ended in a draw because of rain, but it was tantalisingly poised. The West Indies were 2 for 80, chasing 257, when play was abandoned midway through the last day. The highlight of the match had been David Boon's catch in the first innings to get rid of Brian Lara, who had threatened to tear us apart. He'd made 88 at almost a run a ball, spurred on by the drums around the ground every time he hit a boundary (which was often—there were sixteen of them). Then Mark Taylor brought on Steve Waugh, with immediate results. Lara dragged an attempted drive and Boony, who was fielding at midwicket with his feet almost on the pitch, launched himself—as one reporter described it, 'like a Tasmanian salmon'—to catch it in his left hand.

West Indian Steve Bucknor, who was umpiring, was as astonished as everyone else. 'Are you 34 [years old] or 25?' he asked.

It was the first of two on-field incidents that, in my view, show why Australia was about to begin probably the greatest period in its cricketing history. The second happened in the Third Test, at Queen's Park Oval, Port of Spain, where the wicket was so green that the West Indies' captain, Richie Richardson, declared it unsatisfactory before a ball had even been bowled.

It was soon clear why he felt that way. He won the toss, we were sent in to bat and were ripped apart for 128, with Curtly Ambrose taking five wickets and Courtney Walsh three. It was demonic stuff, but amid the shambles Steve Waugh made a stand. He scored 63 of the hardest runs you'll ever see in Test match cricket—he was smacked and bruised all over his body and yet refused to yield to the vicious fast bowling. The two best sides in the world were battling for supremacy and it was awesome to watch.

Things came to a head when Tugga was on 54 and ducked under yet another bouncer. He had been silent until then, but he decided to let off a bit of steam and say something, particularly about Ambrose's habit of staring at the batsmen: 'What are you fucking staring at? Why don't you go and get fucked?' I couldn't hear it from where I was sitting, but I was sure it had the word 'fuck' in some form.

Ambrose, all two metres of him, stormed down the pitch and stood glaring down at an impassive Tugga. 'You talking to me? Don't you fucking swear at me! You can't be cussing me in my own country.' That's what the media reported him as saying, and it sounds pretty right to me.

Richie Richardson ran up from second slip to intervene. There is a famous photo of him pulling Ambrose away with both hands while Tugga watches, not worried in the slightest. Ambrose may have won the battle that day, but Steve Waugh stood undefeated at the end of it. This was Tugga's response after the day's play: 'It's Test match cricket. It's tough. It's not an easy game. If you want an easy game, go take up netball.'

The importance of the confrontation was not lost on any of us in the sheds. I remember the hairs standing up on the back of my neck as I watched. This was a critical moment. I could sense the impact on the other players, senior and junior. It wasn't simply about winning a battle but about being a leader. Although Mark Taylor was still our captain—and he was one I admired—this was the moment when Steve Waugh assumed the leadership of Australian cricket.

The crowd sang joyfully for their hero Ambrose, but we tightened as a group. We realised that if Steve Waugh could stand up so fearlessly to Curtly Ambrose on the greenest wicket we'd ever seen, then we as a team could stand up to the West Indies and beat them.

When we were bowled out Steve came off the ground and, in typical fashion, declared that we could still win the match and the Frank Worrell Trophy. He wanted us to keep fighting even though we were down. We lost the match but Tugga was right about the series.

Many people have noticed my special affection for Steve Waugh, and in a lot of ways that incident with Curtly Ambrose sums up why I hold him in such high regard. I admired him not only for his success as a run machine but for his unbelievable bravery as a leader, and I desperately wanted to emulate him on both counts.

We went to the final Test, at Sabina Park in Jamaica, at 1–1. Everything was on the line and, after somehow routing the Windies for 265, Steve Waugh exacted his revenge on Curtly Ambrose with a magnificent double-century. This was an innings of majesty and occasion, as he and his twin brother, Mark, built a partnership that would enter Test cricket lore.

The strongest memory I have of the innings was actually not of Tugga but of Greg Ritchie, the former Test player who was leading a tour group and had enjoyed the day a little too much. Greg, who was pretty big by that stage, had leapt over a balcony onto the ground and charged out into the middle amid the hordes of locals to congratulate Tugga on reaching 200. It was a moment of unbridled jubilation—Waugh standing with his arms aloft, tired but thrilled, with one of his early Test team-mates in shorts and T-shirt giving him a hug. Thankfully, there was still enough innocence in sport at that time to allow people to stream onto the ground to celebrate such occasions.

There was another memorable aspect of the match. In those times rest days were still in use. I'm very glad they were abandoned a few years later. On this occasion, we lost momentum and it almost cost us greatly. We had the Windies on the ropes by day three, so the series victory was within sight, when we took a day off.

There was nothing positive in the rest day for us because we were so close to achieving our goal and rewriting history. To keep ourselves relaxed, we were bussed up to the town of Ocho Rios north of Jamaica, once a small fishing village but now an important tourist area. It's crowned by waterfalls and beaches—it's where they filmed the movie *Cocktail* with Bryan Brown and Tom Cruise.

While all this sounds very glamorous, we were all too anxious to enjoy it much. It should have been a fun day, sipping pina coladas and swimming amongst the waterfalls, but we didn't have much time to relax—especially after spending most of the bus ride reading fan mail sent over from Australia. There were hundreds of faxes, and we were simply overwhelmed as we sat reading and swapping the missives from home, which reinforced that our victory would not be for us alone but for the whole Australian sporting public.

We were also worried about the threat of rain as we pushed for victory the next day. The storm clouds and lightning had gathered around Sabina Park during the rest day and we had little faith that the old tarpaulin covers could hold back a torrential downpour. If the pitch was flooded, the game would have to be abandoned.

Thankfully, the rain stayed away—but so did our performance. We needed seven wickets, while the Windies needed over 200 runs to make us bat again and perhaps salvage a draw. The latter looked more and more likely through the morning, as our skills abandoned us and we dropped catches like flies. There wasn't much I could do from the sidelines except support the guys as the tension mounted, but I'm certain our fumblings were due in no small part to our incredible desire to win. As I already knew all too well, sometimes the harder you try, the worse your performance becomes.

The turning point came when Brendon Julian ran out Carl Hooper. Brendon, who stands about two metres tall, ran in from the deep, scooped the ball up with one hand and ripped his left-handed throw over the stumps. It was a brilliant piece of fielding that blunted any chance the Windies had of saving the game. Warney quickly followed that up by trapping the left-handed Keith Arthurton LBW with a delivery that pitched in the rough and ripped back to hit Arthurton on the back pad.

Steve Bucknor was umpiring—a Jamaican himself—and he had to judge if the ball was spinning too much. His decision, as usual, seemed to take ages—and due to its huge importance his silent perusal of the moment felt like an eternity. I can only imagine how difficult it was for him, in front of his home crowd, knowing that a decision against the batsman would mean his beloved West Indies would concede the Frank Worrell Trophy for the first time in decades.

When we saw Steve's finger, slightly crooked, waver and slowly rise, our change room erupted. I couldn't contain my glee and I hugged Errol Alcott and slapped Bobby Simpson playfully on his backside. We were all part of something very special.

My diary entry after winning the all-important and historic Fourth Test in Jamaica records:

Boony's rendition of 'Underneath the Southern Cross' was as good as I have ever experienced. Champagne, TV crews, AB in the change room, the Frank Worrell Trophy, men crying—it was simply an awesome celebration in the rooms. The bus ride back to the hotel was fantastic, speeches and singing. Just hanging out with people like AB, Boony, Carl Rackemann, the Waugh brothers and my younger mates is incredible. I love this. I absolutely love it.

• • •

The next day—after a massive night, I'll admit—we flew to Bermuda for a week's holiday, as well as to play what seemed like a couple of picnic matches to us. After reaching the pinnacle of Test cricket at Sabina Park we had a 50-over match against club side St George's. No offence to them, but it was all a bit of a laugh—I even took one of my rare wickets. Our few days there were more about blowing off a bit of steam and enjoying the fruits of a job well done. Most of the trip was spent riding mopeds around the island, much to the frustration of our team manager, the late Jack Edwards, who somehow had to corral our enthusiasm.

I was rooming with Tim May, who is one of the funniest blokes I've ever met. One night he drove his moped into the room, parked it neatly, tossed his helmet casually on my bed and then rolled around laughing at my shock. It was priceless. The ACB then put on a fabulous dinner for us to celebrate our series victory. Jack, who was a great old bloke, found the poshest place on the island but set no boundaries. I think his fateful words were something like, 'It's on the house, boys, so have a good time.'

Did we ever!

The entrées were going everywhere, we flicked caviar at each other across the table like schoolboys, ordered a couple of main courses each, then feasted on every dessert on the menu. Our extravagant feast was washed down with the best red wines and champagne, followed by whiskey and cognac. Warney was the exception. Here we were, eating the best seafood and steak you could imagine, and he ordered a couple of family-size Napolitano pizzas from the takeaway shop next door. The restaurant managers nearly flipped. But pizza was all Warney ever ate on tour, apart from toasted cheese sandwiches, French fries and, occasionally, lasagne—provided it didn't have mushrooms in it. The only green thing that passed his lips was an occasional apple, if he was on one of his health kicks. When you consider that he also smoked a pack of cigarettes a day, it makes you shake your head in disbelief. The guy was simply a freak, an enigma, given that he was one of the greatest sportsmen on the globe.

At the end of the night Jack got the bill and nearly had a heart attack. It was something like US$10,000. He was almost weeping. 'What have you guys done to me?' he cried. 'How am I going to explain this to the ACB?'

Even though we felt for poor old Jack, somehow that only made the night sweeter. Around midnight we ordered a fleet of taxis to take us back to our hotel, then we kept them waiting for three hours, with their meters running, while we continued to party inside, occasionally sending caviar or a pile of chicken drumsticks out to the drivers. Jack had to find another US$500 cash to pay them. Funnily enough, 1995 was the last time the ACB paid for a team dinner like that.

I still find it a little strange that this tour meant so much to me, given that I didn't play much of an on-field role. As I have explained, however, the cricket we played was so exciting and competitive, and—even more significantly—the Australian team forged such close bonds that I have nothing but fond memories of the tour. The way we unified after the early loss of Craig McDermott was invigorating, and the way we fought back after losing the Third Test was a great lesson in never giving in. Of course, the partying after each win was simply unforgettable.

Back home, I chose to do something enduring—get a tattoo of a boxing kangaroo kicking down a palm tree. I had decided to get it done during a karaoke night in Bermuda. My manager at the time was Austin Robertson (who actually managed a few of us), and we were all sitting around having a beer when a few of us vowed to get a remembrance tattoo. In the end, I was the only one who went ahead with it. Austin started doodling designs on a beer coaster, and when I got back to Perth I took the coaster down to a tattoo parlour in Mount Lawley and told the bloke what I was after. He looked at the coaster and told me to come back in a week. By then I was rather nervous about the whole thing, but still determined to go ahead and get it done.

'Are you right to go, young fella?' he asked me.

'Yep,' I replied with some bravado.

'Where do you want it done?'

I gulped. 'On the left cheek of my bum.'

'You'd better drop ya daks, then,' he responded.

I've got another tattoo now—the names of my four daughters running down the inside of my left arm—but even though that piece of body art took three hours to complete, the pain of it was nothing compared to the 45 minutes it took to prick this design onto my backside. Forget being hit by bouncers from West Indian fast bowlers—this was easily the most painful experience of my life. I thought I was being discreet and knew it would be hidden, but I can still recall the feeling of lying face-down, my pants down to my ankles, and gripping the sides of the bench to stop myself from passing out.

Some years later, I bought my dad a tattoo for his 50th birthday. He'd always gone on about wanting one, so I challenged him to do what I had. He came to regret his boasting, and the fact that he'd married a woman with a hyphenated name, because he had a fluttering Aussie flag tattooed into his bum along with my mum's name—Joy-Anne.

I watched Dad's knuckles turn white as he gripped the bench just as I had. Mum thought it was a bit crass, but I think she secretly liked Dad having her name etched there. He went to a corporate golf day a few years later and was in the showers after his round and wondered why all the other men were staring at his backside. He'd forgotten the tattoo by then, but his mates would have had a great laugh.

For me, though, the tattoo was about a moment in time, something that could never be erased. It was the high point of a fledgling career that seemed then as if it could never be surpassed. I had no way of knowing what lay ahead for the team—and for me.

8. Roses

I love roses. I probably got it from my maternal grandmother, Biddy, who had a house in Wembley with several beds of established roses that bloomed brightly in the hot, dry climate of Western Australia. I was with Nanna the day she died in October 1995. I had been sitting by her bed with the family, as she had wanted, before I had to go off and play club cricket for Scarborough. As we sat quietly, I asked her which rose was her favourite. She nominated a pink variety in the back garden, so I went out and clipped the nicest bloom for her. At lunch during the club game, Dad came down to tell me that Nan had died. I obviously knew her passing was imminent but that didn't lessen the pain. Thankfully Mum and her seven brothers and sisters were by her bedside at the end, as was a beautiful pink rose.

By chance, the house I had bought when I was away in the West Indies was around the corner from Biddy's place, and it had a beautiful rose garden out the front. Whenever I was stressed about something, I found it therapeutic to stand there watering the roses in the early morning or late evening. It gave me some space to chill out for a while.

I was out watering them early on the morning of 23 December 1996, while waiting to hear if I had won a long-awaited recall to the Test side, which was midway through a series with the West Indies. The side was cruising, having beaten the Windies in the opening two Tests, but there was talk around that there might be changes.

My hopes rested on the selectors' decision about the young Ricky Ponting. It seems amazing now that he would ever be a candidate for being dropped, but his form at the time had been sporadic and the selectors were said to be thinking of giving him a rest. They had been meeting in Melbourne, which was three hours ahead of Perth, so I knew that the call, if it was coming, would come early. Watering the roses while the day was relatively cool seemed a good way to pass the time.

I was, naturally, on edge. This was my chance to play on one of the world's biggest sporting stages—the Boxing Day Test at the MCG. I'd been in the best form of my life, training like a maniac and having had a huge year for Western Australia. My average for the season to that point was over 142, since I had just scored a double-century against South Australia. There was plenty of media speculation but, as usual, most of it would prove wayward. I'll let Sue take over the story.

• • •

I was five months pregnant with our first daughter, Jessica. We didn't have mobile phones in those days, so Justin had taken the cordless home phone outside. He was trying to keep busy but was extremely anxious about the decision that was being made on the other side of Australia.

It was about seven-thirty in the morning and I was upstairs—a sight to behold, no doubt, in my dressing gown, which covered a growing bulge, and with my hair up in rollers. When the phone rang I expected it would be news about the team, so I came out to the front to watch Justin's reaction. He was standing still and listening intently, the roses forgotten and the hose in his hand gushing water off into the distance. I could hear him repeating, 'No, no, are you serious?'

It was impossible to know in which direction the conversation was heading. Finally, Justin hung up, turned and grinned at me. He was in the team! It had been Geoff Marsh, the Australian coach. Apparently, Swampy had started the conversation by congratulating Justin on the double-century he'd scored for Western Australia. Then he'd asked, 'What are we having for Christmas lunch?' It took a minute for the message to sink in, but by using the word 'we', he meant that Justin would be in Melbourne with the team.

We hugged and danced on the front lawn, Justin spraying the gushing hose around our heads and me still in my dressing gown and curlers, not caring who saw us. The moment was typical of our feelings during Justin's career. We never took anything for granted. Justin was always grateful for his opportunities, tried to make the most of them and expected to have to work hard to stay at the top. It was the same in our family life as well.

● ● ●

I was pumped after Swampy's phone call, but then the fears set in. Instead of the amazing feeling of my debut four years before, I was filled with dread and self-doubt. Was I ready? I'd been battered and bruised against the West Indies in my first Test before touring New Zealand, where, apart from one half-century, I had performed badly. That experience, and not being selected to go on the Ashes tour, had left a big scar. I'd felt like a hero after my first Test, having come from nowhere, but then it felt like I'd fallen and was lying at the foot of the mountain again, wondering if I could ever climb back to the top.

In fact, I'd already had a second chance of sorts, two years earlier on the 1994 Pakistan tour. There, I had made a useful 69 in the Third Test, but it hadn't been enough to secure a permanent place. I had known the match was a one-off because of the injury to Steve Waugh, and perhaps that had allowed me to play with a sense of freedom. When Tugga had returned I had to settle for being twelfth or thirteenth man for another couple of series, including the great 1995 tour of the West Indies. This time, though, I knew the opportunity could be a lasting one. Perhaps that's why it was so forbidding. This time it was for real and I was dreading the possibility of failure.

When you think about it, many young Australian Test cricketers have had similar experiences. It seems to be a normal part of the journey—get them in early, drop them if they fail, then make them claw their way back in. It's as if the selectors are challenging you. 'Here's the challenge,' they say. 'How good are you, son? How much do you want to be in the side? If you want it, you're going to have to come back a better player.' And only the best cricketers can do that.

Exactly this happened to Steve Waugh, Michael Clarke, Damien Martyn, Matthew Hayden and Ricky Ponting. It seems amazing that Ricky has been dropped three times in his career and had to fight his way back in. It seems to be true that failure is an important part of the learning curve, and you become a better, more determined player if you have to earn your place a second, third or even fourth time. Phillip Hughes is the latest young star to experience it. While he enjoyed more success in his first few Test matches than I could have dreamt of, his axing, although tough, may yet be the catalyst for a comeback that could see him eclipse many batting records by the time he retires.

Adding to my fears was another complication, which I haven't admitted publicly before. My hand had been broken as I made my recent double-century. Jason Gillespie had hit me during one of the greatest spells of bowling I ever faced in Sheffield Shield cricket, and while I was never going to own up to a dodgy right hand, I knew I was in trouble. My dilemma was simple. Knowing that opportunities to win a permanent place in the Australian Test team were rare, I didn't want to tell anyone. On the other hand—pardon the pun—my grip-strength was poor and I knew my ability would be compromised.

As I stood in the middle of my front lawn pondering the alternatives, a puddle forming at my feet, I took the only obvious, intelligent and upright course of action—tell no one and plan to bat on Boxing Day with a busted hand.

The team always stayed at the Hilton on the Park Hotel, which overlooks the MCG. When I threw back the curtains on the morning of Boxing Day, I looked down at the happy green and gold masses making their way through the Fitzroy Gardens to the MCG and shuddered. The sight, as wonderful as it was, brought home to me the magnitude of the occasion. Unlike my debut in Adelaide, when I'd had no real time to think about the occasion, this was my first Boxing Day Test. This was different—a moment I'd been dreaming about since I was eleven years old.

A few of us decided to walk from the hotel rather than taking the team bus to the great coliseum. I thought it might calm my nerves.

Joining the throng and mingling with the excitement of this magnificent annual event, many of the fans couldn't quite believe that Steve Waugh, Matthew Hayden and Glenn McGrath—the gladiators they had come to watch—were walking among them. On that day there were 72,000 people, the biggest crowd for 25 years, and for a few minutes, among the zinc war paint, I forgot my nerves as I walked towards the biggest stage of my life.

Of course, the nerves returned—big time—once we were inside the dressing room, and more so when we won the toss and batted on a difficult green wicket. The Australian side was full of confidence, having won the first two Tests, but that was shattered in the next few hours as Curtly Ambrose once again reduced us to tatters. He removed Haydos (who was also on a recall after two years in the wilderness) for 5, Tubby for 7 and Mark Waugh for a golden duck. Tugga came out to join me and to face the hat-trick ball, which he calmly survived.

I was so nervous I could hardly stop shaking. When Kenny Benjamin came on to bowl, I tried to do something about it by hooking him for a big six. Apparently, some of the commentators described it as one of the best shots they'd seen at the MCG. The truth is that it was far from a clean strike. In fact, I had top-edged the ball into the crowd, really, which shows yet again the difference between perception and reality.

We managed to survive until drinks, and as I stood there with Steve in the middle of the heaving stadium, I realised my bladder was full and I desperately needed to go to the toilet.

Tugga was his usual taciturn self and dismissed my problem. 'Mate, if you're not nervous now, playing in front of 75,000 at the MCG against Ambrose, Benjamin and Walsh, then there's something wrong with you.'

He strolled back to the wicket as if nothing could ever bother him and settled down to face another Ambrose over. His words made me feel a little more at ease. I had got into double figures and had a resolute partner at the other end. Then disaster struck.

Tugga played defensively to a delivery, dropping it on the offside, where it rolled towards point. Realising there was an easy single to be had, he called and began running. But I hadn't heard him properly above the noise of the crowd. I was watching the ball but then lost sight of it behind Ambrose, who'd run halfway down the pitch in his follow-through. I hesitated and Jimmy Adams swooped in and got the return to the keeper before I made my ground.

Being run out in a Test match is always a cardinal sin—but being run out now, during my big chance? You must be kidding. I trudged off the ground, full bladder, steaming soul, feeling as if my comeback was in tatters and knowing the demons in my mind would cripple me until the next time I walked onto the MCG to face the fire again.

Surprisingly, the media coverage was unexpectedly supportive. Fairfax writer Peter Roebuck wrote a very complimentary piece:

Langer played really well yesterday, alert at the crease, bravely into position and hooking with swift hands. He seemed to relish the struggle and to belong in the company. It was rotten luck that he lost his wicket in another confusion with Steve Waugh . . . It will be a surprise if Langer does not score enough runs to play his part hereafter. His brain is steady and he is playing his shots.

Sadly for me, Roebuck was wrong—at least for the time being. If the first innings was a nightmare, then the second innings was a farce. Trying to pull Curtly Ambrose through square leg, I got hit in the solar plexus. As I continued to swivel through the shot, the ball bounced off the back of my bat and was caught at second slip by Carl Hooper. Not only had I been winded but I was out for a duck—caught off my stomach. There's a photo of me, my head bowed in utter dejection as I walked off, while the giant West Indians high-fived in the background. All my fears from the front yard in Wembley had come home to roost and, again, I felt as if events had conspired against me. This was it. Test cricket and I were simply not meant to be.

Somehow, I retained my spot for the Fourth Test in Adelaide. I had a chance to redeem myself and, for a while, it felt as if it might be my turn. After bowling the Windies out for just 130, we set about building a huge lead. Matthew Hayden and I looked to be on our way until I played a loose cut and was caught for 19. I didn't need to play the shot, as I'd been scoring comfortably, mostly off my pads. Instead, I had to watch as others achieved what I felt I should have done. Haydos got his maiden Test century and we led by almost 400, before bowling the West Indies out for 204 and securing an innings victory.

It was satisfying to finally play not only in a winning match but also in a series victory, but I lost my place in the side for the final Test in Perth. I walked away feeling that, yet again, I had played my last international.

Roebuck made some other points about me in the same article:

Justin Langer was a tenacious warrior at the [Adelaide cricket] academy and was prepared to carry ironbark across the desert if it would improve his chances of playing for his country. Realising his abilities were not exceptional and yearning to play for Australia, he threw himself heart, body and soul into his work so that observers wondered if he might not be too committed. His career has followed an expected course, a lot of unglamorous shield runs, a Test debut so brave it was almost an epic, a stuttering performance in New Zealand as tension took hold and, now, a resurgence.

He was right in so many ways, although the timeframe for my successful resurgence would be longer than I hoped and he anticipated.

9. The twelfth man

A ndy Bichel is one of those guys you would select to go on a
tour simply because he is a great team man. Both on and off
the field, Andy always gave his all. He was fit and strong, built like
a rugby league player and always ready to bowl another over or add
his sense of fun to an occasion. We were both selected on the tour
of South Africa in February 1997, a few weeks after the home series
against the West Indies was over.

The series was billed as the world championship of cricket, however the First Test was anything but. We thumped the Proteas by
an innings and 196 runs, thanks to Greg Blewett (214) and Steve
Waugh (160), who put on a record 385 for the fifth wicket, before
Michael Bevan and Shane Warne spun the South Africans out for
130. The game finished a day early, and in the wild celebrations that
followed, we decided to take a trip up to the famous Sun City Resort
near the border with Botswana. By the time we got on the bus, the

boys had already been drinking and singing for a few hours, and the party kept going as we set off on the three-hour trip along the N4 highway.

Andy Bichel came to the fore, setting up a bar at the back of the bus, which contributed greatly to the party atmosphere. By the time we arrived at Sun City, some of the boys had been relieved of a few garments of clothing, and the party was really cranking. Thankfully, the team management managed to get most of us off the bus at least semi-dressed, and we eventually collapsed in the hotel to sleep it off.

The hangovers were gone by late morning but the promised sun didn't arrive. Some of the guys played golf and others went to a man-made wave pool. I got up early, encouraged by Tugga and Pigeon, who, as usual, wanted to do something different and so had organised a trip to a nearby game park. For once, I wished I hadn't listened to them. Not only was I nursing a hangover, but it was freezing cold and raining heavily. Even though we could hardly see the promised lions and elephants, the fresh African air was a great hangover cure, and the comfort of being 1–0 up was energising.

I'd been happy to be twelfth man before this tour. I felt I was physically fit, practising and learning a lot from the best. I had enjoyed Pakistan in 1994 and had felt lucky more than entitled when I'd got a call-up for a single Test there, and the West Indies tour in 1995 was fantastic for so many other reasons.

But it's not easy to be outside the playing team, because you become all but invisible. Unless you're in the starting line-up it is really hard to feel part of the action. I tried to be a great twelfth man, and in doing so I learned a lot about being part of a team. I wanted to be upbeat and ready to help out a senior player if he needed something. I believed that by doing the right thing as twelfth man, I would have a better chance of being given a go when my turn came.

If you show you want to be part of something, people will notice. I knew that sometimes players are not given chances because of the perception that they aren't good tourists.

By the 1997 tour of South Africa, however, it's fair to say I was getting a bit anxious about whether I had a future beyond being a reserve player. My figures to that point were not flattering—seven Test matches, twelve innings and an average of just 22.66—but I still held out hope, mainly because of my great form in the domestic competition. But I needed to find a way to make a mark at the international level.

A diary note I made at the time gives an indication of my mindset. The selector Trevor Hohns had told me I was going home and would miss the one-day series.

Feel very disappointed; that bitter, sick, tearful feeling that I've felt before. Mainly worried about missing out on another Ashes tour, which is now totally out of my control. Every day can't be a good one, I suppose, or you'd never appreciate the good ones as much.

I sometimes imagined I was standing at the doorway to a glamorous room, watching those inside having a great time at a party. One of the guests suddenly beckons me in. I enter hesitantly, too shy to take one of the beers offered by the attendant waiters until someone shoves a glass in my hand. The first sip is ice-cold, as delicious as it looks, and I begin circling the room, hoping to join a conversation. Again I am beckoned and I join the fringe, laughing nervously at a joke and sipping my beer.

Then I open my mouth to speak but my story flops as I fumble the punchline. The room is suddenly silent, the music dies away and the men all stop drinking and look at me. A waiter appears at my side and takes back my half-finished beer, before leading me firmly back to the doorway. He doesn't close the door but leaves it tantalisingly ajar, enough for me to peer back inside to see the party restart. As I watch, I am almost knocked over by two other young men who have been beckoned inside. All I can do is watch and practise my story, in the hope that I will get another invitation.

All imagination aside, the realities of my life had changed dramatically by this time. I was no longer the kid who looked like a schoolboy in 1993 against the huge West Indians. I'd had a few seasons of first-class cricket under my belt, a few tours as twelfth man and, more significantly, I was now married and expecting the birth of my first child. Sue and I had been wed the previous April. I remember panicking when Sue wasn't pregnant after a month, but it happened quickly enough and, as it turned out, we had nothing to worry about in the fertility stakes—we have four beautiful daughters.

I knew before I left for South Africa that I would be cutting it very fine to be home in time for Jessica's birth. I'll let Sue take over the story.

● ● ●

There was never a question about Justin going on tour, even though Jessica (we didn't know her sex before she arrived) was due so close to the last Test there. We had both chosen a path in life, we'd tasted the excitement of Justin playing Test cricket, and so we were prepared to mould our family around its demands.

Everything had gone really well through the pregnancy. I was comfortable and had plenty of family support when Justin left in mid-February. The baby was due in late March so, if all went to plan, Justin would return after the last Test in South Africa with a few days' grace.

But things changed when my obstetrician revealed that he wouldn't be around if the baby came over the Easter weekend, as seemed likely. There had been a lot of movement and 'things were happening', as he put it, so I had two choices—sit still with my legs crossed for three days, or be induced on Holy Thursday before he left for his out-of-town family holiday.

I chose the latter, which meant Justin had to change his flights and rush back almost as the match was finishing. Apparently, the flight the ACB had booked meant he almost had to travel around the world to get home, and even then he might miss the birth. Instead, his team-mates each put in and bought a new flight to make sure he got back in time.

Justin arrived home a few hours after I was induced. On the next day—Good Friday—the doctors delivered our baby while his kids sat in the car outside with their bags packed for their holiday. Thankfully, she was a girl—I'd already decorated her room in lemon and spearmint green, with little white geese stencilled around the walls, thinking it was unisex.

I remember watching Justin with his new daughter as she was being weighed. Jessica was looking up at him with her big dark eyes, and you could tell that they bonded at that moment. Justin was smitten.

● ● ●

Jessica was just four weeks old when I left for the next tour—my first Ashes in England. I remember going into her bedroom, leaning over the cot and kissing her on the head. I was wracked with guilt and hadn't calmed down by the time Dad came to get me and take me to the airport. I got in the car, sniffing and trying to hold back the tears. Dad took one look at me and said, 'What's wrong with you? Got a cold or something?' I was beside myself but couldn't bring myself to admit it.

Jessica was born with a capillary haemangioma, also known as a strawberry mark, in the middle of her forehead. On the day I left it was the size and shape of a small freckle, but within weeks it had grown into an angry red and purple lump. Thankfully, as she grew the mark all but disappeared, but it was very scary for Sue and me at the time. Having to leave them made clear to me the sacrifices required not only of professional sportsmen and women, but also of others who have to travel frequently.

• • •

My glee at being chosen in the squad for an Ashes tour was quickly swallowed by my continued frustration at not making it past twelfth-man duties. I was being given chances to play in tour matches against county sides, made a few half-centuries and even a big 150 not out, but it simply wasn't enough.

England won the First Test at Edgbaston, the Second Test at Lord's was drawn and we won the Third Test at Old Trafford. Sue and Jessica had joined me as we arrived in Leeds to play the Fourth Test at Headingley. I thought I was a chance to make the team, but the night before the match it was announced I had missed out again. I felt totally dejected.

As it happened, there was a world club championship of rugby league being played at the time and a number of Australian teams were in town. I felt like drowning my sorrows a bit and, with promises to Sue that I'd be back in an hour, I headed downstairs to meet up with some of the rugby boys. My namesake Allan 'Alfie' Langer was there, as were the Walter brothers and the hulking figure of Mal Meninga, who shoved a pint of Caffrey's Irish Ale in my hand and listened politely to my tale of woe.

Eventually, after three pints, he suggested we call Steve Waugh and get him to come down from his room to talk it through. I couldn't contemplate calling down one of our most senior and respected players the night before such an important game, but Mal insisted. 'I know Steve, and I also know he is the sort of bloke who would want to help,' he said, reaching for the house phone.

Tugga duly appeared a few minutes later in his tracksuit pants— he was probably ready for bed. 'What's up, boys?' he asked casually, sitting down. He didn't seem upset by the call at all.

Mal didn't mince words: 'Young fella here is worried about his future and getting a chance. I thought you might be able to help him out here.'

We spent the next half an hour thrashing things out—the atmosphere and the lubrication were enough to put me at ease and have my say. Steve could make no promises, but that wasn't the point. The fact that two sporting legends had taken the time to listen to me, and encourage me to have faith in my ability, meant the world, and was perhaps the first indication of Tugga's interest in seeing me realise my potential. I would have to wait, but it would be worth it.

10. Six-second Steve

As we prepared to tour Pakistan in September 1998, we knew that Australia had not won a first-class match there, let alone a Test, for almost four decades. We had been performing well at home and had won several series overseas, against the West Indies, England and South Africa, but success on the subcontinent remained elusive. Despite history being against us, we had a quiet confidence about our chances, and this time I was in the playing side.

A combination of my continued good domestic form—another three centuries and an average close to 60—and Australia's problems in finding a permanent number three since the retirement of David Boon in 1995 meant I was being given another chance. In the five years since my debut, I had managed nine Tests and had a dismal batting average of barely 22. By contrast, I had toured seven times as a reserve, twice to Pakistan and once to New Zealand, Sharjah, the West Indies, South Africa and England. As one commentator put it, I had knocked on more doors than a Red Cross worker. Keith Stackpole, the former Test opening batsman, reckoned that all I needed was a bit of luck.

I kept telling myself that too. My comeback against the West Indies eighteen months earlier had been a train wreck, although not all of my own making. The First Test at Rawalpindi reminded me of my Boxing Day Test, with Wasim Akram trapping me first ball with one of his inswinging yorkers. I didn't get a chance to redeem myself in the second innings. Steve Waugh (157) and Michael Slater (108) gave us a big first-innings lead, and then Stuart MacGill spun Pakistan out twice to give us a momentous victory.

Amid the celebrations that followed at the Australian Club, I ended up having a few beers with Mark Waugh. He'd scored a duck in the game too, but he listened silently to my worries and then patted me on the back.

'Statistics and averages,' he scoffed. 'All you have to do is go out in the next innings and score a century, then everything will be okay.'

'That's all right for you to say,' I protested, before he cut me off.

'It all balances out,' he assured me in his typically nonchalant but honest way. 'You get a couple of ducks or low scores and then throw in a few hundreds. Don't worry about it so much.'

I watched him saunter off and realised the sense he was making. My thoughts should be about my next innings, not what had just happened. I was in a side that wanted me, and it was only a matter of time before I would prove myself. I just had to keep the demons of self-doubt at bay.

A little later I was in the bathroom, talking to myself in the mirror. It must have looked hilarious, but thankfully there was no one else around. I was trying to give myself a pep talk. This was what I had been working towards, and I didn't want to play domestic and county cricket for the rest of my career. Test cricket was the goal, but I was messing it up. I had to look ahead and be positive. The Second Test, at Peshawar, was going to be my moment.

Ten days later, we won the toss and opted to bat first on a yellowish flat pitch. But instead of the comfortable start they expected, Mark Taylor and Michael Slater had an awful time in the first hour as Shoaib Akhtar, who had come into the side to replace an ill Wasim Akram, bowled a sensational opening spell, which was regarded as one of the quickest ever in Test cricket. In the eighth over, after facing 27 deliveries for two runs, Slats got an edge off Shoaib.

I walked out to face the executioner. I knew that this was it. I was already standing on the edge of the cliff; another failure would almost certainly push me over the edge. Not only was I nervous about my position in the Test team, but I was facing the fastest bowler in world cricket for the first time. Shoaib steamed in with the crowd baying for another wicket. He sent down a full-pitched rocket that smacked me hard on the pads. The world seemed to stop as I looked up at the umpire.

The West Indian Steve Bucknor had a reputation for being rather deliberate. 'Six-second Steve' always took his time when considering an appeal. The key to Bucknor's decision was his head rather than his finger. If he nodded, you were gone. If he began shaking his head, you were reprieved.

Six seconds doesn't sound like a lot of time, but at that moment I felt like I was holding my breath underwater with someone standing on my head. Everything seemed to be happening in slow motion, from Shoaib's gut-wrenching appeal to Bucknor's tilt of the head as he calculated the mathematics of the ball, the pads and the stumps. Surely it couldn't happen again—another first-ball duck to a fabulous delivery. Surely the cricketing gods must balance the ledger and let me live.

I was drowning in front of a huge crowd, like Houdini in a tank of water struggling to free himself from a straitjacket. Was it the end? Only one man knew, and he was taking his time deciding. As I struggled to hold my breath, Bucknor's head finally began to move—sideways.

'Not out,' he boomed in his deep, deliberate voice.

I was saved and Shoaib was furious, stalking back to his mark in the distance and tearing in even faster than before. *Bang!* He tried to bounce me on the flat wicket and the ball sat up. I saw my chance and rocked onto the back foot, smashing the ball past point to the boundary.

Shoaib was angry and in my face; I could feel his breath on my cheeks. This was war. I suddenly felt alive and fantastic. I banged my bat a bit harder on the ground and embraced a buzzing in my toes, an electricity that I knew would allow me to counter the enormous energy being focused against me. It was a great feeling. The ball seemed bigger and my feet lighter.

As Tubby and I settled in, the pitch became easier and the bowling more erratic. Stumps was called early on that first day because of bad light, which left me stranded on 97. I had a night to sweat on my possible first Test hundred. I had done enough to have made my mark, but those extra three runs the next morning meant everything to me. The magical three figures is a mark that all batsmen desperately want against their name—97 or 99 just doesn't mean the same thing.

The next morning there was another delay, this time for rain, so I was nervous as anything when we finally got back out into the middle. I couldn't feel my hands, they were so numb, and although

I'd rehearsed in my dreams how I would score those runs, it didn't exactly go to plan. After a long and fidgety wait, all I could manage were three nervous lap-sweeps off the spinners. This was hardly the Cinderella moment I had envisaged, but I didn't care because I'd got my first Test hundred and no one could ever take that away.

As I noted in my diary that night—and later wrote on the back of my bat—my physical and emotional response was pure relief rather than elation. It was like the exhaustion you might feel when you stagger to the top of a mountain and collapse at its summit, unable to relish the view.

More nervous than I expected . . . century came off a misfield. Thinking and worrying about my hands, feet, right shoulder and head instead of thinking about the basics of watching the ball and letting my body and technique take over. Too much thinking . . .

How typical of me. I'd just scored my first Test century and all I could do was admonish myself.

When I was finally out for 116, Tubby and I had set an Australian record for the highest stand against Pakistan. Our 279 runs had been scored at almost four per over, and my innings of over six hours at the crease contained ten boundaries. I had arrived as a Test batsman five years after making my debut, although it was hidden to some extent because Tubby went on to make 334 not out, tying Sir Donald Bradman's highest individual Australian innings. In the end, the only thing I got out of it was a new nickname—'Arthur Morris', since that great left-handed opening batsman is more remembered for being at the other end when the Don was bowled for a duck in his last Test innings in 1948 rather than for the 196 he scored to help Australia win the game.

I didn't care. I had finally got back in the door and I knew that I belonged. In a strange way, the Third Test, at Karachi, confirmed it even more. We were 1–0 up and pushing for a historic series victory. In contrast to Peshawar, where we'd drawn, the pitch was quite difficult and both sides were dismissed for under 300 in their first innings. By the third day we were 28 runs ahead and pushing to set a challenging target. But we had to guard against a collapse, since that would give Pakistan a chance to win the match and square the series.

Tubby and I batted through 50 overs against a determined attack. As we walked off unconquered, he looked at me and seemed to nod, as if to tell me he had seen the skill and determination he needed to, in order to think of me as Test material. I finally had his respect. I felt as good that night as when I had scored the century in Peshawar.

The next morning was an incredible contrast as Wasim Akram began reverse-swinging the ball. The previous evening I'd been playing confidently and could see another hundred coming, but when we resumed I had no idea. Akram's brilliance made me feel like I was playing French cricket; I poked and dabbed without scoring for more than an hour before I was run out for 51.

Despite a century by Mark Waugh—thus proving his own theory—the match ended in a draw. But the series was won, and at last, at long bloody last, I had taken the next step and had a Test century to my name. More importantly, I had finally earned the respect of the two Marks—Taylor and Waugh—who, I always felt, considered me an impostor in the baggy green cap.

While this was happening, something even more important was occurring at home. I may have scored my first century but, as Sue explains, we were about to have our second child, Ali-Rose.

● ● ●

Maybe I should have been paying more attention, but I really didn't feel like being at the Carine Tavern with Justin's parents, Colin and Joy-Anne, where they watched Justin get his first Test century. My reluctance was twofold. Firstly, as I explained earlier, I was very superstitious when it came to Justin and cricket, always blaming myself if he got out while I was watching or listening. But I was also heavily pregnant with Ali-Rose—she was born three weeks later—and I didn't want to be too far from home.

I was at a neighbour's place having lunch when Colin called me with the news. My reaction, probably like Justin's, was sheer relief more than anything else. The early days were a rollercoaster. The fact that he was finally back in the Test side was a big thing for us, and with an expanding young family, some permanency was comforting in so many ways.

The local newspaper had taken a photograph of Joy-Anne leaping excitedly from her seat as Justin scored the runs he needed. Later, a television station called me and asked if I would re-enact watching him, sitting in front of the TV and then leaping in excitement (despite the belly), so they could dub in the appropriate vision. I'd heard of some dumb media stunts before but this took the cake. I'd missed the moment and even the smoothest of reporters wasn't going to talk me into a re-enactment.

● ● ●

The decline of Pakistani cricket—with no international cricket at all being played on their home turf these days—is very sad. I have so many wonderful and enduring memories of playing there. But the security situation is such that the city in which I scored my maiden century, Peshawar, the capital of the country's north-west frontier province, is now a no-go zone for most people, let alone an international cricket team.

There are times when being at the centre of the publicity machine that surrounds the Australian cricket team is difficult. Occasionally, our actions have been taken out of context, or even entirely misunderstood. I remember one glaring example from that 1998 tour of Pakistan. We had arrived in Peshawar a few days before the Second Test to give us time to prepare. A side-trip was also planned, which we thought would be a cultural experience. Some of these trips involved the arts or the local society, but others, such as the trip I made with Steve Waugh into Trenchtown in Jamaica, were quite dangerous. On this occasion, we were invited to go into the mountains and see Pakistan's tribal life firsthand. It sounded exciting, so eight of us, including Glenn McGrath and Tubby, decided to go.

We made a bumpy two-hour bus journey into the Sulaiman Mountains, heading for the famous Khyber Pass, the gateway to Afghanistan, which has been an important trade route and passage since 326 BC, when Alexander the Great marched his army through it to reach India. The omnipresent danger was clear from the armed guards—members of the Khyber Rifles in their mustard-coloured uniforms—who led and followed our bus. Although we'd been given assurances of safety, there are no guarantees in this region. Still, we felt that was part of the adventure.

The law in this part of Pakistan is black and white. On one side of the dusty road there is government land, with its laws and controls and shops selling the usual array of foodstuffs, clothing and electrical goods. On the other side there is tribal land, where the shops are free to sell anything. There are no rules—it is a place where a man is judged simply by the size of his gun. The men sit together in groups, each holding a machine gun. I found the culture both frightening and fascinating.

We looked down through the amazing canyon and towards the valley beyond, where so much blood has been spilled in creating and then re-creating the area's politics. The clash of geography and history was quite overwhelming. We were treated to a display of dancing and even a Pakistani bagpipe band, and we posed next to an anti-aircraft gun that was last fired during the Russian–Afghan wars in the 1980s; it was still pointed towards the city of Kabul.

Finally, we were taken to a rifle range. It seemed the obvious thing to do; if you go to the Barossa Valley you visit wineries, but here at the Khyber Pass you visit rifle ranges. We jumped at the chance to fire a Kalashnikov machine gun. Half a dozen targets were set up on a rocky cliff and we each fired off a few rounds, feeling the *thump, thump* against our shoulders as the rounds ripped into a distant cliff. Being a farmer, Glenn McGrath was the only regular shooter among us, but I was pleased with my effort and posed, smiling, with Gavin Robertson, a New South Wales spinner, for a photo. Sadly, it found its way into the Australian media, and that's when the trouble started.

The image was picked up by the anti-gun lobby at home, mainly because the AK-47 guns we were holding were apparently similar to some of the weapons used in the Port Arthur massacre a few years before. In hindsight, it was perhaps thoughtless of us to have been photographed with the guns, but of course there was absolutely no malice in our actions. In fact, the opposite was the case, in that we were sharing the local culture and accepting local hospitality.

Cricketers are sportsmen, not politicians—and I would suggest our national players are mostly very good ambassadors for our country. We have, at times, been subject to unfair scrutiny, but I suppose that comes with being public figures.

I remember the storm of criticism when we stood for a minute's silence on the day Sir Donald Bradman passed away. We were in India, and we decided as a group to wear our baggy green caps as a sign of our respect for the great man. Yet some in the media wrote that we were being disrespectful because we *didn't* take our caps off during the short memorial ceremony.

Sometimes I am sure the world has gone mad, but one thing I learned very late in my career was that media coverage, as hurtful and ignorant as it could at times be, tended not to be personal. But the fact remains that if the media or others in public positions are going to voice criticism of the Australian cricket team, then they should do it with as much thought and care as they are demanding of it.

11. Bat tragic

Kim Hughes was my boyhood hero. Not only did he come from my neighbourhood, but he wielded his arrogant, flashing blade like a knight in a fairytale as he slays the ugly dragon—in other words, the Poms or the mighty West Indians.

My first bat was a Kim Hughes Slazenger Black Cat, which I bought with my own pocket money when I was nine. In my eagerness, I took it to school that morning and strode into the nets brimming with confidence. It felt great in my hands and I began to play some shots as my hero did—I hit cover drives on one knee, I danced down to the spinners and I smashed flamboyant cut shots through the offside. Then I pulled a delivery and swung around violently, slicing a chunk out of my new bat on the metal stumps behind me. I was devastated and raced back to the store, where they put pigskin around the blade so I could keep using it. I reckon that's when I became a bat tragic.

In December 1980, a few days after my tenth birthday, I went to the WACA to watch a Test match against New Zealand. I sat right on the fence at deep point, eagerly banging on the metal sponsorship signs with the other kids to make as much noise as possible in support of the players. Australia was cruising to victory with Hughes at the wicket. John Bracewell was bowling from the members' end, and Hughes launched his front leg down the pitch to a full and wide delivery and smashed the ball straight towards me. It smacked into the sponsor's sign with a satisfying clang, ending the game with victory for Australia. All I could think of was that Kim Hughes had hit the ball to *me*.

A few months later, Dad was at a charity auction and managed to buy one of the bats Hughes had used to score a Test century. It took pride of place in his study, and I would often sneak in to look at, touch and even hold the icon, which was signed and studded with red marks from his shot-making. My brothers and I would plead with Dad to let us use the blade in the backyard, but he always scoffed as he ordered its return to the office sanctuary. And so there it remained, tantalising but forbidden.

One day in 1983, I decided to 'borrow' the bat for one of my junior cricket matches. Why did I take it on that particular day? I don't know—that's like asking the kid why he took the chocolate from the kitchen.

The match was at Marri Reserve in the northern suburbs of Perth, and I was playing for the Sorrento/Duncraig Cricket Club under-14s. Mum always dropped me off in the car park at the top of an embankment, then I'd walk down the steep hill with my gear and sit at the bottom, waiting for the game to get underway. I was all nerves that morning, excited by what I had done and what I expected would happen. It was a beautiful blue Perth summer morning, the air pungent with the scent of freshly mown and slightly dewy grass.

My team batted first and I was to come in at the fall of the first wicket. When the moment arrived, I carefully removed the bat from its cover and set off for the middle, wearing my yellow cap, white shorts and Puma Sheffield shoes. I was conscious of the weight of Kim Hughes' bat in my hand—it was too large and heavy for me, especially with the weight of his Test heroics ingrained in its willow, yet I was determined to put it to use.

It made a satisfying thud when I took guard and settled in, waiting for the opposition kid, who no doubt was channelling Dennis Lillee. The day was warming up and so was my batting. I waited patiently for the inevitable half-trackers, which I dispatched through square leg with my favourite short-arm pull shot. Kim's willow responded perfectly, and I'm sure the opposition kids were sick of chasing the red leather to the boundary and beyond.

I was in heaven, living a fantasy that had everything but the atmosphere of an MCG crowd. It didn't matter, though, because I was hearing the fans cheering in my mind as I raced past 50, then 60, 70, 80 and 90. Centuries were rare in junior cricket, if only because of the short matches, but nothing was going to stop me and Kim's flashing blade.

Bang, bang, bang! The crowd went wild, the imaginary scoreboard flashed up the three figures and I was euphoric. My first Test . . . I mean, my first northern suburbs under-age competition century. This was real—not backyard cricket with the neighbourhood kids, but a proper hundred—and I knew I would never get sick of the feeling.

● ● ●

I tell that story as the background to another significant moment in my career, which happened fifteen years later—my first Test century against England during the 1998–99 Ashes series. It happened at Adelaide, only this time I was finally entrenched in the side.

My first Test century in Pakistan two months before had been followed by a couple of half-centuries, including one in the first innings of the First Test against England in Brisbane. We had arrived in Adelaide 1–0 up after thumping the English inside three days at the WACA. By this stage Ricky Ponting had also firmly established himself in the side and we were great mates.

Ricky and I were about the same size and liked the same gear—Adidas shoes, Kookaburra bats and Oakley sunglasses—so we used to swap things like a couple of teenage girls. Ricky, for example, used to get these light running shoes with red stripes down the sides; we called them 'race horses'. He had so many pairs that I used to ask him if I could have one he'd worn a few times, knowing that he didn't like wearing the same pair for too long. I actually liked them a bit old and loose. I'd give him bats I didn't like and vice versa. Occasionally, if he had a bat I fancied, I'd nick it from his bag and wait until he noticed. By then, though, it was too late to take it back.

Over the years, I reckon I would have scored five or six of my Test centuries with bats I'd borrowed or nicked off Punter. Most blokes had a favourite bat which they used until it fell apart, but I used to change mine every session. If I got to lunch or to tea, then rather than continue with the one that had been working really well, I would swap. I can't really explain why. Probably it was a bit of superstition that became part of my routine. Also, I always thought that, since bats were my main tool of trade, it was no use having five of them sitting in my cricket bag unused.

In Adelaide that year, as we were preparing to take on the Poms again, Ricky suggested I have a hit with a smallish bat of his. It was a bit light for him but I found it really suited me. I had been brought up to use lighter bats—two-pound-seven or even two-pound-six— encouraged by the Meulemans, in particular. I took Punter's bat out with me and scored a century against the old enemy. It was a memorable Test—I was made man of the match and we secured the Ashes. Sadly, the bat split after that innings, but, like all the bats with which I have scored centuries, I have it displayed in a cabinet at home. The walls of my cellar are lined with autographed bats from every team in which I played.

All my century bats have a short message written on them to remind me of the occasion. For example, the inscription on that 1998–99 Ashes bat reads, 'An absolute rocket of a bat given to me by Ricky Ponting before the game. A sensational blade.' The 1998 Peshawar bat says, 'All I can say is what a relief,' while a bat I used in Hobart later in 1999 is rather cryptic: 'Bat with the clicky handle. You just never know, mate, you just never know.' I'll explain that one a little later.

● ● ●

I was never afraid to seek advice, but at times I surprised myself in doing so. In August 1994, just before I left on a tour of Pakistan in which I didn't play a match, I wrote a letter to Sir Donald Bradman. It began:

Dear Sir Don,
I feel a little shy about writing this letter, but I felt that you may be able to offer me a little advice which may help me achieve my goal of becoming a very successful Australian Test cricketer.

I described myself as a predominantly back-foot player who could handle the quicks and spinners, but who was finding it difficult to manage the rhythm of the medium-pacers. I asked him how he used to prepare mentally and physically for a game.

Sir Don replied just two days later:

Dear Justin,

Thank you for your letter. You flatter me by suggesting that an old octogenarian like me can help you with your cricket. When I finished playing, I summarised my thoughts in my book The Art of Cricket, which deals with all facets of the game, and if you haven't got a copy I think you will find it worthwhile. Also I made a video on the art of batting, and this should be available almost everywhere. My success in the game was, I think, more a matter of natural ability than any-thing else. I did not do anything special—I did not take any measures to fit me physically other than live a normal and sensible non-smoking and non-drinking career—and I relied on the practice nets to work out any chinks in my batting. You mention specially the medium-pacers and a slight problem you have with them. Against them, I always started to move just before delivery by going slightly back and across. In fact, the main basis of my batting was playing back because I think this gives the batsman greater flexibility in making shots and taking the initiative than the forward player, who becomes stuck in the groove. I supposed the one outstanding feature of a good player is his ability to concentrate and to impose his will on the bowlers. I always played cricket for fun and because I loved the game. It never became a boring pastime. I am sure you have the right attitude and I congratulate you on your success so far. Follow your own instincts and don't be a slave to coaching.

I wish you good luck in the future.

Kind regards
Don Bradman

I was blown away to receive such a gracious reply. The things that got me were the first line and the last lines—that I was flattering *him*, and his advice that I should follow *my* instincts. The former was a lesson in humility, the latter a lesson in self-confidence. Both are required to succeed.

Allan Border, 2nd Songmaster, 1984–85

JL: Can you remember Bacchus passing the baton to you?

AB: I honestly don't remember ever getting up onto the table and leading the song as it has traditionally been done over the last 15 or 20 years. It was January 1984 and Bacchus had announced his retirement, so we all decided to hop into a few beers that night to celebrate what had been a great career. I reckon it was that night that we had the conversation to try and preserve the song.

JL: When do you remember singing the song?

AB: Well, I've wracked my brains since you asked me and I can't remember the song until Boony did it in 1989 in England after we won the First Test at Leeds. While it has become one of those fantastic Australian traditions it was still very flimsy back then. The truth is we didn't win a lot of games in that period before '89. I don't know how we even remembered the words because we had sung it so few times. One of my favourite images, which was captured, is of Boony on the table singing the song. I would love to hear Boony's account of how he resurrected the song, even remembering the words. Maybe he researched it from Bacchus. There was a little dead period which coincided with a real lull in our performances. Guys were coming and going from the team, or maybe the tradition was broken with World Series cricket. We lost our way a bit in that time and some of our great traditions got shelved: those very special moments like the cap presentations. Because of World Series cricket, all the guys who had the tradition moved to a different side of the fence and all the young guys like me just didn't know any better and it took a while for it to reappear. We definitely took our eye off the ball for a few years.

JL: Do you think the song is important?

AB: Oh yeah, I think it has become a really good tradition. The song is now a must-do thing when you win. The handing over of the baggy green cap, and the team song, are absolutely fantastic to ensure the traditions of Australian cricket.

12. Trenchtown

The 1995 tour of the West Indies had been memorable because of our great team achievement, but the 1999 tour would be a personal turning point for me. The cricket was as close and exhilarating as four years before, but this time I was in the middle of things, on the field as well as off. The series began at Port of Spain in Trinidad, where we won easily, rolling the Windies for just 51 runs in their second innings—their lowest score in 71 years of Test match cricket—thanks to Glenn McGrath (who took 5 for 28) and Jason Gillespie (4 for 18).

The Test had finished a day and a half early, which meant two things. Firstly, we had more time to celebrate that night, and secondly, we had an extra day in town with nothing organised. The next morning, slightly the worse for wear but still exhilarated, we headed to a small island for lunch. In the afternoon, some of the blokes chose to stay around the beach and take it easy, but a few of us decided to head offshore for some big-game fishing.

Steve Waugh, Matthew Elliott and I were sitting up the top of the boat with the skipper as we headed out of the bay towards open sea. The conversation turned to seasickness, because we could see a long, slow rolling swell in front of us. Being a West Australian, I grew up on the ocean, and this looked much like the swell through Gage Road off Fremantle. Tugga had a boyhood in Sydney and reckoned he was prepared, but Matthew was from Melbourne and I'm not sure what sort of experiences he'd had at sea. Anyway, he insisted that he'd be fine but twenty minutes later he began to yawn. Tugga and I looked at each other, knowing what was coming next. Yawning is almost certainly followed by a huge vomit.

Sure enough, within ten minutes or so, Matthew was hurling all over the place and couldn't stop. For the next three hours, as we trawled without success for sailfish, he remained curled up in the foetal position, vomiting repeatedly. There could have been nothing left in his stomach. Eventually, the captain called it quits and said we'd turn for home, at which Matthew sat up for the first time and whispered, 'Thank God for that.'

Right at that moment, all three lines went off together—*zing!*— as they were taken by three giant fish below the surface. This is what we'd been waiting for all afternoon. We jumped into action but the fun lasted only a few minutes, as one of the fish crossed the other three lines and they all snapped.

The skipper wasn't dejected. 'Well,' he said, rubbing his hands together, 'that's just what we wanted. We can't let them get away now. I think we'll hang around for a while.'

'No, no, no,' Matthew groaned, collapsing back into a heap.

We continued to trawl for another hour, while Matthew continued to dry-retch in the bottom of the boat. We didn't catch a thing, having not even a nibble after those thrilling few minutes of action.

Eventually, we headed back to the marina, much to Matthew's exhausted delight. He stepped—or crawled—ashore and was the happiest man alive. But the fun wasn't over. We then had to get on a bus to be taken back to the hotel. We had to stop at least five times so Matthew could throw up whatever was left. I have never seen a sicker human being in my life.

● ● ●

Kingston, the capital of Jamaica, is not a sleepy backwater, as some other venues were, but is a strange mix of vibrant success, with its famed reggae music, and a whiff of danger that you can almost taste the moment you step into the street. Danger was exactly what I found on the day I arrived.

We'd unpacked, had a brief training run and familiarised ourselves with the venue, Sabina Park, and by late afternoon I was peckish. I decided to walk up the street to a burger place I'd spotted from the team bus. It was only a few hundred metres away and the streets were buzzing with people, so I wasn't worried for my safety.

As I began walking a big Jamaican man fell into step beside me. When I say big, I actually mean huge—he was probably as tall as Curtly Ambrose, was covered in tattoos, probably weighed 140 kilograms and had arms the size of my legs. He said nothing as we walked and I kept my head down, hoping he would go away.

But he waited outside the burger shop as I ordered, and then fell into step with me again as we walked back. By then I was walking a little quicker.

When we got back to the hotel, he said his first words to me. 'That'll be ten dollars.'

I looked up at this mammoth man with his hand stretched out and asked the obvious question: 'What for?'

He looked down at me impassively. 'Security.'

I paid him, waiting until I got back to the safety of my room before trying to work out whether he was protecting me from others or from himself.

The Test at Sabina Park was just as confusing. Brian Lara went out to toss the coin with Tugga. To say he was under the pump from the cricket-loving West Indies would be an understatement, and it looked like this could be his last Test as captain. He confirmed as much to Tugga, saying, 'Thank god this will be the last time I ever have to put up with this shit.' Beware the wounded tiger!

We began very shakily (me included), and Steve Waugh's century was the only shining light as we were bowled out for 256 on the first day. The only good point was that we had an hour or so to bowl at them; as always, this meant we had everything to gain and the West Indies had everything to lose.

They were 4 for 37 at stumps and it looked like we were going to run over the top of them, as we had in Trinidad. But Brian Lara had other ideas, launching into one of his greatest innings the next day. He scored 213, dominating a 322-run partnership with Jimmy Adams (94) to turn a likely deficit into a 175-run lead. Then we collapsed, thanks to a great debut by an off-spinner named Nehemiah Perry, who took five wickets, and the West Indies squared the series with an emphatic ten-wicket victory.

The match was over early on the fourth morning, which meant we had a spare day in Kingston before moving on to Barbados for the Third Test. There was nothing to celebrate that night, and instead of having a few beers in commiseration with the boys, I ended up going to dinner with two of our chief destroyers, Jimmy Adams and Nehemiah Perry.

I'd known Jimmy for a few years; we were linked by a common association with my batting coach, Neil 'Noddy' Holder. His friends lived in a big white house in the Blue Mountains that overlook the city of Kingston and had views out across the ocean. We sat around having a laugh after dinner, and for some reason Jimmy began telling me about Kingston's infamous ghetto area, a suburb called Trenchtown. The stories he told about the drugs and gang warfare there made it sound like the scene of a Hollywood movie, a world away from the seemingly carefree style of the West Indies Test side and their equally flamboyant followers. Instead, Trenchtown was a slum of concrete houses, a place most outsiders, especially white men, wouldn't dare to enter.

I got home about one in the morning and was roused the next day at seven-thirty by a phone call from our team manager, Steve 'Brute' Bernard.

'Sorry to wake you so early, JL,' he began, as I struggled to wake up. 'Tugga's going into a place called Trenchtown today and thought you might like to go along.'

I was awake in a shot. This must be a prank call, I thought, but how could they have known about my conversation the night before? But Brute insisted he was serious. As usual, Steve Waugh wanted to get out and see the real world and, as only he could do, he'd managed to 'get permission' from the local warlords to visit. It sounded unbelievable but I was keen to go and see for myself.

I had a sense that I was going to see the equivalent of the Bronx in New York, but it was quite different. The area sits, dry, flat and baked brown, between the city centre and the coast. It's bounded by three main roads and a major cemetery, beyond which you can just hear the sounds of the ocean, but in fact the beach is taken up with concrete shipyards and docks.

For many music lovers, Trenchtown is the home of reggae and reverberates with the raw sound and bitter lyrics of musicians like Bob Marley and Peter Tosh, who were boyhood friends in the neighbourhood. Marley lived in First Street and life was horrendously difficult. He often starved and at one stage slept on a wooden bench.

It was evident from the moment we arrived that it would have been a mistake to venture anywhere near Trenchtown without the clearance—the invitation—Tugga had gained. The men were big and, although friendly, were clearly on edge. This was their turf, and we didn't belong. But they relaxed a little after a while and even let us take some photos, happy enough to meet some famous sports people. We took photos with our digital cameras, and even the big gangsters were blown away by the fact they could see themselves instantly. Suddenly there was a competition to see who could show off the biggest scars and war wounds for the camera. I remember the roughness of their faces, but mostly I remember the kids, a dozen of them playing in an abandoned car not far from Marley's old home. They seemed happy but they had almost nothing, and they knew it. It was something I always struggled with.

Thanks largely to Steve Waugh, I have seen many of the poorer areas of the cities where we've played Test cricket. It never failed to leave a mark on me, reinforcing the fact that I am a lucky man to have lived the life I have, and to have had the opportunities to achieve the most I can.

The Third Test, at Kensington Oval in Bridgetown, Barbados, was as amazing as the Second but for different reasons. Steve Waugh, as was becoming his habit in the West Indies, plundered the attack before suffering a bitter LBW decision one run short of his first double-century. Ricky Ponting also made a century and, after dismissing Brian Lara cheaply for once, we managed to take a 161-run first-innings lead. We seemed to be cruising towards a draw, at worst, which would ensure that we would retain the Frank Worrell Trophy after our grinding series win four years before.

But Courtney Walsh and Curtly Ambrose destroyed us yet again with their height and venom, reducing us to a second innings of 146, which gave us a lead of 307. It still seemed big enough, though, and with the Windies at 5 for 105, and later 8 for 248, we looked like we'd win comfortably on the fifth-day wicket. But Lara again had other ideas.

It's difficult to admire someone when they are carving you to pieces, but his innings was of such quality that I found myself in as much awe as desperation as he single-handedly created one of the great Test victories. The crowd danced with delight as Lara dispatched Jason Gillespie through the covers just after tea to bring up his 150 and win the game. He had scored half his team's runs and leaped into the throng of delirious fans, who stormed the ground to kiss the pitch. The Windies had won the game by a single wicket and gained a 2–1 lead in the series with one match remaining.

A decade later, Lara's remains one of the best innings I have seen. Like Shane Warne, the only way to describe Lara is as a freak—he was a cricketing genius. If I were down to my last dollar, I would pay to see him bat. He was a nightmare for opposing captains because of his ability to hit the ball into the gaps at will.

He was also the greatest sweeper of the cricket ball in the history of the game—in my time, anyway. He'd lap it fine, so we would put a fielder there to cover the shot. In response, he would sweep hard in front of square leg, so we would place another man there. You could almost see him smiling as he watched the changes, then he'd score a boundary just behind square or through midwicket, forcing us to strengthen the legside with another man. That field adjustment would, of course, give Lara gaps elsewhere, and sure enough he would soon step back to give himself room and carve the ball through the offside.

The whole thing was like a game of chess, played in his unique style. He ignored the textbooks, instead playing with a distinctive high backlift and an emphatic movement across the wicket. As Sir Donald Bradman had written to me, you should 'never become a slave to coaching'.

The whole of the West Indies partied hard that night. Just three weeks after being routed for 51, their team was now favoured to take back the Frank Worrell Trophy. We were forced to rebuild. Our team meeting the night after the Test was pretty heavy. We had to acknowledge that our team unity and direction had suffered because of overconfidence. We had expected to win, we'd relaxed too much and so we were now in trouble. Steve Waugh took the lead, as a captain should, and demanded that things change. He never used to say much, even when he was angry, but the dozen or so words he delivered then left no one under any illusions about the consequences, should we fail to live up to our team expectations.

We agreed to institute the 'Ian Chappell rule': what happens before midnight is your business, and what happens after midnight is the team's business. Tugga hated the idea of curfews but he had no choice. We had to regroup and win.

The biggest revelation, though, was the seemingly outrageous decision to drop Shane Warne for the final Test. Warney's form hadn't been great, but leaving the game's greatest spin bowler out of your side for such an important game looked suicidal. Shane certainly felt aggrieved by it, publicly threatening to retire and brooding about it for some time afterwards.

Although I would never consider myself in the same league as

Warney, I can understand his feelings, having been dropped several times. In particular, I know the psychological impact that having your value questioned can have. What made it worse was that, as vice captain, he'd sat through the selection process with Tugga and our coach, Geoff Marsh, and been forced to plead for his place. But the truth was that we couldn't play two leg-spinners against Lara, who was almost single-handedly murdering us, and Warney had only taken 2 for 268 in the three Tests to that point. By contrast, Stuart MacGill had taken 7 for 220, and would take another five in the final Test.

Shane's later recollection in his autobiography resonated greatly with me. He wrote:

It hurt me greatly to be dropped. I felt that my overall record in tough situations and big matches should have counted in my favour. All the way through my career I had produced when it mattered and I thought the selectors should have backed me.

The pitch on day one made life difficult, and we barely reached 200 runs on the first day. Thanks largely to Tugga and some lusty late hitting by Colin Miller, we staggered past 300 for our first innings. In reply, the West Indies made just 222, despite another amazing innings from Lara, who, in contrast to his careful and skilful century in Barbados, clubbed us for 100 off just 84 deliveries, with fifteen fours and three sixes. His second 50 was scored off just 21 balls.

Queenslander Adam Dale (he was actually a Victorian) had been brought into our side to replace Jason Gillespie, who'd been injured. It was only his second Test, and he found himself bowling against the rampant Lara, who took a liking to his normally tight swing bowling. Adam bowled one over to Lara early in his innings and was spanked for ten runs. He was taken off, and he was probably wishing he could stay out of the attack.

Just after tea, though, Tugga brought Adam back on. By this time Lara had scored 77 from just 73 balls and looked, as one commentator suggested, as though he had a plane to catch. This is how Cricinfo.com's ball-by-ball coverage described the next over:

35.1 Dale to Lara, FOUR, on drive.

35.2 Dale to Lara, SIX, pulls it away over the forward square leg, how predictable.

35.3 Dale to Lara, no run, woah! There's an unusual event, saved in the infield at mid on.

35.4 Dale to Lara, FOUR, hammered thru the mid off, the fence was lucky to contain that one.

35.5 Dale to Lara, FOUR, full toss, Dale was totally rattled, outside the off stump, slams to the long off boundary, one bounce over the rope.

35.6 Dale to Lara, FOUR, pulled thru the mid wicket, yet again, another 4. That's 22 off the over, amazing stuff.

What a hammering—22 runs off the over. Lara had now scored 99 from 79 deliveries. Thankfully, he was out a few balls later after getting his century.

As for Adam Dale, the poor bugger was ashen-grey when we got back to the change room. He said he wasn't feeling well, had almost fallen asleep and had no energy. A few of us thought that was an excuse and that he simply wasn't handling the pressure. In retrospect, though, our assessment was totally unfair. We found out a couple of days later—after he'd bowled in the second innings and taken three wickets for the match—that he had contracted pneumonia. I doubt Adam remembers the match fondly. He'd had to bowl on a flat wicket with no swing against the great Brian Lara, who had just come off two of the great Test innings. Not only that, but he was crook as a dog and ended up in hospital. There is no fun in that.

Our second innings would be a turning point for me, however. I had scored my first Test century in Peshawar, Pakistan, the previous October, then I'd followed it with a century in Adelaide during the 1998–99 Ashes series. I'd been proud of these, naturally, but I still had a nagging doubt in my mind about whether I belonged in Test cricket. Was I really good enough? This time I scored 127 when it mattered most, with my team 2–1 down in the series. My innings was the difference between us presenting a formidable challenge to the West Indies or handing the match to them on a plate. Not only that, but I was playing against Courtney Walsh and Curtly Ambrose on their home turf.

They were an awesome combination. I hated facing Walsh. He was as accurate as Glenn McGrath but probably a yard quicker, and I had no idea how to score a run off him. Ambrose was a nightmare—the smiling assassin. In my first Test I drove him down the ground for three runs, and I reckon that was the last time I drove him in the fifteen or so Tests I played against him. If he hit you on the body, he'd smile; if you played and missed, he'd smile; and if you hit him for four, he'd smile. If he got you out, he'd do his double hand-clap, and if you happened to glance back at him on your way to the pavilion, he'd be smiling. When I reached my third Test century just before drinks on the fourth morning of the match, it was the moment I finally proved to myself that I was good enough to be at this level.

The sporting world is full of clichés. We often advise young guys as they're coming through the ranks to 'back themselves'. What does that mean, anyway? Are we suggesting they go out and slog the ball in the hope that nothing will go to hand? Of course not. It takes time and experience to understand the concept of self-belief, not just in cricket but in life. Until you've been in the middle—in the cauldron—and felt the pressures and devised your own way to handle them, the words don't mean much. On that day in Antigua, against the best and when it mattered most, I learned that I could trust myself.

We lost our last eight wickets for just 83 runs, but the 388-run target we'd set was always going to be difficult for the West Indies. By stumps on the fourth day they were 4 for 105, and with Lara back in the pavilion another grandstand win seemed highly improbable. It became all but impossible when Jimmy Adams was out in the third over of the final day. In the end, they were all out for 211.

Our celebrations were hefty, as you would expect. We'd been mightily challenged, fought back and won. One of the things I love about Test cricket—and it's something people often don't understand—is that you have to work so hard for success. That's why we celebrate hard. In this series, we'd been a bit complacent and had had to reassess, knuckle down and work really hard to ensure we retained the Frank Worrell Trophy. I enjoyed Test series like that a lot more than when we were winning easily.

13. Bulawayo Express

There are times when the hard slog of training, dieting and planning for Test cricket has to give way to something a little less strict. It's one of the reasons our celebrations after a victory were so important; they were a few hours when we were free to let our hair down, without the constraints of diet and behaviour—to a degree. We were permitted to feel as if we had achieved something special.

Times have certainly changed from the day I first stepped foot into the Australian change rooms. Back then, my first meeting with my new team-mates had been at the bar of the Hindley Park Royal in Adelaide. A few pre-game beers were pretty much the routine of many of the senior players, as were a few beers and a club sandwich at the end of each day's play.

These days however, there is no such freedom as the players dedicate themselves to the task ahead. Cold beer has been replaced by the strict hydration therapy of water, sports drinks and massage, while video analysis and exacting strategic meetings have eclipsed the good old days of a chat in the bar to nut out the best way to get over the line during the upcoming contest.

That said, there were still a few rare occasions where our pre-match preparation took a twist. The story of the Bulawayo Express is a great example. It was a night that even the Ice Man—our captain, Steve Waugh—reckoned was one of the most enjoyable of his serious and illustrious career.

It was October 1999 and we had arrived in Zimbabwe for a couple of matches, including a one-off Test match—the first ever between our nations—and three one-day internationals. As important as the twenty-day tour was for the international game, it would be true to say that none of us were really looking forward it. It was coming off the back of a tough six-week tour of Sri Lanka, where we'd lost the series 1–0 and Geoff Marsh had announced his resignation as Australian coach, so we were looking forward to getting home.

Adding to our reluctance was the fact that we had arrived in the capital, Harare, after a marathon 38-hour flight through five countries, apparently because of a sponsorship deal. Tugga was ropeable when we got off the plane. This is what he told the local media; it gives you an impression of what sometimes happens behind the scenes:

I actually thought it was Wednesday but someone told me it was Thursday, so that about sums it up at this stage. I don't know, but it will probably see me out; any more trips like this will see me out. It's ridiculous. It takes me seven to ten days to get over [the jet-lag] and that's when the Test match finishes, so to me it doesn't make sense.

I felt the same way. My form in Sri Lanka had been terrible, with Murali having me all at sea. Without doubt, the toughest bowler I ever faced in Test cricket was Muttiah Muralitharan. He gave me more sleepless nights than Shoaib Akhtar, Curtly Ambrose or Courtney Walsh ever did. Obviously, Murali couldn't hurt me physically, but he definitely got to me mentally—I had no idea how I should play him. The harder I tried, the worse it got. I couldn't pick him out of the hand, so in the end I just tried sweeping everything. He was a magician. His action was such that my mind was in a frenzy every time he sent his magic dust down the wicket.

On the one hand, I knew he was going to spin the ball away from me, as an off-spin bowler; but on the other, his wristy action looked as though he was going to bowl leg-spinners and bring the ball back towards my stumps. Imagine my confusion—I know the ball is going to spin away, but something in my brain keeps telling me that the ball should spin back in. All in all, this confusion had created my worst nightmare, resulting in a top score of 32 and an average of a bit under 13. My confidence was shot. I was tired, missing home and my young family, and generally feeling pretty sorry for myself.

Still rubbing the sleep out of our eyes and trying to loosen our backs from the flights, our first match was a lead-up game against a President's XI in the regional city of Bulawayo. With its rather forbidding name—which, roughly translated, means 'a place a slaughter'—Bulawayo is a multicultural city of over a million people. It uses at least three languages and is the hub of Zimbabwe's fragile business community.

The match was a three-day affair. Although we were using it to acclimatise to our new surroundings, we were already match-fit—or match-weary, to be more accurate. We were more interested in visiting the famous Victoria Falls than in playing another game of cricket before the Test match. Stuart MacGill, who was twelfth man in the tour game, was put in charge of organising a trip to the Falls. We had 72 hours between the tour match and the Test back in Harare, so Stuie was under a bit of pressure.

We batted first against the President's XI, and, after an unusually cold start to the day, the skies cleared by mid-morning and the sun warmed the ground. The blue skies and clear air of Bulawayo were a welcome change from the tough Sri Lankan conditions, and it was nice to play against lesser opposition on a hard and bouncy pitch. Any reprieve from my Sri Lankan experience was a pleasing one, and with every passing minute at the crease I was able to relax and find some of the touch that had been eluding me. I ended up top-scoring with 148. The Waugh twins both made centuries in the second innings, Damien Fleming and Shane Warne cleaned up the Zimbabweans and we won inside three days by 244 runs.

In between running out the drinks, Stuie MacGill had investigated the best way for us to get to Victoria Falls. He suggested taking the evening train through the night, seeing the Falls, then flying to Harare on a privately chartered aircraft later the next day. The only difficulty was that we would have to head straight to the station from the ground if we were to make the train.

When we got to the station, Stuie had everything sorted. He'd bought the tickets, and had some eskies filled with cold beer, spirits and soft drinks, and another with what might have passed for party food—sandwiches and chips and the like. It wasn't exactly a healthy diet, but there weren't many other options and, hey, this was Stuie's first crack at being a tour coordinator.

Joining us on the trip were Steve Waugh, Ricky Ponting, Matthew Hayden, Glenn McGrath, Greg Blewett, Simon Katich, Matthew Nicholson and our fitness trainer, Dave Missen. The fact that our captain came along may be a surprise to some, but Tugga loved these side-trips. He actually encouraged them, instilling in us the sense that we should get out of our comfort zone and actually *see* the places we were visiting.

For Steve, touring wasn't just about cricket; it was also about experiencing life and the world around us. It was too easy to sit in a comfortable hotel and ride in air-conditioned buses to our venues and dinners, where we were locked away from the real cities outside. The Vic Falls trip was a bit like seeing the Taj Mahal in India, Trenchtown in Jamaica, Robben Island off Cape Town, South Africa, where Nelson Mandela had spent 27 years behind bars, and the slums of India. All these places were fascinating in their own ways, and I always felt I would be a fool to ignore the opportunity to see them.

Within the first half an hour on the Bulawayo 'Express', we quickly realised that this trip was going to take a lot longer than a few hours. Victoria Falls was over 400 kilometres west of Bulawayo and the train was chugging along like an old man with a Zimmer frame. We seemed to stop at every tiny town on the map, and often just to allow a train to pass the other way. Not that we were complaining, mind you.

We had a bar set up in one carriage and a game of cards going in the other. Those who weren't playing sat around relaxing, listening to our one and only CD, *The Best of the Eagles*. Our surroundings were straight out of the British colonial empire—wood-panelled carriages with brass fittings, built in Britain and still carrying the 'RR' logo of Rhodesian Railways. It sounds more luxurious than it really was, because the carriages hadn't really been maintained and consequently were a little rattly and rickety, but their effect was mesmerising.

Our gentle progress through the darkening African bush, where elephant herds wandered across the railway lines and prides of lions peered nonchalantly at us from beneath the trees of the great national parks, was taking us to another world. What struck me most, as the sun melted away, was the richness of the African night—the beautiful black, velvety African skies were studded with a million stars. These breathtaking skies, combined with the pungency of the dirt outside, were as inebriating as the cocktail mixes coming from Stuie's makeshift bar.

Nature and the cabin room activities weren't the only attractions along the way. As the evening wore on, we began to notice a common theme amongst the locals as we pulled into the stations of towns like Hwange and Dete—their headwear. It was like a fashion parade outside our windows, with most of the people milling around wearing variously sized and extremely colourful hats. Then someone came up with the idea that we should have a hat contest.

Things became competitive, and we hung out of the windows offering people money for their hats. Our efforts to secure the best hat caused such a commotion that the passengers in neighbouring carriages began to notice what was going on. Before long, we had people lined up outside our cabin offering to sell their hats, sparking an impromptu auction.

I bought a jaunty black and white cap from an African guy who must have been twice my size. It cost me 400 Zimbabwean dollars, which at the time was the equivalent of about US$20, although nowadays it'd be worthless. On that joyous night, however, both buyer and seller were very pleased with the deal.

I don't think we ever chose a winner, but the auctions and the fun of our dress-up party lightened the mood even further. In fact, it turned into a full-blown party. We'd been giving Stuie a bit of stick earlier in the night about his organising skills—particularly about the lack of 'express' in the Bulawayo Express, but as it turned out, and in contrast to our plane flights from Sri Lanka the week before, this long-haul trip was a blessing in disguise. We sat back, relaxed and enjoyed each other's company. I still wear my 'baggy black and white' occasionally as a reminder of a very happy night.

Normally, I would never have done something like this before a Test match, but I'd had such a rotten time in Sri Lanka that I knew in my heart that I needed some downtime. Sometimes it takes a degree of courage to let go and simply go with the flow, especially when you're not performing at your best, but it can actually pay dividends. For me, the wide-open plains of Africa, with its big skies and jacaranda trees, which reminded me so much of home, was the perfect tonic.

Others had different reasons to get away. Matthew Nicholson, for example, had been brought into the side for the Bulawayo match but had had an absolute shocker, bowling eighteen wides and five no-balls. To his credit, and instead of hiding away, he came on the trip for the mateship and the chance to put his bad days behind him. MacGill and Katich had played almost no cricket during the entire tour, so they, too, needed something to help them feel part of the group.

Scientifically, it might not have been great preparation for a Test match, but I learned that night that methods of preparation can vary. The power of the night's camaraderie would be of more benefit than another team meeting or net session. We were chugging through the African veldt in a rickety old train, munching on Cheezels and, as the night wore on, drinking warmish beer. The carriage turned into a virtual nightclub on the other side of midnight, filling with other passengers who came to join us as we partied. At one stage I crawled into a bunk bed to try to catch a few winks, but I gave up because of the thick cigar smoke that clung to the ceiling.

The train finally pulled in at the Victoria Falls station around seven the next morning. There's a photo of me and Tugga sitting at a table as we arrived. I'm wearing the hat I'd bought, and my sunglasses cover the telltale bloodshot eyes of a big night and little sleep. There are some locals peering through the windows at what must have been a carriage full of sick white blokes.

We stumbled off the train into the sunlight and staggered to our hotel, which laid on the most amazing breakfast you'd ever seen. It was just the thing we needed. Our tiredness disappeared and we perked up for the walk across to the Falls, me still wearing my funny hat. The trek was worth the effort. Mosi-oa-Tunya, which means something like 'the smoke that thunders', is one of the Seven Wonders of the World—a giant curtain of water with a constant deep roar, which plunges into a gorge and creates a plume of misty, cooling spray. For us, the icy sprays of water offered welcome relief from the sun and the hangovers of the night before.

In the early afternoon we retired to the hotel courtyard and flopped in easy chairs for a few hours of much-needed sleep before the flight to Harare, which, thankfully, was uneventful. We arrived back from the 1300-kilometre round trip just in time for our team meeting, much to the relief of our stand-in coach, Allan Border, who was worried he would have to lead his first pre-Test as coach without his captain and a number of his senior players.

The meeting went smoothly, but we found out afterwards that our luggage hadn't arrived from Bulawayo. Apparently, the van had been delayed by a flat tyre somewhere between the two cities, leaving us to attend an official function that night at the Australian High Commission in T-shirts, jeans or shorts, and thongs or runners. But our less than official attire fitted perfectly with our relaxed state of mind from the previous 48 hours.

Our performance on the field wasn't affected, though, and we beat a gallant Zimbabwe by ten wickets inside four days. Perhaps Cheezels, Zambezi Lager, silly hats and all-night train journeys should be used more often in Test preparation! It's hardly likely, in these days of professionalism, but it could be worth a try—it was definitely perfect for us on that great night in beautiful Zimbabwe.

14. You never know

Maybe I was destined to be a Test batsman for Australia. It's a big call, but look at what happened on the day I was born— 21 November 1970. South African great Barry Richards scored 356 for South Australia at the WACA in a Sheffield Shield match against Western Australia. It was one of the great first-class innings, and the match was a showpiece of the sport, including players like Ian and Greg Chappell, Rod Marsh and Dennis Lillee. If I draw the bow a little longer, my Test number was 354, which makes the effort of Richards—who opened the batting, by the way—all the more prophetic. Ian Chappell made 129 in the same innings but it was obscured by Richards' brilliance, just as my first Test century in Peshawar would be when Mark Taylor made a triple-century. My batting coach, Bob Meuleman, was also in the side that day, as was Tony Mann, who would ring me 23 years later to tell me I was playing for Australia.

Okay, enough already. My birthday falls in the cricket season, which was great for presents when I was a kid, but not so as an adult because I was rarely at home to celebrate. There were many times I was playing and even batting on my birthday, and while I had some decent birthday knocks over the years, only one stands out as memorable.

My birthday couldn't have been further from my mind when I arrived in Hobart in November 1999 for the Second Test against Pakistan. I was coming off my rotten tour of Sri Lanka a few months before; I'd then wasted a promising innings against Zimbabwe with a runout. I'd also been dismissed early in the First Test against Pakistan at the Gabba. The media was on my back, my place was under question, and once again I was doubting my ability.

It was Steve Waugh who noticed how much pressure I was under. The team was having breakfast the day before the Test when he pulled me aside. Tugga never used to talk much, but when he did it was serious. We sat down away from the others.

'I don't want you to read anything in the press or listen to anything they say,' he said, obviously aware that journalists had been calling for my head.

I looked at him and thought, 'That's easy for you to say.'

'The important thing is that I want you in the team, your teammates want you in the team, John Buchanan wants you in the team and the selectors want you in the team,' he continued. 'You're the best number three in Australia, and I want you to go out there and show us why you're in the team.'

I was stunned, but so grateful. Tugga didn't have to do what he did. Great leader that he was, he had recognised that a member of his team needed a boost, even if it was in private. Here was the captain, this legend, telling me that I was wanted in the side and I was his man.

We had a net session later that day. After my hit, I walked past Tugga, who was doing a quick media conference before heading back into the change rooms.

As I passed by, one of the reporters asked him, 'Do you have a message for Justin Langer, because his place in the side must be under threat?'

Tugga hadn't seen me, and I felt embarrassed that the question had been asked within earshot of me. I put my head down and kept walking. But I heard his answer nevertheless: 'Yeah, I have a message for Justin. Stop reading your shit.'

I kept walking and didn't hear his other comments, but apparently he repeated what he'd told me that morning. Not only was he praising me in private, but now he was publicly backing me. I had to repay his faith.

I was given another boost when my father, Colin, came to Hobart the night before the match. I suspect he reckoned I needed a boot in the arse, to sharpen me up for the game. He called it a morale boost, but that usually meant a few comments like, 'Don't feel sorry for yourself. It's all in your head—it always is.'

Silly as this might sound, I found it one of the comforting things about Dad. Mum was a softie who took me to every game and kept a scrapbook with every article ever written about me, while Dad was a successful businessman, a handy player himself and as tough as nails. Their good-guy-bad-guy act always worked a treat.

We bowled out Pakistan for 222 on the first day and made a good start in our innings, so I should have felt pretty good when I walked out to bat on day two. Instead, I was really nervous. Not only was I under pressure for my place, but I was also facing one of the best bowling line-ups in the game. It was a bit like when I'd faced the West Indies in my first Test back in 1993. Pakistan had Wasim

Akram, the best left-arm fast bowler of all time; the Rawalpindi Express, Shoaib Akhtar, the fastest bowler in world cricket; and Waqar Younis, the world's best reverse-swing bowler. They also had a superb spin attack, led by Saqlain Mushtaq, who was the first off-spinner to master the doosra.

That day Dad had turned up dressed in black trousers and a black shirt. The one thing he forgot—apart from his sense of colour—was a tie, which was a problem when he was invited into the committee room for lunch. I ended up lending him my team tie, the bright red one we wore with our striped green and gold blazers. When I went out to bat, I could see him standing at the window in the rooms in the direction of square leg, his red tie standing out like a beacon against his black shirt. Every time I looked up, there was my old man.

I took centre guard and looked up. Waqar was off his long run, not unlike Ian Bishop years before. He started steaming in and I began mentally repeating my mantra, 'Head forward, watch the ball, head forward, watch the ball.' I knew this could be the beginning of the end but I tried not to be distracted.

But as Waqar approached the wicket and turned side-on to let his fireball go, I held up my hand and stepped away, apologising profusely. I had no choice; a seagull had flown over my head and, believe it or not, dropped something on the pitch in front of me, just short of a good length. Here I was, my Test future on the line, with Waqar running in from Melbourne, and this happened. I couldn't believe it.

I don't know if the TV cameras picked it up but I could see something square and yellow sitting on the pitch. It was a bloody slice of Kraft cheese. 'You've got to be kidding me,' I thought. I picked it up and wondered what to do. I couldn't drop it off the side of the pitch because the gulls were feeding. Instead, I flung it like a Frisbee back behind the infuriated wicket-keeper.

I had to go through my process again, nervous as hell, my heart pumping, my cricket life on the line. Yet somehow I realised that the bird's intrusion might have been a lucky break. After all, the seagull was the symbol of the Scarborough Cricket Club, where I played my junior cricket and I'm a life member. (I must add here with some shame that, in 2004, during a match in New Zealand, I killed not one but two seagulls with a full-blooded cut shot. It was an accident, of course, although I could later quip that I'd managed to kill two birds with one stone.)

Anyway, having disposed of the cheese, I took my guard in a much more positive frame of mind. As I did so, a piece of advice that Steve Waugh had been hammering me with came to mind. 'Get out at them, get out at them,' he'd been saying. What he meant was to seize my destiny with my own hands; to take the challenge to the bowlers, rather than letting them dictate to me. To trust myself—in particular, my technique and my instincts.

I watched Waqar turn at the top of his mark and steam in again. This time I was ready and positive. The ball was full and straight, I stepped forward and—*crack*—smacked the ball straight back past him for four runs. I felt alive again, and I was away.

I batted pretty well, moving past a half-century. I thought I was on my way to a ton, but I got a rotten decision and was given out, caught at bat-pad, for 59. I was filthy about the decision, and the umpire, Peter 'Porky' Parker, knew it. Still, it was a welcome score at a tough time. Then I watched as we collapsed from 1 for 191 to be all out for 246. We had a lead of 24 but it should have been much more. Pakistan was back in the game.

By chance, Porky got in a lift with me at the hotel that night.

We didn't socialise with the umpires during a match, for obvious reasons, but it was impossible not to have some form of interaction off the field. As we were riding up to our respective floors, he turned to me and confessed he'd made a mistake that day with my dismissal. The decision stood, of course, but he was admitting to being human. His words, as I recall them a decade later, were simple: 'Sorry, mate—I messed that one up. I'm really sorry.'

I waved him away, pleased that he had at least acknowledged the error and hoping that my luck might change.

• • •

A century by the laconically brilliant Inzamam-ul-Haq put Pakistan in command of the Test on day three, and a stubborn last-wicket partnership early on day four boosted their innings to 392, setting us a target of 369 to win. It was a herculean task under any circumstances. Only five teams in the history of the game had scored more to win a Test match, and Australia had only scored more than 300 to win five times in 120 years.

Michael Slater and Greg Blewett put on 39 for the first wicket, then I came in at number three. Greg and I put on another 42 and were going steadily; we felt we were in good shape to make a fist of the chase. But then the wheels began to fall off. It's often more realistic to think of a score with two extra wickets down, and that's exactly what happened. Our 1 for 81 became 3 for 81 in no time.

Greg got out to seam bowler Azhar Mahmood for the second time in the match, then Mahmood removed Mark Waugh with his next ball. Steve Waugh and I slowly pushed the score to 125 after tea, but then it happened again. Tugga got out, then Ricky Ponting came and went within a few balls, scoring his second duck of the match and his third in a row. Now we were 5 for 126, still needing 243 more to win and with no recognised batsmen to come. The situation looked pretty hopeless. To compound matters, I was nursing a crushed finger courtesy of Shoaib, who'd hit it with a full toss clocked at over 150 kilometres per hour.

To be honest, at that moment I was thinking about my own position in the side rather than of winning or even drawing the match. I'd scored 59 in the first innings and was on the verge of another half-century. If I could hang around and perhaps be not out at the end, then I figured I'd be alright for the next Test.

Gilly, who was coming through the gate, was only in his second Test match. Even though he'd made a good impression in Brisbane, nobody could have foreseen the amazing impact he would have on the game. If he or I got out, only the tailenders were left to keep the best bowling attack in the world at bay.

Trying to be positive, I greeted Gilly with, 'C'mon, mate. You never know. If we hang in here we could make history.'

Realistically, I was hoping we could make it through to stumps, which was an hour or so away. The forecast on the last day was for plenty of rain, which meant we might be able to save the game with some gutsy batting and a bit of luck.

Gilly nodded, smiled and then went about blasting 45 off 54 deliveries in that last hour of play. It was a portent of things to come over the next decade, as he turned a backs-against-the-wall situation into one with a skerrick of hope. I walked off having battled my way to 52. We were 5 for 188 and needed 181 more to pull off one of the game's greatest victories.

I was pretty pleased with myself as we headed back to the hotel, which looked out over the Hobart docks. I took Dad out that night for fish and chips by the dark, glassy water of the harbour. Gilly and

Steve Waugh joined us, but instead of being tense and worried, the expected downpour the next day seemed to relax us. I was so convinced that we'd probably saved the Test, and that I had probably saved my own place in the side, that I even allowed myself a glass of red wine over dinner. Well, after all, it was my 29th birthday.

I don't remember talking much about the game, and Dad remembers it the same way. He has never relished the limelight of having a son in the Australian Test side, always preferring to support me from the background, but I know he enjoyed being in the midst of something special that night. As things turned out, it was very special. After dinner I headed back to the hotel and slept like a baby.

Gilly watched the movie *Jerry Maguire* before he went to bed. He must have been more confident than me, because he was contemplating a victory dance like Cuba Gooding Jnr's if we won.

When I woke up the next morning, I drew back the heavy drapes and, as the Poms say, it was cracking flags. Instead of overcast skies and steady rain, the skies were blue and the clouds high. There would be no rain today. I had been lulled into a false sense of security by a weather forecast that was dead wrong. Now I knew we had a fight on our hands.

There wasn't any great excitement in the rooms that morning. Everyone felt the same—that the elements were conspiring against us because the promise of rain hadn't eventuated. How strange—cricketers wanting rain! In spite of this, I was relaxed. I'd made a few runs, I was used to the pitch and I had a sense of the game. I felt pretty good as Gilly and I walked out onto Bellerive Oval.

We decided to count the target down and see how far we got. I was counting the runs in lots of ten, and Gilly was counting the minutes in the same way. It helped keep us thinking and acting as if we had a chance. Counting time meant we were still in the game, and counting runs meant we were closer to victory.

The Pakistanis played into our hands by opening with their fourth-string bowlers, medium-pacer Azhar Mahmood and off-spinner Saqlain Mushtaq. I am still surprised about their decision on that fifth morning. With Waqar, Wasim and Shoaib at their disposal, the last thing I expected were some 'sighters' from Azhar Mahmood. Even though he was whippy and reverse-swung the ball, his slightly slower pace allowed us to play ourselves in. By the time the quicker men came on, we were set.

When I was on 76 I got a big nick to a delivery from Wasim Akram. I had swung hard and the sound could be heard around the ground. Dad heard it, my team-mates heard it—even the seagulls heard it! But I looked up to see umpire Parker shaking his head. Wasim was ropeable.

For years afterwards, I insisted that the sound everyone around the ground had heard was a dodgy bat handle. But it's been ten years now, so I'm prepared to admit here that, yes, I did nick the ball. It was a break that went my way, and I don't regret for an instant waiting for the umpire to make a decision.

It was only when we survived to lunch that I realised we really had a chance to win. The mood back in the sheds was more like that of a football change room. Everyone was pumped and telling us we could win it. They had music playing and even Tugga was agitated, tossing an orange worry ball from hand to hand. After lunch I walked out onto the ground with a newfound belief, as if I had the collective energy of all my team-mates.

Soon after play began I got hit on the chin by a Shoaib Akhtar bouncer. It hurt like hell but I just turned and grinned at him. There's a photo of it somewhere. I look crazed, my grin only made worse by a missing tooth I had from an injury early in my career. I always took the plate out when I batted because I couldn't chew gum otherwise. It left a gaping hole in the front of my mouth which made me look like a crim.

Gilly came down to have a chat. 'Mate, you're crazy,' he smiled.

I just looked at him. 'I love this stuff, Gilly. Bring it on! I bloody love it, and I'll smile at him every time he hits me because we can win this, and he knows it now.'

And that's exactly what happened. Shoaib kept hitting me and I kept smiling. It didn't matter—I knew we were going to win.

Gilly and I began talking between deliveries. The countdown had become a real race now, because we could see the finish line. When we were twenty or so runs from victory I did a fist-pump and made a Lleyton Hewitt 'C'mon' sign to the change room. It was completely out of character but my emotions were running so high. It was exhilarating. I had forgotten about my own glory because the team victory was so close.

Disappointingly, I got out with five runs to get, trying to hit Saqlain out of the park. But I wasn't upset—we had won. As I left the ground, I hugged Dad, who was still wearing my red tie. I felt a bit like Pat Cash climbing up into the stands after he won the 1987 Wimbledon men's singles final. I'll never forget the look on Tugga's face as I walked back into the change rooms. He was like a proud uncle, not saying much but with a look that said it all—I gave you the green light and you proved I was right. We learned later that the game had interrupted Parliament, and Prime Minister John Howard even wrote to us. It was such a freakish event.

As it turned out, it was probably my best Test innings. I had been lucky to survive the caught-behind chance, and Wasim had been justified in feeling aggrieved on the field. But, to give him his due, he later publicly accepted the decision and said his team had been beaten not by the decision but by the best batting partnership he'd seen during his illustrious career. It was a very sporting gesture from a true champion.

We celebrated well into the night in the change rooms. We blew the roof off the place singing the team song, then left in the team bus, most of us still in our whites and spikes. Where did we go after such a victory? McDonald's, of course! After all, it was not the night for healthy eating or sensible carb-loading. It must have been quite a sight, the Australian cricket team rocking up unannounced, all wearing our baggy greens and some of us still in our spikes and obviously a little worse for wear. We sat around eating Big Macs and laughing our heads off. I still can't believe that didn't make the TV news somewhere.

15. Straps, caps and slaps

One of the traditions of the Perth Test was a pre-match formal dinner. These events were part of the off-field expectations, if you will, of members of the Australian team; to be perfectly honest, they could be tedious. But they could be pleasant and even, on occasion, instructive, as I experienced on my return to Perth for the Pakistan Test of November 1999.

There is a myth about playing in a home Test. Yes, you get to sleep in your own bed and see your family, but the flipside is that you don't actually have much time to catch up with friends or be at home. In 1999, this was particularly true, as the weight of expectation and the demands for our time intensified after the heroics of Hobart. Gilly and I were wanted everywhere—we were two Perth boys who'd 'done good'.

Nevertheless, I arrived at the formal dinner in a great state of mind. It made a nice change not to worry about my place in the side, although I was still aware it was only really as secure as my next innings.

The guest speaker that night was the great Ric Charlesworth, the Bradman of the hockey field, a gold-medal-winning Olympic coach, a Sheffield Shield cricketer, a parliamentarian and a GP to boot. I'd met Ric a few times before, so after his speech I went over to shake his hand and say hello.

I didn't get the response I expected. Instead of a smile, he looked at me with a frown on his face. 'What on earth do you think you were doing in Hobart?'

'What do you mean?' I stammered, a bit taken aback after a week of plaudits.

'You got out with five runs to get. What were you thinking? You were soft, you made a mental error, and you should have gone on to finish the job for the team. You can't afford those lapses if you want to be a champion.' Ric's expression was deadly serious, and I walked away stunned.

I could have simply dismissed this as a rant from a former champion, but I realised pretty quickly what great advice it was. I was very lucky during my career to have had several levels of support, from my immediate family in the first place, but also from others such as Charlesworth, Noddy Holder, Steve Smith, Nigel Wray and the Meulemans, who always reminded me to keep perspective in the good times. Steve Waugh always insisted that the best approach was to level out your emotions so that you didn't plunge into a depression when things weren't working, but also to keep your feet on the ground when things were great.

I remember the 1999 Perth Test well, firstly because my run of good form continued, but not before I was reminded of just how good the Pakistan attack was at that time. We bundled them out before tea on the first day for 155, but Wasim Akram and Shoaib Akhtar then reduced us to 4 for 54 in the next hour. Ricky Ponting joined me at the crease, which was a very tense moment, given his run of three ducks in a row. You could sense the crowd holding its collective breath, waiting to see if Punter could break the sequence and rescue Australia from a precarious position. He answered the question very quickly with a perfect on-drive that rocketed to the boundary and signalled his intent.

The only thing that disturbed the next seven hours of play and a record 327-run partnership was the fastest over I ever witnessed. I use the word 'witnessed' deliberately, because I was standing at the non-striker's end for the six deliveries Shoaib slung at Punter, who still reminds me of how I always politely declined the single we could have taken as each ball spiralled above his head to the wicket-keeper, Moin Khan.

While waiting for Shoaib to walk back to his mark, I'd stroll down the pitch with a grin on my face to let Punter know just how quick the last ball had looked from where I was standing. The speed of a bowler is, of course, judged through the air, but visually you are struck by the pace off the wicket. I was so in awe of Shoaib's deliveries, which were taking off like aeroplanes, that I was giggling like an idiot. Those who remembered back that far likened Shoaib's speed that day to Jeff Thomson's during the 1974–75 Perth Ashes Test, when he destroyed England.

We survived Shoaib's spell and then shredded the bowling. Punter answered his critics with a chanceless 197 to take man-of-the-match honours, and I was on a roll, scoring 144 to secure the man-of-the-series award. After so many years in the wilderness, I felt like I had finally arrived.

● ● ●

Everything was going well for me off the field as well. Jessica was an energetic two-year-old, and my second daughter, Ali-Rose, had her first birthday during the Pakistan series. We needed a bigger home. Sue and I had been looking for a while but nothing seemed right. What I really wanted was a place near the ocean. I figured that if I was going to tour for seven months of the year, then I wanted to come home to something that would help me relax. Watching the sun set over the Indian Ocean every night would be perfect.

The problem was the price of real estate along the coast. Everything seemed beyond our financial comfort zone, but Dad had other ideas.

I had a two-week break between the end of the Pakistan series and the first of three Tests against the Indians, so I decided to stay in Perth for a few extra days. Dad called me up and said he was sick of waiting for me to find something. 'Meet me here and let's do it my way,' he said, and hung up.

I knew better than to argue with him, and when I arrived a while later I could hear the printer in his office churning something out.

'Here,' he said, shoving a letter in my hand. 'I need you to sign 30 of these.'

> *Dear homeowner,*
> *My name is Justin Langer. I'm interested in buying a house in your area. I'm a private cash buyer. If you are interested in selling your home, please contact me on this phone number.*

I was horrified, but Dad insisted that we were going to do a letter-box drop from Sorrento to Scarborough, targeting older and smaller homes that might be in our price range and could eventually be redeveloped. I tried to resist but it was no good.

Sue came along as we drove around for a couple of hours, stopping the car long enough me for me, hiding under a hoodie and sunglasses, to shove my note in a letterbox. Dad was driving and Sue was taking notes of the houses, but both of them were taking the piss out of me and beeping the horn to embarrass me even further.

We had two letters left and decided to drop them further south in the suburb of City Beach. It was just wishful thinking, really, given the prices there, but I braved another round of car-honking and posted the letters at two small houses with ocean views. Our task over, we went back to Mum and Dad's place, where I tried to regain my composure with a couple of Vegemite sandwiches.

As we sat there having a laugh about the morning's events and debating whether anyone would call, the phone rang. Mum answered and a woman hesitantly asked for me. She lived in one of the two City Beach places, and the letter had prompted her to think about her future. She and her husband were in their seventies, their kids had all grown up and moved out, and their house and garden were getting a bit much to handle. Hesitantly, I asked if we could come and have a look at the house. She told me she would need a couple of hours 'to tidy up a little bit', but soon enough we were back at the house having a cup of tea and cake with the owners, a retired judge and his wife.

The house was great. The backyard was huge and the front had a view over a park, with City Beach sparkling in the background.

As we left, the judge took me aside. 'I don't know yet if we want to sell, but in case we do, I just wanted to warn you that I reckon the place is worth $450,000 but my wife wants $500,000.'

I tried not to gulp. Even at his wife's price, the place was a bargain and within our price range. Sue and I hardly slept that night, and neither did Dad. At six o'clock the next morning, as I arrived at the gym for a boxing session, he rang with another order: after training, I had to go home, shower and put on a suit, then front up to the house and offer them $550,000.

'But Dad, that's $50,000 more than they asked for,' I protested.

'Trust me,' he replied. 'Just trust me.'

I did as he said and was back in City Beach a few hours later. The judge answered the door in his shorts, his chin covered in shaving cream.

'Ah, Mr Langer—I thought I might see you again,' he said, inviting me inside.

I waited while he finished shaving, then he asked me what I wanted. I was more nervous than when I was facing Shoaib Akhtar a few days before. I blurted out dad's suggestion. 'Sue and I love the house and we want to offer you $550,000.'

He studied my face, thinking for a second, before reaching out with his right hand. 'I'm a man of my word,' he said. 'You have a deal.'

Dad was right. Sue and I had our dream home and, although my mates still accuse me of getting a bargain, the judge and his wife got more than they'd expected as well. At the time, living close to Perth's sunsets seemed like a fantasy, but now, having retired, I know the true value of following that dream, which has made the sacrifices of leaving my family for so long each year worthwhile.

I'll give you an example. Last November Ali-Rose turned eleven and we had a birthday party at home after school. My youngest, Gracie, turned four the same month and we had a little birthday party for her a few days later. It was the first time I had ever been to one of my kids' birthday parties. Mel Gilchrist came over with her daughter and Gilly was supposed to come over as well. I hadn't seen him in a while and was looking forward to a couple of beers. An hour or so later he gave me a call and was still at home:

'Listen mate, sorry but I'm not coming over today,' he said.

'Fair enough. What's up?' I asked.

'Mate, I'm floating around in the pool with my boys and, to be honest, it has been a very long time since I have done this, just the three of us. I'd rather be here with them if that's okay.'

I understood completely.

● ● ●

As a captain, Steve Waugh was in some ways a contradiction. He was a leader and a man of ideas, but his quiet nature often meant he appeared tentative when suggesting them to others. The first Test of the new millennium, which began on 2 January 2000 at the SCG, was a case in point. Tugga, always a lover of cricket history, had the great idea of marking the Test against India by wearing velvet skull-caps like those worn in the first Test against England at the SCG in 1901. 'You have to remember where you've come from so as to know where you're going,' he later said.

But instead of simply announcing the decision as captain, he asked what we all thought. Of course, everyone agreed, and although we were a bit dubious when they arrived because they looked so different, we happily wore them in what was a momentous match.

The rest of the series, which we won 3–0, was a bit of a blur because so much had happened over the summer. We comfortably won the first two matches, in Adelaide and Melbourne, and came to Sydney with the words of our new coach, John Buchanan, ringing in our ears. In the WACA dressing rooms he had simply asked us, 'What do you guys want to be known as? The Invincibles, the

Dominators or the Unbeatables? I'm telling you, this team has the ability and the depth of talent to win every single Test match it plays.'

It seemed an incredible thing to say—ridiculous, really—but here we were, a few weeks later, with six wins on the trot and the expectation that we'd continue to win in Sydney. We had decided not to worry about names—let the media handle it—and instead tried to concentrate on what Tugga described as 'the road less travelled'. He meant we should strive to do the unexpected, to go the extra yard and create a mindset and spirit within our team which would set us apart from every other Test side.

Sydney was a critical part of that process. We tore through the Indians on a rain-interrupted first day and dismissed them early on day two for just 150. Tugga warned us that the early going on the fresh wicket would be tough, but he insisted that if we got through the first few hours then things would get easier.

During a rain delay on day one, the ultra-marathon runner Pat Farmer had visited our rooms. I was amazed by his ability to run so far and asked him how he prepared mentally. He told me that as he laced up his runners, he visualised finishing the race, so that when he went through the hard times during the race he always had that picture in his mind. I had a terrible record at the SCG up until that time, so he suggested doing something similar and establishing a picture in my mind of exactly what I wanted to achieve. That night I visualised being in the baggy green when I reached a century.

Tugga was right about the conditions. We lost a couple of early wickets on day two, then I settled in with Mark Waugh for a century partnership, although I felt lucky to have survived the first hour. I couldn't seem to get a grip on the pitch and I was nervous, playing and missing outside the off stump or nicking the ball through the slips. I was almost out on several occasions before, having struggled to reach 40, I chopped a no-ball onto my stumps.

The bowler, Javagal Srinath, was furious, and I don't blame him. I'd had a lucky escape, and I knew I had to find a way to gee myself up or I'd be out very quickly. I decided to stand up a bit taller in my stance and tap the bat less to improve my balance. The difference was immediate and from that moment I hit the ball beautifully. My timing had gone from awful to amazing.

Srinath couldn't handle it and spent the entire time telling me I was the worst batsman ever to play Test cricket. However justified he thought that was, it only made me more determined. As I approached my century, I remember discarding my helmet and calling for my baggy green skull-cap, because I wanted to record the three figures in the cloth cap. Having done so, I went back to common sense and put the helmet back on.

We bulldozed through India again on day three and won by an innings and 141 runs to record our seventh straight victory. India's highlight was a breathtaking second-innings century by V.V.S. Laxman, who showed for the first time that he fancied the Australian bowlers. There were some other great achievements too. It was Mark Waugh's 100th Test, Ricky Ponting scored a great century and Glenn McGrath took ten wickets for the match. I ended up scoring 223, beating the record score by an Australian against India, which had been set by my childhood hero, Kim Hughes.

The celebrations afterwards were, to say the least, a little unorthodox. They probably haven't been revealed publicly before now. The SCG cellars are situated beneath the lower end of our change room. After a win there, at a certain point one of us would bang on the floor. When the staff below were ready, they would tap their ceiling three times and we would go downstairs and have a red wine with them. We had a great time that night and were still there at midnight carrying on.

Because winning was becoming a habit, Ricky Ponting, our songmaster, was looking for new ways to sing the song—a tradition which has continued to this day. He announced that we were going to do it on the pitch. This was not unheard of (we'd done it at Lord's and the MCG), but what was different this time was the costume— Punter told us to wear nothing but our jockstraps and baggy green skull-caps.

It was a scene that any newspaper photographer would have loved to capture—the entire Australian cricket team in the middle of the SCG on a beautiful summer's night, singing our team song almost naked. To make matters worse, we ended up running around for the next twenty minutes trying to slap one another on the arse—childish, I know, but it was one of the most hilarious nights of my life.

16. Best in the world

There were a couple of perceptions about me which I have always wanted to challenge—in particular, that I was a dour left-hander and that I only began to score more freely after I became an opener. I worked hard to improve my scoring options and pace early in my international career because, as I explained earlier, I realised my own shot-making was limited.

Our arrival in Auckland in March 2000 for a three-Test series against the Kiwis was particularly significant for me. It was seven years, almost to the day, since my Test career had been interrupted, and a lot had happened personally in that time. I was now approaching my 30th birthday, I was married with two kids, and I was a more seasoned player with a growing confidence. I'd been very successful over the past summer, including two centuries and a double-century in my last seven innings. I was also scoring more quickly.

One of the areas I had been working on was how to play spin

bowlers. I'd always felt that was a weakness in my game and I found it particularly hard to score against them. I could sweep them and perhaps play a cut shot if they really bowled rubbish, but apart from that I really floundered. I decided to do something about it, and for more than a year before that tour of New Zealand I had been ending every training session by getting someone to toss down some off-spinners or left-arm spinners so I could dance down the pitch and hit them back over their heads. Basically, I was practising hitting sixes. I was always looking to improve different areas of my game, but my ability to dominate spin bowling was a high priority if I was going to make a mark on international cricket.

The first Test in Auckland was a turning point for me, in this regard. Although it was a low-scoring match, it was the moment that I finally had the guts to bring what I had been practising onto the field. It was a dry, spinning wicket, so as soon as the left-arm spinner Daniel Vettori was brought on, I began coming down the wicket and hitting him back over his head.

The boys in the change rooms were laughing because they knew what was happening, but the watching media—not for the first time—misunderstood my actions and thought I was being reckless. Far from it. I hit nine boundaries, including a six, in a run-a-ball 46, while the team's total was 214 at three runs an over. The second innings was a replica of the first—I scored 47 runs, including five boundaries (two sixes). While I was disappointed not to have nailed a big score after two good starts, I was invigorated because I knew my hard work in the nets had finally become a viable option in the middle.

I kept up the tempo in the Second Test at Wellington, which we won to record our ninth straight victory, by scoring 57 in the second innings, including five fours and a six. I was a completely different player to the scared boy who had toured in 1993. This time, I had control of my game and the confidence to play my shots.

By the time we got to Hamilton for the Third Test, I was as chilled out as I would ever be before a game. I had exorcised my demons and felt secure in the side. In front of the change rooms at this lovely little ground, there is a big rose garden. Every morning, I would pluck a bloom and smell it, reminding me not only of home but also of my own peace of mind.

The match didn't start well, though. We knocked New Zealand over for 232 but then were 5 for 29 and in big trouble. I was sitting with Steve Waugh in the change rooms and worrying about what had just happened, including my own dismissal for just 4, but he was nonchalant.

'Don't worry,' he said. 'We'll be right. Someone will get us out of this.'

I was flabbergasted by his faith, but he was right. Damien Martyn and Adam Gilchrist put on 119 for the seventh wicket and we ended up with a 20-run lead instead of a sizeable deficit. We then knocked them over for 229 and so needed 210 for consecutive victory number ten.

It was not going to be an easy task on a greenish pitch. I went in at 1 for 13 and was almost out cheaply when a ball from Chris Cairns came off my body and rolled precariously close to my stumps. I had to make a change at that moment, find a cue that would make me refocus on the task.

One of the things I am often asked is what I look at as the bowler is running in to bowl. Greg Chappell talks about watching the bowler's face and then, like a camera, gradually zooming in on the ball as it comes out of his hand. I took that idea a step further that day. Worried that I wasn't watching the ball closely enough—'like a

Fresh face: I made my first-grade debut for Scarborough in 1985 at the age of fifteen. The great Dennis Lillee was a team-mate, and my childhood hero Kim Hughes the opposing captain.

Smiling: The look on my face was probably relief after a fiery Test baptism in 1993 against the West Indies. Keith Arthurton, Desmond Haynes and David Boon can all see the funny side too.

Guinea pigs: Shane Warne holds a tube of KY gel which he, New South Wales batsman Jason Young and I had to use during a hydration experiment while at the Australian Cricket Academy in 1990.

Cheers, boys: David Boon leads the team song after we beat the West Indies in Barbados in 1995. We always sang with cold beer and warm gusto.

Caviar anyone? It's little wonder the ACB stopped hosting celebration dinners after our extravagant effort after beating the Windies, at Bermuda in 1995. The expression on Slat's face probably sums up behaviour that night.

Pure joy: My first century against the Old Enemy at the Adelaide Oval in 1998. We retained the Ashes that week although Steve Waugh, as usual, looked calm about the whole thing. Hamish Blair/ Allsport/Getty Images

Morning after: Tugga and I arrived in Victoria Falls after a night on the
Bulawayo Express in 1999, a little worse for wear but with wonderful memories.
Note my baggy black and white cap—I've still got it.

Reprieve: Umpire Peter 'Porky' Parker bats away Wasim Akram's appeal during
the famous 1999 Test in Hobart. It was one of the most significant moments
in my career. I can admit now that, yes, I did nick it but there were plenty of
decisions which would go against me. Jack Atley/Allsport/Getty Images

Legacy: Steve Waugh left an indelible mark off as well as on the field. In 2001 we visited some of the children at Udayan, a children's home in Calcutta. Steve is patron of the girl's wing of the home, which educates and cares for children from leper colonies. Hamish Blair/Allsport/Getty Images

Smack, six! What better way to bring up a century in a Boxing Day Test against England in 2002. I went on to make my highest score—250. It just doesn't get any better than this. Hamish Blair/Allsport/ Getty Images

The sanctuary: Relaxing with a beer in the change rooms with a cold beer and my team-mates during the first Ashes Test of 2006–07. I didn't know then, but three of us would soon retire. Hamish Blair/ Getty Images

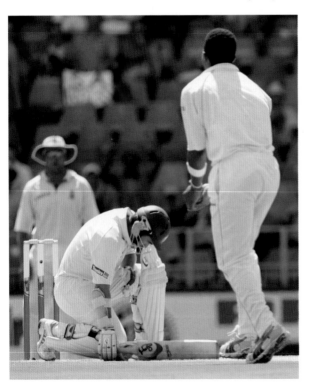

Lights out: My 100th Test match in April 2006 came to a quick end when I was hit in the head by South African quick Makhaya Ntini. Of all the times I got hit, this was the worst—physically and psychologically.
Hamish Blair/ Getty Images

Me and my mate:
The picture says
it all, really. The
gladiator and his
sidekick, arm in arm,
acknowledging the
crowd, after my last
Test at the SCG. It's
not just skill that
creates a partnership.
Our on-field success
was made possible by
our mateship off it.
Jack Atley/ Bloomberg/
Getty Images

Revenge is sweet:
It was a fairytale
ending, retiring
having won the
Ashes in a 5–0
sweep, alongside
two of the game's
greats—Shane
Warne and Glenn
McGrath.
David Hancock/ AFP/
Getty Images

Friendship: Sue's friendship with Mel Gilchrist and Kellie Hayden meant as much to her as my friendship with Gilly and Haydos.

Fashion tragic: Dad's unfortunate attire during the famous 1999 Test at Hobart against Pakistan only added to the drama and joy of a great victory. You can almost hear him asking if it was okay to remove the red tie.

hawk', as Sir Vivian Richards had told me in 1995—I concentrated on watching it from the moment the bowler turned at the top of his mark. I had never consciously done this before, and although I tried it on a few occasions afterwards, it never worked like it did that day.

I pounded my way to a run-a-ball, unbeaten century. That night Steve Waugh said this about me to the media: 'At the moment today he is the best batsman in the world.' Tugga's comments made the headlines, and the thought that I had gone from a scratchy, plodding batsman to a more fluent run-scorer was a great thrill. The headlines and Steve's comments were an amazing compliment—one I shrugged off publicly but felt proud of privately. I had scored 952 runs in the ten matches we had won since Zimbabwe, including four centuries, and at an average of over 63. The team was on fire and so was I. Life couldn't get any better—but, as I soon found out, there can be danger in too much success.

● ● ●

From Hamilton I jumped straight on a plane to England, where I was due to play county cricket for Middlesex. It was my third season for the club, and therefore my sixth straight season of cricket. I was in great form and continued to smash runs in England, scoring almost 1500 runs at an average of over 61. But I was worn out and something had to give.

My footwork was getting a bit lazy, I knew, but I was getting away with it because of my confident intent at the crease. I was standing on top of the mountain looking down, but I could sense a crash coming, as though I had forgotten to secure the safety ropes before my descent from the summit.

The season at Middlesex ended well but I couldn't wait to get home to Perth to see my family. It had been a great season but I needed some time and space. I wasn't going to get any. As I walked through the arrivals hall to get my luggage, the realisation hit me that I didn't have time to rest. There was yet another season on the doorstep.

I suddenly felt weary. As I collected my bags from the carousel, I had an awful sense that I had to start again—yet again—and I knew my batteries were empty. I began the 2000–01 season with successive ducks against Queensland in a Pura Cup match, and they were followed a few days later by a third duck, this time against South Australia in a one-day match. Suddenly my world was changing.

Some negative newspaper headlines quickly appeared. 'Langer clanger' read one after the Queensland match. The South Australian match was reported the next morning under the headline of 'Langer form raises doubts', which made me angry. A few months earlier I had been hailed as the form batsman in the world, and I'd carried that form in England. Why would I suddenly be doubted?

The problem was that I had forgotten the little things that made the big things work. Success had made me complacent about my footwork patterns and routines.

Looking back now, I can see why the media was raising questions. Some of the observations were legitimate, but it was still difficult to cop. Often an article might be written with some finesse but the headlines are usually very black and white—and let's face it, that's what most of us read. The impression of those few words can far outweigh the balance of any article.

In any case, the result was that I felt under pressure even before the first match of our five-Test series against the West Indies. I even noted in my diary how I breathed a sigh of relief when I got a quick single to get off the mark in a club match for Scarborough against

Bayswater. 'After all the cricket I've played in my life, that single run was a huge relief,' I wrote.

My poor form continued in the first half of the West Indies series. I scored 3 and then 5 in Brisbane and Perth, with no chance of a second-innings redemption in either match, as we crushed the Windies twice to record our eleventh and twelfth consecutive wins, equalling the world record.

My abiding memory of the Second Test in Perth was Glenn McGrath's hat-trick. He had snared opener Sherwin Campbell and the great Brian Lara off successive balls, then off the next ball I took a catch at short leg to get rid of Jimmy Adams. It left the West Indies at 4 for 19, and every fielder rushed in to congratulate Pigeon in a wave of arms and legs. I love the photo of the moment, which shows us as a team, our arms linked in the middle of the ground, with McGrath at our centre like a totem pole. It typified the team and its spirit, and showed why we were so dominant and set so many records.

The thing I remember best about the post-match celebrations (and there are bits I don't recall) was the reaction of John Buchanan. He was a great bloke, a lanky father figure who shared the occasional beer and joke with us but was generally at the edge of our shenanigans. He would sit bolt upright in a corner, his legs crossed neatly, nursing a beer, the froth lining his moustache as he quietly pondered what lay ahead. At times he would gaze around with a small smile on his face, like a farmer surveying his abundant wheat crop or his herd of prize Herefords.

I had known Buck from our days at Middlesex, when he was coach there. We even shared a flat together for a while when we first arrived in the UK, and we always got on well. I knew what he was about and I liked his coaching style. He knew he was in the midst of one of the most talented groups of players in cricket history, so he never tried to teach us about the technical side of the game, but he was able to guide us and create strategies to ensure we made the most of our talent. He had sparked the notion of us winning every game in those same WACA change rooms less than a year before, and it was in his vision—and his courage to sell his vision—that our success lay.

Rivalling Sydney's straps and caps celebrations, the tradition of the team song took another course that night. Punter decided that it was such a special occasion that everyone should lead a verse. As a result, we sang it twelve times over the next few hours, which represented both each victory and each member of the team that had won the Perth Test. There were several renditions at the ground, including the one I led as the team gathered on the WACA pitch, there was another at the hotel before we went out, and then one on the bus as we headed to the Leederville Hotel just north of the CBD. Slats led another one onstage at the hotel in front of a roaring crowd of delighted local patrons, who will never again get such a close look at the Aussie team celebrating a famous victory.

I regained some form after Perth, but in a sense the damage had been done. I spent the whole summer being negative, or at least not as focused as usual. The truth is I wasn't living in the moment, but was always thinking of the future or the past. I kept telling myself to hang in there and get past the Windies and the tour of India, which came a few weeks afterwards, so I could use the three-month break between India and the Ashes tour to have a rest and get back into shape. While this theory was generally sound, it also had a major pitfall. Because I was struggling for runs, I instinctively felt that it was because I was losing my fitness. To curtail this, I ended up training harder and wearing myself out even more. I hit more and more balls to 'get it right', but really I should have been resting and backing my game.

My drop in form challenged my sense of self-belief. I had always associated being fit and being healthy together. Not only was I wearing myself out physically, but I'd also hit thousands of balls in the nets, adding to the problem, which added to my cycle of despair. Instead of accepting the ups and downs of form, I drove myself constantly, with a fear that mediocrity was not acceptable, particularly to the media.

In retrospect, I would have been much better off to have kept some perspective and saved my energy for our matches. This was a lesson I really only learned in the past year, when I was captain of Somerset. I went to see a well-known nutritionist in the UK.

'You're very fit, aren't you?' he said, 'but I can tell without even looking at your blood sample that you're not very healthy.'

I was a bit taken aback and asked what he meant.

'I can see it in your face and your eyes. It happens sometimes to people who constantly train hard. They end up wearing their bodies out and become unhealthy.'

He went on to explain the importance of getting the balance right between training and recovery, and then showed me how nutrition plays a vital role in maintaining great health. His insights and strategies have had a profound impact on my life today.

● ● ●

By the time we got to India at the end of February 2001, I was tired and playing as if I wanted to get off the ground as quickly as possible. Getting to 50 was my aim, the sooner the better, instead of building an innings. I find that when I am tired I want things to happen quickly, and when they don't I get frustrated and uptight. At Test level there is no room for this attitude because ultimately you will come unstuck. And I did. My figures from that tour show my state of mind—I clubbed 22 boundaries and five sixes in just five innings, which really wasn't my style. During the previous summer, I had been scoring quickly but it had been due to my sharp focus. The difference then was that I was cashing in on my starts and scoring hundreds. I'd always seen myself as a marathon runner rather than a sprinter, but in India I was exhausted and wanted to get to the finish line as quickly as I could.

Even though I was on edge, we won the First Test, in Mumbai, to stretch our winning streak to sixteen. India rolled over for 176 and, while we were in some trouble at 5 for 99, Matthew Hayden and Adam Gilchrist came to the rescue and racked up a 197-run partnership at a run-a-ball rate. Haydos had spent some time in India before the tour relentlessly practising because he felt he had a weakness against spin bowling, and it paid dividends with a courageous century. Gilly played with his typical flamboyant style to put us in charge, and there was nothing to suggest we couldn't continue our winning ways.

Eden Gardens at Kolkata is a cauldron, a coliseum filled with 100,000 people every day of the match. The conditions are hot, the air thick with humidity. Even in this hostile atmosphere, however, Steve Waugh is a demigod, loved not only for his skills as a cricketer but also for his charity as a human being. On the outskirts of this amazing city of fifteen million people, Tugga visits, supports and helps raise funds for a home for children—particularly young girls— from families with leprosy.

We visited Udayan before the Test. It remains one of the most moving experiences I have had in all my life, particularly since I have four young daughters myself. Throughout India we saw kids on the streets, begging for food to survive and owning nothing but the clothes they wore. At Udayan these disadvantaged kids have a chance to be normal, playing and sleeping in bedrooms no different to my kids' rooms.

In one sense, Kolkata is one of the worst places I have seen, but equally I have never been more moved than when I visited it. India tends to have this effect on you; it's a sad and confronting, yet mesmerising, contrast between rich and poor. Visiting the Taj Mahal was a perfect example of this. We travelled in a rattly little minibus through the most appalling poverty to see one of the world's most lavish and amazing structures.

It seemed a matter of fate that Tugga would get a century in that Kolkata Test—it was his first in India. I remember him running down the pitch, his arms in the air in pure joy, as the enormous, swaying crowd went wild, as though our captain were their own. One-nil up in the series and with the captain leading the way, we made 445 and knocked India over quickly for 171. Our huge lead set up what everyone assumed would be victory number seventeen—and our first series victory in India for 35 years.

There has been a lot of criticism since then about Tugga's decision to enforce the follow-on, but at the time the argument to do so was overwhelming. We were on a roll, and when Jason Gillespie got Sachin Tendulkar out in the second innings they were 3 for 115, still almost 160 runs behind. Victory seemed just a matter of time. While there were some ominous rumblings late on day three when V.V.S. Laxman cut loose, dispatching Warney effortlessly and scoring a great century, they were still so far behind that it seemed impossible for them to mount a serious challenge.

With victory in sight Michael Slater turned up on the fourth morning with a boxful of big Havana cigars, while Tugga had somehow procured a case of Southern Comfort and some other festive refreshments. It's possible we spent the morning preparing for our expected party instead of the day's play. All we needed were six wickets and a series triumph in India would finally be ours.

We got none. Laxman and Rahul Dravid batted all day and didn't give us a single chance. I remember coming in to the rooms at tea, slumping in the change room and trying to dredge up some energy. The best plan we could come up with was to bore Laxman out by stacking the offside field and bowling wide outside his off stump. Glenn McGrath had the first over after the break, with seven men on the offside and just one guarding the legside. He duly bowled outside the off stump and Laxman seemed to block the ball defensively. Instead, it rocketed through the offside and had hit the boundary pickets before any of us could raise our heads. At the other end, he was playing Shane Warne, who was bowling around the wicket into the rough, as though he was batting on a first-day wicket at the WACA. We realised at this point that, no matter what we did, this wouldn't be our day.

Tugga tried everything, including nine different bowlers. Ricky Ponting bowled a few overs, and Matty Hayden and Michael Slater both had a trundle too. Then, for the last over of our most trying day in Test cricket, he turned to me. 'Go on, Lang, you have a go.'

'It's reached that low, has it, Tug?' I grimaced. 'Okay, give me the ball.'

I'll admit here to being one of the worst bowlers ever to turn his arm over in the Test arena, but in fact that could have been an advantage. As a batsman, I hated facing the part-timers because you never knew what was going to happen. They could bowl rubbish, which was likely, or they could sneak a ball through which caught you unawares. I'd got Mike Hussey out twice in grade cricket back in Perth, and I once had the great Jacques Kallis LBW in a first-class match at the Gabba. Laxman and Dravid were both tired and wanting to get into the change rooms to celebrate. Maybe I stood a chance.

I'd spent hours in the nets over the years, mainly with guys like Damien Fleming, trying to learn how to swing a cricket ball. This was my chance. I trundled in, hoping to swing one of my medium-paced pies and trap Dravid LBW. He flicked it off his pads for a single and strolled through.

Laxman looked at me with disinterest as I tried to swing the next one away towards the slips and let it go through to Gilly. The same happened with the next delivery, which didn't swing at all and passed by harmlessly.

Laxman was now almost asleep. Maybe he wasn't thinking clearly—if I swung one back into him, he might leave it and I'd bowl him. It was a good plan, except that, even as he dozed, Laxman paddled it for a single.

Two deliveries left—I was running out of chances. Dravid blocked the next one for another single. One ball left. One chance to impress, and Laxman, having made 265, could barely keep his eyes open. A bouncer was out of the question without breaking my toes, and a slower ball was impossible. The yorker was the only one.

I ran in, concentrating on the base of off stump, and bowled the perfect delivery, full and straight. Laxman didn't move—he didn't need to. The ball cannoned into his blade and bounced quietly into the offside. Dravid didn't even bother calling for the single.

I didn't bowl again the next day. In fact, it would prove to be my one and only over in Test cricket. Laxman eventually made 281 and Dravid 180, giving us a target of 384. We fell well short, as Harbhajan Singh took six wickets. India's victory, quite rightly, ranks as one of the greatest in the game—they not only ended our record winning streak, but also became one of the few sides to win after being forced to follow on.

Our change room was silent, a scene of utter disappointment, cigars and whiskey forgotten. We knew that even if we had held on for a draw, we would have been better off than we were now.

In a surreal twist, we actually didn't spend too long inside the rooms but were drawn back onto the ground by the scene outside. The noise was overwhelming, and we emerged to see thousands of fires ringing the arena as the more than 50,000 spectators still at the ground began lighting newspapers to celebrate. The scene was dreamlike in the fading light, and we watched the Indian players charging deliriously around the ground.

Despite a great double-century from Haydos, India also won the next Test, in Chennai, thanks largely to another amazing performance by Harbhajan, who took fifteen wickets for the match. How the game can change. A week or so earlier, we'd been one day and a few wickets away from our seventeenth straight victory and a historic series win. Instead, India was celebrating one of the great triumphs of all time.

I finished the series with an average of 32, which was better than Mark Waugh's, Ricky Ponting's and Adam Gilchrist's, yet I arrived home with a sense of foreboding. We had become the most successful side in history during the tour, but we'd lost a series we should have won. Nothing was said but change was in the air; as usual, I felt I was being targeted. It didn't help that I was tired, and somehow I seemed to be surrounded by people telling me how brilliant the series had been.

'But we lost,' I'd always reply. 'Isn't winning the point?'

'Yes,' they'd say, 'but what a contest!'

Australian Test cricketers train and compete on the basis that winning is everything, urged on by the media, which argues that anything less is failure. I love the fact that Australians love an underdog and want close, exciting games like that Indian series and the 2005 Ashes series, but it was difficult to understand why so many people actually seemed *happy* that we were beaten. The Australian cricket team always took great joy in victory, but we were also good losers—not only because we appreciated great competitors but also because we used defeat as motivation to win the next time.

Leaving India and finally getting the break I had craved since arriving back in Perth from England six months before, I wanted to chill out and concentrate on what I did best—train and train and train. I wanted to forget about the demons of disappointment and try to be so fit that I could run through brick walls by the time I got on the plane to England.

I was also delighted to be home for the birth of our third child. When Sophie finally popped out after a long labour, I realised that any plans I might have had for a male Test cricket heir had been dashed—and it was confirmed four years later by the arrival of daughter number four, Grace. Seriously, though, I wouldn't swap my girls for anything, and I'll follow with enthusiasm whatever they pursue in life, as my parents have done with me and my siblings. (That's not to say I don't chip away at Sue to have a crack at a number five son!)

Like Sue, I loved the time immediately after the birth. Life seemed to glow, not just because of our newborn child but also because we could be a complete family with our other kids—Jessica, who had just turned four, and Ali-Rose, who was two. Being at home with no pressure was bliss. It was a time I would cherish even more after returning to the harsh realities of international cricket.

David Boon, 3rd Songmaster, 1985–96

JL: What are your recollections about being songmaster?

DB: It was handed to me by Allan Border when he was made captain. I still hold very dear to my heart that I was the person who did that for about a decade.

JL: Did you always do it in the change rooms?

DB: Yes, but things have modified over time. I was quite impressed with the way it was held back a little bit, taken somewhere else or even back to the hotel. I liked the initiative to make a comment about each player's contribution to the victory before the song started.

JL: When did you sing it?

DB: We always sang it within fifteen minutes of the game's completion. Sometimes there was beer flying everywhere and it was a bit loud. We liked to do it then so that the opposition could hear it and we could rub our victory in a bit. I firmly believe that's where it belongs and not in public.

JL: Do you know much about the history of the song?

DB: Nothing ever used to happen when Australia won a Test match. We would go back and have a beer in the dressing rooms and celebrate in the normal fashion. Rod Marsh decided that something should be occurring. He took a great Australian poem and, with a few word changes, made a little song. I think it is fantastic.

JL: Can you remember singing it in 1995 in the West Indies?

DB: I can. I was a bit sad, in a way, because Allan Border had fought so hard and so long but had never enjoyed the success we had just experienced. We sang it quite loudly and robustly in the dressing rooms and back at the team hotel. It was repeated a few times, which was not the norm.

JL: So what did being songmaster mean to you?

DB: There are two things that clearly stand out, over and above the actual honour and the privilege of playing for Australia. One is what the baggy green represents. No one can ever take that off you. The other one is singing the song. Everything you have worked for comes together in that dressing room. Irrespective of whether somebody may have failed in that game or succeeded in that game, you have won a cricket match and everyone comes together. No one sits in the corner. It is all together.

17. The shekels

It is no secret that I was a fan of Steve Waugh as a captain, a player and a friend. He was critical in saving my career by helping instil in me a belief in myself. But the truth is my feelings towards the skipper weren't always rainbows and butterflies. I had gone to England for the 2001 Ashes series fresh and ready after three months off. My tour of India had been mediocre, but after 41 Tests I felt my place in the side was secure. I had even been named one of Wisden's cricketers of the year for 2001.

But a sequence of events conspired to bring my career to the edge. In the lead-up to the First Test, at Edgbaston, I had a run of outs in tour matches, firstly against the MCC and then against Essex. At the same time, Damien Martyn, who had been in scintillating form during the one-day series, was blazing away, scoring centuries in the same matches. There was a little bit of speculation about my position, which was annoying, but I didn't really think about it until two mornings before the Test. I was getting ready for team training when there was a knock on my door. Tugga was standing outside. He didn't come in.

'Mate, we're leaving you out,' he said. After briefly explaining the situation, he looked at the floor and then turned and walked off.

I stood there gobsmacked. I felt like my guts had been ripped out and were spilling on the floor. Here was the bloke who had always backed me, and now I'd been betrayed. It was a shocking moment. I walked back into the room and slumped into an armchair as an avalanche of thoughts crushed me. What would people think? Was it the end of my career? How would I tell my parents and friends? How could I face my team-mates?

To make matters worse I had to get on the team bus 30 minutes later, and sit there while Tugga told the rest of the team. Upon arriving at the ground, I would have to summon enough enthusiasm to do a net session in front of the media, who would have got wind of the change. Before practice began I asked Tugga if we could have a word.

We stood aside from the others and I implored him to give me a reason. I couldn't understand what had happened. I was his man—the year before, he'd described me as the best batsman in the world. I had never let him down. On I went.

Tugga listened and shrugged his shoulders. 'Yeah, I know, mate, but Marto's in amazing form and Punter can move up and slot in at number three. It's just the way it is.'

And that was it. The conversation had probably lasted three minutes, most of which had been me begging for a reason. He walked away thinking everything was sorted, but I was left floored. My world had ended. I didn't know what to do so I buried myself in fitness; running 100-metre sprints with our fitness coach, Jock Campbell. I was already fit but I nailed myself. I reckon I ran

50 of them that day, and then for the next five weeks I trained like a maniac. It was the only way I knew to let out my frustrations.

It was great news for Marto, but it's tough to congratulate someone when they've taken your place in the side. It was true that he'd been in great form, particularly in one-day cricket—a team in which I didn't play.

Another element made it even more difficult to accept. Marto was a mate, but we had a rivalry that stretched back to our junior days in Perth, so our friendship was always tinged with a competitive edge. I suppose there was some symmetry in what had happened, given that I'd taken his spot in the side in 1993. But it didn't make the situation any easier. I couldn't look anyone in the eye, especially Tugga but also Gilly, who was vice captain, and John Buchanan, the coach. I felt betrayed, like Shane Warne had a couple of years before in the West Indies.

We won the Test in a canter, with Gilly scoring a classic 152 at better than a run a ball. Tugga got 105, as did Marto, who justified his selection by scoring his maiden Test century off 165 deliveries with fifteen boundaries. Damien was sublime at his most fluid, and all his skills were on show. Warney spun out England twice, supported by McGrath and Gillespie, and we went one-up.

I put aside my disappointment and joined in the celebrations, which continued the next day. In our post-celebration swagger, we all donned our baggy greens and travelled down to London to watch Pat Rafter play the Croatian giant Goran Ivanisevic in the final at Wimbledon. It was a very funny day, especially when we arrived and were making our way to our seats on centre court. We heard a huge roar from the other side of the stadium and all looked up, expecting to see Rafter and Ivanisevic coming onto the court. Instead we saw our travelling Aussie supporters, the Fanatics, still decked out in their green and gold and cheering us. There was another cheer before the game got underway, this time as the US actor Jack Nicholson arrived with a couple of women on his arm. He had his trademark sunglasses on and waved to the crowd with a flick of his wrist, as if he were the queen. The only downside of the day was that Pat lost in five sets.

The pattern continued in the Second and Third Tests. Marto scored a half-century at Lord's as Australia won by eight wickets, then helped us win a tense seven-wicket victory at Trent Bridge and retain the Ashes. In the meantime, I could hardly get a run. The harder I tried, the worse it got. There was no way I was going to get back into the side and I became more and more angry.

Things came to a head in a match against Sussex between the Third and Fourth Tests. Tugga had pulled a calf muscle, and it looked as if he'd be out of the next Test and also the rest of the series. It seemed I might find a way back, at least temporarily. But I needed to perform well in the Sussex match to stake my claim.

It was a strange three-day match, during which both sides made abrupt declarations to get a result. In the first innings I was batting with Gilly, who was captaining the side. I was trying so hard but everything I hit went to a fielder, while Gilly was effortlessly carving boundary after boundary through the covers. He was making the bowlers look second-rate, yet I was making them look like Wasim Akram.

In the second innings I missed out again, and this time I left the field a broken man. When I got back to the change rooms I tore strips off Gilly. He was one of the selectors who dropped me and his brilliance was now highlighting my woes. 'Look what you've done to me,' I stormed. 'You can all go and get fucked!'

I threw my bat around the room and blamed everyone but myself.

It was a scene I sincerely regret. We got changed and boarded the team bus. I sat with my cap pulled down over my eyes, refusing to even look at anyone. As far as I was concerned, it was all over. This was the end of the road. I wanted to retire.

We got back to Brighton, where we were staying, and John Buchanan pulled me aside, insisting that I go for a beer with him. At first I resisted churlishly, saying, 'No, I'll work it out for myself.' But then I agreed with an equally blunt response: 'Yeah, whatever.' I followed him down to the bar with Gilly.

My rage got started again, and for the next hour I spewed out all the anger. I was shouting and crying. 'They were fickle but I'd never let them down before. I trained harder than anyone, and yet just because Marto was in good form they dumped me!'

Eventually, Gilly made his escape. I had a few more with Buck and we went back up to our rooms. He gave me a hug before we parted. It made me feel that I'd been understood, or at least heard.

I don't remember much of what happened next. I sat in my room and phoned Sue, then Mum and Dad and a couple of mates. I must have sounded suicidal, because the following morning Sue called back to announce that she was coming over on the next flight, bringing our daughter Sophie, who was only a few months old. Nothing I could say would dissuade her.

That night I had dinner with Tugga to try to straighten things out. This time I was quieter and he realised the mistake he'd made. When we'd first talked, he had thought everything was clear. This second, longer conversation made him understand that it wasn't.

Tugga called it a great lesson, but there was no turning back time. The team was up and playing well, and I wasn't. The best he could do was to tell me not to give up. 'You never know what opportunity might be around the corner,' he insisted.

Sue arrived the next day and I immediately relaxed. We went to Headingley, where Simon Katich came into the side for Tugga, whose calf injury hadn't healed. Marto scored another century—118—but we lost the match, after a daring declaration by stand-in skipper Adam Gilchrist and a wonderful century by English batsman Mark Butcher. We were 3–1 up with one Test to play.

There was nothing I could do. I had probably played my last Test, but I had my family and friends back on my side. They loved me and I knew things would be okay. Sue stayed a week, and by the time she was due to go home I had accepted what had happened and was ready to move on. Regardless of my situation, I was feeling happy again and was at ease about the future.

Even though I had been really down, I had sensed that my predicament was having an impact back at home. But it was only later that I found out about a bet between Sue and Dad. I'll let Sue explain.

● ● ●

Justin losing his place in the Australian side at the beginning of the 2001 tour was probably the lowest point in our cricketing life. I say 'our' because I always felt so much a part of his career, almost as if I was out there with him. But what happened to him on the field directly affected the rest of the family, and this appeared to be the end of the road at Test level, at least on a regular basis. We had just committed to building a house, among other things, and the loss of his place in the side would also have an impact financially if his Test career was over.

Justin was devastated and I was sitting at home with a new baby. Should I go to be with him, or would that simply complicate things? He was still on tour and I had always stayed at home when he was away.

Amid the gloom, Justin's father, Colin, was the optimist. We've always had a fun, teasing relationship, and he boldly declared that he had no doubt his son would be back. Not only that, but he insisted Justin would be opening the batting before the tour was over. I dismissed the notion entirely. It seemed impossible to fit him back into such a successful team, and they were hardly going to drop Matthew Hayden or Michael Slater—or so it seemed.

Colin dared me to take a bet of 100 gold shekels that he would be right. After asking what a shekel was and learning it was a gold coin, I accepted, even agreeing to his terms that it be delivered in a calico bag. When we saw each other over the next few weeks, he would start singing this ridiculous song he'd made up; the lyrics went something like this: 'Have you been to the shekel shop, collecting shekels do not stop . . .' Colin would sing it to antagonise me, which at least created some lighter moments in an otherwise dire few weeks.

Things got so grim that I decided to go to England for a week to be with Justin. I couldn't stay home when he was feeling so bad, even though Sophie was so young. I took the next flight to the UK— after pleading with the Passport Office because my passport had expired and Sophie didn't have one—and we spent a few days talking and coming to terms with the future.

By the time I had to return home to Perth we both felt better and had accepted the situation. On the morning of my departure, we were in our hotel room. I was packing and Justin was getting ready for training when the phone rang. It was Steve Waugh. He had news. Michael Slater had been dropped and Justin was back in the side, this time as an opening batsman.

Justin hung up and we danced on the bed like lunatics, just as we had five years before on the front lawn at Wembley when he'd got his first recall. We'd been given another chance.

I flew home that night, deliriously happy but unable to tell anyone as I was on a plane. Sophie and I arrived back in Perth on a Saturday afternoon. I was jet-lagged but determined to pay my father-in-law his money and clear the debt as quickly as possible.

But there was a problem—the banks were closed. I drove to an ATM, withdrew $100 and went around to a couple of dozen neighbourhood shops, gradually breaking down the notes into one-dollar coins. Somehow I managed to find a calico bag. I scrawled '100 shekels' on it, tied a bow around the top and then drove to the Langers' house.

'There's your 100 shekels!' I said to Colin triumphantly, banging the bag down on the kitchen table. He's still got it, and occasionally—just to keep the banter going—I'll try to hit him for a loan of a few shekels.

● ● ●

Tugga's message to me over the hotel phone had been typically concise. 'I reckon you'll do a good job for us, mate,' he'd said. 'I always thought you'd make a good opener.'

I didn't really understand the situation with Michael Slater, although I was aware there had been problems with his marriage. There was a strange morning when he missed the team bus and there'd been a couple of confrontations, but I had no idea of the team leaders' concerns about him until I read Gilly's account. He and Tugga had made the decision with the other selector, Trevor Hohns, to drop Slats and reinstate me.

At that moment in the hotel room with Sue, though, all I could think of was the personal reprieve. I vowed to Sue before she left that, if nothing else, I would have fun and enjoy what we both still thought could be my swansong in Test cricket.

Two of my best mates had booked a trip to England for the final Test of the series. Their tour had been booked twelve months earlier, when I was still cemented in the Test team. Despite my absence from the team, they decided to keep their booking and come to England for a week with the boys. Imagine their delight, though, when they rang me on arrival to discover I had been picked for that final Test. In their enthusiasm, they searched for the odds on me scoring a century in my comeback Test, which were pretty long, but they put a bet on anyway.

I went to training, which was tough because Slats was understandably angry. Having been in his shoes at the start of the tour, I knew exactly how he was feeling; but, like Marto in the First Test, I was also pumped to be back into the action. John Buchanan threw some brand-new cricket balls at me, but, as had been the case all summer, I was batting like a busted arse. It was that bad.

Then I stopped, suddenly aware of what was wrong. I had to relax. I was so uptight that it was impossible to move. Instead, I stood as still as possible and relaxed my shoulders and hands. When Buck started throwing the balls again, I smoked them. My feet were dancing again and I felt alive for the first time in six weeks. Had I found the solution to all my woes? The next day would tell.

Tugga won the toss and decided to bat. As I sat in the change room putting on my gear, I had to keep reminding myself of what the morning meant. It was a chance—my last chance—but it was also an opportunity. One perspective meant stress, the other delight. The serious stuff hadn't worked and I had to try something different.

I got up, one pad on and no shirt, and turned on the music box. Some Cold Chisel number came on and I started dancing around the change room. Everyone must have thought I was crazy. Damien Fleming started smiling and laughing along with me—maybe he understood what was happening. I finished getting ready and stood at the door, still dancing on my feet. 'C'mon, Haydos,' I called. 'Let's get out there and have some fun.'

As I stood on the balcony and looked down towards the ground, I spotted Geoff Miller, an England selector, with a really serious look on his face. Geoff is normally a funny guy and is a great after-dinner speaker. I started laughing and smiling at him. He noticed and broke into a broad grin. I started saying good morning to people in the crowd, then to the England players as I walked out onto the ground, and finally I cheerfully greeted the umpires. Everybody was wondering what was going on.

Although I was smiling and relaxed, I scratched around and had got to about 7 when Andy Caddick bowled a short ball straight at my body. I saw an opportunity to play a full-blooded shot, got into position and pulled as hard as I could. It was one of those shots that should go for four but, if you're unlucky, goes straight to a fielder. And, as had been my luck all tour, that's what happened. Caught at silly mid-on. My innings seemed over until I noticed the umpire—no-ball! A break had gone my way.

Another one came along when Phil Tufnell was brought on to bowl spin. It was the turning point for me—and for Phil, because in fact it would be his last Test. I'd been telling myself to relax through-out the innings, and now I really did. My innings had climbed into the forties by then and I felt confident and ready to pounce on this opportunity. I knew that if I got after Phil early, he had a tendency to drop his head and worry about the situation. In his second over

I hit him for six to bring up my half-century, which had taken 113 deliveries.

My next 50 took just 64 deliveries, including three boundaries in one over from Tuffers, and I brought up a century that would not only save my career but actually give it a rebirth I could never have imagined. I'd also done the right thing by my mates in the stands, whose winning bet on me helped fund their week in London. I am still waiting for the commission.

A couple of overs later I was back in the change rooms, not out but retired hurt. Caddick hit me in the head with the second new ball and I was carted off with a bad gash—blood was pouring out of my ear.

I lay in the medical room, sore but laughing. Everyone thought I was mad and I was rushed off for precautionary X-rays. Sue rang, all worried, but I was fine. A blow to the head was nothing. For five weeks I'd struggled to find a place in the world I loved, and now, given the chance, I'd just scored a Test century. I might have been lying on the physio's bench tattered and torn, but I was the happiest bloke in the world.

18. Nature boy

If there is a weakness in cricket administration, it is the inability to communicate with players, especially when delivering 'bad' news. Too often condescending clichés, like 'knocking on the door' and 'next cab in line', are used to escape the uncomfortable situation. As a player, I found it was eternally frustrating not to have meaningful conversations about selection. I copped it at both ends over the years—good and bad—and there was nothing worse than silence at the other end of the phone line, or hearing that clichéd rubbish.

Through the latter part of my career, Trevor Hohns did a great job as chairman of selectors. He was generally fair, tough and consistent, but like most selectors, his communication could have been better at times. They all promised to improve but rarely did. I mention this as constructive criticism, because it is an important aspect of management that is often overlooked; in the end, it makes it harder for younger players, in particular, to cope with the inevitable ups and downs of a career at the elite level.

I experienced first-hand—with Somerset in England—just how difficult and thankless a selector's job can be, but it only confirmed my belief that eye-to-eye, honest and constructive feedback, while hard, is crucial. When a player gets dropped, the feeling is excruciating. Being told the areas where he can improve is essential so that he sees a pathway back into the team. This doesn't happen enough.

My greatest frustration came at a pivotal moment in my career. Opening the batting for the Test side in 2001 could have been a fleeting chance, even though I scored a century in my first outing at the Oval. I had no idea if I was just a stop-gap measure while Slats copped a slap on the wrists or if the selectors were considering me as a permanent opener. After all, I had played nearly all my cricket at number three.

When I'd been dropped at the start of the tour, I had tried to raise the issues with Tugga, who'd asked if Trevor Hohns had spoken to me. He hadn't, and the silence lasted almost two months. It was only after I had scored 96 as an opener for Western Australia in the first game of the Sheffield Shield season, playing against Trevor's state, Queensland, that he tracked me down to talk about the coming series against New Zealand.

I was in the side, which was great news, but I was still disappointed that it had taken so long to have a conversation about my future. I'm sure things could have been made easier, and my decline less rapid, had I been given more guidance by the men in charge. Enough said.

For all my frustration during the Ashes tour, the summer of 2001–02 would be an amazing one, firstly at the expense of New Zealand. From the moment we arrived in Brisbane for the

First Test in early November, Haydos and I were celebrating our partnership.

We wanted to highlight the fact that we were mates—close mates, like brothers—and yet we were also very different, which made the combination a very powerful one. I was a back-foot player who liked playing square and Haydos was a thumping front-foot player who loved to hit straight. If the bowlers weren't already confused by bowling to left-handers whose strengths meant bowling different lengths, then our height difference would also be unsettling.

Those interviews were fun, but it was on the pitch that we left our mark. Just as perceptions about me as a grafter and a fighter were set in stone in my first Test back in 1993, our partnership on that first day in Brisbane set the tone for the next six years, tattooing onto the brains of administrators and the public that we were closely bonded as mates and intent on playing exciting cricket. It all might have been very different given that there was a loud appeal against me in the first over. I was probably lucky to survive, to be honest, but after surviving the hiccup we laughed, hugged and high-fived our way through the first day, each scoring a century and together breaking a 40-year-old world record for the first wicket by left-handers by scoring 224.

At one stage, as we chatted between overs, I told Matty that it felt like we were playing backyard cricket, not out of disrespect for the Kiwi bowlers but simply because we were having so much fun.

His response was typical: 'Mate, if you think this is like backyard cricket, look at the little crest on your left chest.' He jabbed his finger at the Australian emblem on my shirt, then kissed his own badge, went back to the crease and bludgeoned another boundary.

Our closeness was best illustrated when Haydos got his century.

As one scribe later wrote, we embraced 'like old soldiers'. That's exactly how we felt about each other.

I often describe the mateship within the Australian team as being like that of the Anzacs. I say that with respect and admiration for an Aussie spirit defined in war, but also in the belief that we should all aspire to it in our own lives.

Haydos summed up our friendship well at the end of that first day's play. 'We share a lot of common values and we have both had pretty similar careers, in some ways,' he said to the press. 'We have had big highs and big lows, and we have always been there for each other during the low times. During the low times, when you look around, that's when you see your mates.'

Our dream start continued in the Second Test in Hobart. I scored another century and Matty made 91 as we built a 223-run opening stand. Contrary to the way we usually played, however, this time I was the one who came out firing. At one stage I'd scored 58 runs off as many deliveries while Haydos only had a single. I have a photo of this moment, which I still use to tease him about who was the 'block artist' in our partnerships.

The reason for my blazing start that day could have been a recipe for disaster. Despite my success in the previous few Tests, I was searching for something to help me score a bit more freely. A couple of days before the match, I was having some centre-wicket practice and decided I was going to try to bat like Gilly by extending my grip further up the handle and swinging more freely. Jason Gillespie was bowling and I kept pulling him over midwicket for six. By the end of practice I reckoned I *was* Adam Gilchrist—and I gotta tell you, it was a great feeling!

We batted first and I was dropped when I was on 5—another lucky break. I told Haydos I was going to take advantage of it and bat as I had been practising. Incredibly, I started hitting perfect cover drives, which had always been my weakness. At the Cricket Academy years before, Warney used to take the piss out of me because he reckoned I couldn't hit a cover drive. He was right. Even though I had hit thousands of them in practice over the next few years, I'd never been able to get it right in a match.

On this day in Hobart, however, everything changed. I probably hit half a dozen boundaries through the covers that morning. I felt like rushing off the ground and phoning my batting coach, Noddy Holder, who'd been patiently helping me for years. I wanted to tell him that all our work together had paid off. What was once my weakest shot was now a strength. I was hitting it instinctively, and over the next few years it would actually become my signature shot.

That day reinforced how I feel about coaching. The psychology of sport, in particular, has always fascinated me. At the elite level, coaching isn't so much about changing a player's stance or how he holds the bat; rather, it's about unlocking his mind so that he can play every shot. I will always remember Don Bradman's words of wisdom in his letter to me: 'Don't be a slave to coaching.' He was not suggesting that I ignore technique, but that I listen to and trust my instincts.

I realised another important thing that day. A number of my most satisfying innings, including my first Test century and my first as an opener with Matty Hayden, came when I was at rock bottom, feeling either flat or as though it were my last chance. In those situations, I had found the ability to let go rather than tighten up, and it had paid dividends. The secret was unlocking my mind. I had to play with courage—I had to be prepared to fail in order to succeed. I also realised how you needed a bit of luck to be successful; at the Oval I was caught off a no-ball early, at the Gabba I got a decision going my way in the first over, and at Hobart I was dropped on 5. On every occasion my luck helped me seize the opportunity to cash in and score a hundred.

● ● ●

One of my favourite times with Haydos was when we toured South Africa in early 2002. We were both in a great frame of mind as we were coming off a 3–0 whitewash of the Proteas during the Australian summer. We'd had a pair of double-century opening stands in that series, and Haydos had scored a century in each Test. I'd scored two centuries myself—116 in Adelaide and 126 in Sydney. The latter had been particularly pleasing: Steve Waugh had been insistent that he needed a big opening stand as the pitch was difficult and the Proteas had a great attack, led by Allan Donald and Shaun Pollock.

Haydos continued the domination in the First Test, at Johannesburg, belting a belligerent century to set the tone for the series, even though it was later overshadowed by Adam Gilchrist scoring the fastest double-century in history—204 off just 213 deliveries—as we crushed the Proteas by the ridiculous margin of an innings and 360 runs.

Between Tests we visited a game park, staying in five-star tents in the middle of the bush. We arrived in the evening, checked in and then sat around a huge bonfire, having a feed and a few beers to end the day. That in itself was amazing, but Haydos in particular found it exhilarating.

We all went to bed for the night, happy to be in the safety of our tents. Like most people in the African bush for the first time, we half-expected a lion to come leaping out of the darkness at any moment. I was reading or watching TV when I suddenly heard a whooshing sound, followed by a howl. I got up to see what was going on.

Out the back I saw some outdoor showers, which were set up behind screens and on boards. Haydos was lathered up under a great jet of hot water, scrubbing away with delight under the velvet blackness of the African sky.

'The nature boy is back! The nature boy is back!' he was yelling, throwing open his arms as though he was trying to haul in the gazillion stars that winked like diamonds.

I didn't bother interrupting him; he was enjoying himself way too much.

South Africa had been forced to make some changes for the Second Test, at Newlands in Cape Town. They brought in three new faces, including a youngster named Graeme Smith. He was big and strong with good balance and body language at the wicket, but we weren't too bothered. His grip seemed to suggest that he was a very strong onside player and, therefore, quite limited. Our opinion hadn't changed after he made only three in South Africa's first innings as they stumbled to 239.

Haydos and I were in the mood to crush their spirit and from the outset we were scoring at almost a run a ball. At one point we were standing mid-pitch between overs when Smith, running from his position in slips to the other end, barged straight between us. It was needless and provocative, and we both gave him a mouthful before the umpire, Steve Bucknor, stepped in. We wondered who this arrogant young punk thought he was. Our doubts about him were entrenched three years later when he toured Australia, this time as an opinionated captain whose team was crushed, yet again, by 3–0.

(My view changed in my 100th Test when I was felled by a bouncer from Proteas bowler Makhaya Ntini and Graeme phoned to ask how I was doing. For the captain of the opposing team to make that phone call really showed some character, and I haven't forgotten his act. Notwithstanding his early bravado, Smith has also become a successful captain and a fine batsman. I watched with admiration as he batted against Australia with a broken hand in the most recent series between the sides, and I thought his unbeaten 154 at Edgbaston last year to guide South Africa to its first series win against England in four decades was outstanding. He has captained Somerset, as I have, and is renowned as a strong leader and a good person—attributes I really admire.)

The Second Test had extra meaning, not only for the series but also to decide top spot in the ICC's new ranking system. A quirk in the system had meant that South Africa was the number one team, even though we had trounced them in Australia, so we had to win at Newlands to regain the spot.

We knocked them over for 239 in their first innings and then scored 382 ourselves. South Africa fought back and showed some backbone to make 473 in their second innings. So we needed 331 to win, a tough task over the final day and a half of the Test. Haydos and I made a century opening stand, and when he got out we were 2 for 201 and cruising, but then three more wickets put the game back in the balance.

Then Adam Gilchrist, who had made 138 in the first innings, walked out to join Ricky Ponting. Paul Adams, the unorthodox leg-spinner, was bowling and had just taken the wickets of Steve Waugh and Damien Martyn. The crowd was baying, sensing that the game had swung back in the South Africans' favour.

Gilly took guard, looked around the field and waited for Adams, who came into bowl. Suddenly, Mark Boucher, the South African captain, stopped his bowler and ordered a field change. The crowd howled again. Adams walked back to his mark, turned and ran in, but Boucher stopped him again. It was obvious he was trying to unsettle Gilly. In the dressing room, we were really feeling the tension as well. There was just so much riding on the game.

At last Adams ran in and bowled. Gilly jumped down the pitch and smashed the ball for four. The tension released like a popped balloon. The crowd sank back into their seats and we relaxed, knowing we were going to win. 'It's okay, Gilly's away,' someone said.

That night we celebrated big time, first at the ground and then in a huge restaurant and bar at the top of Table Mountain, which famously looms over the city. After an hour or so the owner closed the bar so we could continue our celebration alone, and Punter, who was songmaster then, led the team song. What a place to do it, overlooking this spectacular place we'd just conquered.

If that wasn't good enough, the owner then told us he had something special—he would let us ride on top of the cable car down the mountain. You've got to be kidding, I thought. The thing travelled more than a kilometre up the mountain, turning so it gave people the best view, and he was suggesting we travel down on top of it.

Looking back on it now, I still can't believe we agreed to do it, but we all climbed on top. Thankfully, it had a small railing. The ride was unbelievable, and Haydos made it unforgettable. He stripped naked and climbed onto the rails at the front, draping himself in an Australian flag, then flung out his arms and yelled out an almighty cry like he was Leonardo DiCaprio in *Titanic*. I can't remember who coaxed him down or how, but we were all alive the next day and ready to move onto our next challenge, the nature boy included.

• • •

Rory Steyn is a tough South African who runs 100-kilometre marathons for fun and guards celebrities for a living. He was our security man every time we were in South Africa. I met Rory during our 2002 tour. We immediately hit it off and I was particularly intrigued about his relationship with Nelson Mandela, whom he had been assigned to protect on Mandela's release from prison in 1990. One night over dinner, Rory told me about his experiences. Initially, he had been insulted by the assignment to guard Mandela.

'I took it as an insult to look after a black man—particularly Mandela, who represented everything I had been raised to oppose,' he said. 'But I found this man with a gentle, intelligent face and demeanour. I thought I'd only have to wait a day or so before he dropped the facade. I waited for a week, then a month, a year and then a decade, but he did not change. It was not a facade. Nelson Mandela, with his humility and ability to forgive, was able to completely change my programming.'

After hearing Rory's story, I read Mandela's own account, *Long Walk to Freedom*, and I visited the shantytown of Soweto a couple of times to run cricket clinics for kids. But I wanted to see the scene of Mandela's greatest personal struggle—Robben Island, where he spent eighteen of the 27 years he was imprisoned. The island sits a few kilometres off the coast of Cape Town. In a way, it reminded me of Rottnest Island, off the coast of Perth, not only for its location but also because of its history as a prison and in the sense that it is always within eyesight of the city but somehow sits on the fringe of your consciousness.

A group of us went there before the Third Test. The visit was truly inspirational and showed us the psychological strength one man could have. The prison cell where Mandela had spent 23 hours a day for so many years was just a tiny room. He was allowed just one letter and one visitor every six months. He counted sand grains to keep his mind alive and studied law through an external program run by the University of London. I think about Nelson Mandela's spirit often. For this man to emerge and forgive the way he has is simply amazing.

● ● ●

Steve Waugh, believe it or not, was under a cloud for that whole series. If you look at his career statistics, it is difficult to find a period in which he really struggled, but in South Africa he was under some pressure and, it appeared, was even considering retirement. He had a run of outs, which came to a head when he was bowled by spinner Paul Adams in the Second Test at Cape Town.

As we got on the team bus to go back to the hotel that night, I noticed Tugga sitting by himself, cap pulled down over his head. It reminded me of the way I'd felt the year before when I had been dumped from the side at the beginning of the Ashes tour. I sat down next to him and put my hand on his shoulder. 'It's a lonely old world, isn't it, skipper?' I said. It was a conversation starter as much as anything. I knew the value of talking to someone when things got tough, so I wanted to see if he wanted a pair of ears to help him get through this period.

I understood completely how he felt. I was a grafter and the struggler among an amazing collection of players, so I knew how each of them felt when they inevitably went through a bad patch.

The other major downside of the tour was a now infamous incident to do with Gilly. Anonymous and ridiculous rumours had begun to circulate about whether he was the father of his two-month-old son, Harry. It was an awful set of circumstances, especially with the First Test in Johannesburg approaching, and yet Gilly went out there and played one of the all-time great innings—his 204 off 213 balls.

He had gone out to bat towards the end of the first day, feeling very emotional, in front of a hostile crowd. There was one section of idiots who were waving placards alluding to the paternity issue. Despite this, he battled his way through to finish the day on 25 not out.

That night a couple of us went to dinner with Gilly because we wanted to let him know he had our support. I got back to my room afterwards and decided to write him a letter, which I then slid under his door.

I've always been a big writer of letters, probably because of my great mentors, my dad and Nigel Wray, who had given me great support in my early days. Dad taught me about the power of thankyou notes, impressing upon me that the recipient would always remember if you sent one and would never forget you if you didn't. Making a phone call is great, talking face-to-face even better, but a letter is something permanent.

I wrote to Gilly that he had control over his feelings and reactions, and that the important thing was that his family and friends knew the truth. I included a quote from John's Gospel, which says simply that 'the truth shall set you free'.

At the end I wrote:

Don't let ignorance control your spirit. See you at breakfast.

JL

PS: It's not every day that you get a chance to score a Test century.

The rest is history.

19. Highway to hell

Leadership in elite sport is most often displayed rather than spoken and emerges in adversity rather than triumph. Steve Waugh's confrontation with Curtly Ambrose in 1995 confirmed to the team that he was the natural successor to Mark Taylor, and Ricky Ponting did the same thing against Pakistan in October 2002.

It was a controversial series from the beginning, with the First Test played in the Sri Lankan capital, Colombo, and the next two in neighbouring Sharjah because of the politically unstable climate in Pakistan. Before the Colombo match we were worried about the possibility that Pakistan, having brought their own groundsman to the neutral venue, might prepare the pitch at the P. Saravanamuttu Stadium in favour of spin. Instead, they won the toss and put us in to bat on a shaved pitch, trying to knock us out with pure pace.

It was an eventful first over. I was dropped off the first ball of the match, Haydos was out off the fifth and then I was hit in the head off the sixth. After that Punter and I carved them up with a 183-run partnership. My form had continued from Australia, but I missed out on a century and was sitting in the change rooms watching when Shoaib Akhtar came back into the attack. He'd been bowling at close to 160 kilometres per hour that morning and, now refreshed, he upped his pace again. Ricky had been seeing the ball so well that, approaching a century, he was batting in the baggy green rather than a helmet. Then Akhtar hit him in the head.

It is probably a moment that Punter doesn't remember, but for the rest of us watching it was hugely significant. Punter didn't go down, instead shaking his head like he was dismissing a fly and then settling over his bat to wait for the next delivery. The whole thing sent tingles up my spine and reminded me of watching Viv Richards playing against Dennis Lillee and Jeff Thomson when I was a kid, when Viv refused to trade his fading maroon cap for one of the helmets that were coming into use at the time.

Like Richards two decades before, Punter was dismissing the fastest bowler in the world. It was as though he were asking, 'Is that the best you can do?' He went on to smash his way to a big ton. It signalled to me that this guy was ready for leadership.

While Punter was beginning something special, the tour also signalled the end of another special career. Mark Waugh was left out of the Ashes squad, which was announced a few days after the Third Test, and immediately retired from international cricket. I sensed during that last series against Pakistan that he felt like he was coming to the end of his career. It was as if his enjoyment of the game had run its course. Although my friendship with Steve Waugh is well documented, I also had—and continue to have—a strong bond with Junior, which probably stemmed from our great differences.

I was a big fan of Mark. He made the game look so effortless and I made it look so hard. I was a training workhorse, whereas he famously declared one day that he was a Rolls-Royce cricketer. 'You leave a Roller in the garage during the week and take it out at weekends for show,' he said. While his brother Steve was an ice man who demanded that the side train harder in the heat of Sharjah, Mark would have scoffed and applied a little extra suncream to his lips. You shouldn't take this as arrogance, though, but rather as his self-deprecating humour. Mark said these things and acted this way as much to take the mickey out of himself as anything else. While Tugga's stern outlook made him look like a worrier, it was always Mark, with his coolness, careful hairdo and sweatbands, who got the cold sores.

We used to laugh when watching the brothers bat together, always wondering what they might be saying to each other out in the middle. From what we could see, they said very little, always meeting mid-pitch before turning and walking back to their respective ends like two soldiers on guard duty. I asked Mark once what they talked about.

He laughed. 'Mate, we've shared bunks since we were one year old. What could we possibly have to say to each other that hasn't already been said?'

Mark often joked about their childhood in Bankstown. 'Other kids had Tim Tams and Drumsticks but we had Milk Arrowroots and Twin Poles.' He told stories of family dinners where there were six lamb chops on the table to share between five people. 'We'd eat the first chop really quickly so we could have a chance of grabbing the spare one before anyone else. Guess who won all the time—that fat bastard over there,' he'd laugh, pointing at his older brother.

We won the First Test by 41 runs. The two Tests in Sharjah were both over very quickly—thanks to Warney, in particular—as we crushed a dispirited Pakistan. If they had lasted the full five days I don't think any of us would have survived. I never played in conditions like it again. The temperature inside the stadium was over 50 degrees Celsius and the humidity was at 90 per cent. It was so hot that Andy Bichel, who was as fit as anyone in the side, could only bowl two overs at a time before needing a rest. He ended up taking ice baths and hallucinating in the change rooms.

Despite this, Tugga insisted that we actually up our performance so that our opponents felt our psychological dominance as much as our physical pressure. It was an amazing thing to ask of his side—the road less travelled, he liked to call it—but he got it. In the middle of this cauldron we would jog to our fielding positions between overs to show the opposition we weren't affected by the heat.

The tactic worked and we rolled a dispirited Pakistan side for 59 and 53 in the Second Test and then won the next by an innings and 20 runs. Yet Sharjah was a difficult place to be, not least because the state has a total prohibition on alcohol, so we couldn't enjoy a cold beer after the scorching days. We found ourselves on the highway every evening travelling about twenty kilometres across the border to Dubai.

After we demolished Pakistan in the Second Test, my form dropped a few notches. I was out cheaply in the first innings of the Third Test but Punter and Tugga both made centuries and we posted a formidable 444, before a rampant Shane Warne destroyed Pakistan's batsmen.

But not everything Warney bowled was perfect. I was fielding at bat-pad on the third day when Pakistan's middle-order batsman Hasan Raza pounced on a short ball and hit it straight at me. I instinctively turned away but was struck on the back of the head, and I dropped like a lead balloon. I'd been hit a few times before, but this one was like the lights going out, even though I was wearing a helmet. Apparently, I was unconscious on the ground for two minutes before I got up and walked, dazed and nauseous, to the change rooms.

Our medical staff were worried and decided to get me to hospital for a precautionary brain scan, and that's when my problems really began. They put me in a neck brace and on a stretcher. As the attendants were loading me into the ambulance, they pushed a bit hard and I whacked my head on the wall inside it.

With our security officer, Reg Dickason, in the back with me, we headed off down the highway to the hospital in Dubai. The driver completely ignored the speed humps, sending me bouncing on the stretcher in the back every time we went over one at 100 kilometres per hour. By the time we got to the hospital, I reckon my concussion was actually worse than when I was hit in the head.

Reg went off to see the hospital administrators but the ambulance officers had other ideas. They unloaded me, still on the stretcher, and tried to wheel me into an elevator that was clearly too small for the trolley. In their vain attempts to squeeze me into the lift they kept banging my head against the elevator wall—until they gave up and tried the stairwell instead. Ignoring my pleas to stop, they ended up carrying me up this staircase, my head pointing down and banging against the stretcher rails.

Reg reappeared, realised what was going on and started yelling at these two clowns. Eventually, they loaded me back into the ambulance and took me back to Sharjah to another hospital, where the brain scans thankfully revealed nothing wrong other than concussion, mostly caused by the trip!

After the Second Test, I was in the wars again. We were intent on celebrating our great victory, which had taken less than two days, back in Dubai. I remember having a few beers and a cigar while talking with Darren Lehmann, then the world suddenly went black. I had passed out.

I woke up to find Steve Waugh and Jock Campbell, our fitness trainer, helping me up off the floor and walking me out of the bar and into a taxi. I have never been so drunk in my life, yet I had only had two or three beers. I had seriously underestimated the impact of the heat on my body and paid the price—we stopped every few hundred metres on the way back to our Sharjah hotel so I could vomit on the beautifully mown green verges along the highway.

● ● ●

My history with the Dubai/Sharjah motorway started on my first trip to the United Arab Emirates and while I have kept this last Dubai incident quiet for more than 15 years, I suppose our ten-year rule can come into play. It was April 1994 and we were in Sharjah for a tournament called the Austral-Asia Cup, played between six nations from the region including India, Pakistan, New Zealand, Sri Lanka, Australia and a team from the UAE. It had been played every four years since 1986, but because of the increasingly busy international schedule, this would be the last time the tournament was played.

We had arrived a few days before and things had got out of hand the night after our first match, against Sri Lanka. A group of us had been celebrating in Dubai and rolled out of the bar. Our attempts to get all of us into one taxi failed, so we split into a couple of groups.

On the way down the highway we started to get pretty silly. I was reaching over the driver and beeping his horn and we were yelling out to cars as we drove along the highway with the windows down.

I'm not making excuses here, and looking back it was pretty embarrassing, but we thought it was hilarious—boys will be boys. A long white limousine went past at one stage and we started gesturing out the windows to the darkened windows. We had no idea who was inside but it seemed appropriate to recognise the contrast between our battered cab and their luxury.

The limousine pulled ahead and we forgot about it, instead signalling to our driver to pull in at a Kentucky Fried Chicken store so we could get a late-night feed. Just before the store a police car was waiting, with its blue lights flashing. It ordered our cab to pull over. Then we noticed the limousine, and our driver started shaking his head and muttering: 'What have you done. This is very bad, very bad.' Apparently there were two Arab sheiks in the limo who, naturally enough, had been offended by our hi-jinks.

The driver got out of his taxi and spoke to the police, then got back into the car, did a U-turn and followed the police back to Dubai. We started to feel uneasy about the situation, realising that something had got out of hand. The driver was questioned in one room while we waited. When the police and the driver came out of the room, there was more talking and the driver then pointed to me. He seemed to be indicating that I was the one at fault. My problem was compounded because I was sitting with my legs crossed and, inadvertently, pointing the soles of my shoes at the police officer. This, I later found out, is an insult to Muslim people in the UAE and the officer started yelling at me at the top of his voice.

I had gone from drunk to stone-cold sober in seconds and, realising I had to say something, began to protest politely and plead our ignorance as the idiots we were. The senior officer then spoke in halting English. He knew who we were and, at that moment, he intended to hold us overnight in the cells before deporting us. We would not be playing the next game and therefore we were in a world of trouble.

The arguments went on for an hour or so and eventually they were persuaded to let us go. The driver was told to take us to our hotel. We got back to the hotel without further incident and gave the guy every cent we had. I had learned a life-changing lesson about respecting other cultures. Things could have turned out so much worse; maybe it was time to start growing up and taking things a little more seriously.

20. As good as it gets

Meditation has been a big part of my life since 1993. It began from a simple conversation with former New Zealand opening batsman John Wright back on my very first tour. He suggested it might help me to relax rather than get so wound up emotionally by Test cricket and personal performances.

In the weeks after my disappointment at being dropped from the team and even the squad for the 1993 Ashes tour, I noticed an advertisement in the local paper for meditation classes. I needed something positive to focus on and decided to give it a go. In the years afterwards, I have tried many different types, including transcendental meditation, which focuses on a mantra, a Buddhist form that concentrates on breathing, and even meditating to a symbol, such as a burning candle.

In the summer of 2002–03, when England toured Australia, I was using the last of these three techniques and concentrating on the symbol of the Christian cross. I had no particular reason for this other than it was a symbol I knew well. I was raised in a Catholic family and have turned to faith at different times in my life, so the cross was a strong symbol to meditate on, and I was doing just that as we approached the Melbourne Test match.

The thing I miss most about Test cricket is crossing over the boundary to begin play on the first morning of a big match. There is something fresh and exciting about the whole thing, particularly at a venue like the MCG on Boxing Day. On the morning of 26 December 2002, the crowd already numbered over 75,000. We were 3–0 up in the Ashes, the sun was shining brightly and as Haydos and I came onto the ground the U2 classic 'Beautiful Day' was playing. It was pure bliss as the crowd roared in expectation, and I reached over and put my arm around Haydos in an instinctive embrace.

I remember saying to him, 'Mate, how good is this? How many people get to do this in their lifetime?'

It must have looked strange to those watching. Opening the batting for Australia in a Boxing Day Test is a very serious affair, and yet here were two opening batsman laughing on their way out to the middle of the ground.

I got to the wicket and went through my usual routine, using my spikes to scratch a line roughly twenty centimetres behind the crease so I could get some grip on the pitch with my bat. The wicket was fresh and I had to work harder than normal to get some traction. Then I asked the umpire for middle stump and scratched a line lengthwise, again having to work hard to get a proper mark on the pitch. When I looked down I realised I had scratched a perfect cross in the turf.

It seemed to be an omen of some kind, particularly given my

feelings as I'd walked onto the ground, but as sharp as I tried to be, the morning session was really flat for both Haydos and me. We went to lunch with only 88 runs on the board at an unusually slow run rate, but at least our partnership was unbroken.

Then everything changed. We doubled our score in the first ten overs after lunch as I found my range and Haydos started to bludgeon the bowlers. At one stage he wandered down the pitch to talk to me. The medium-pacer Craig White was bowling and Haydos was getting impatient.

'If this was a one-day game I'd be hitting him back over his head,' he fumed.

'Well, just do it and get it out of your system,' I told him.

The next ball he flat-batted White back over his head for six, then he hit the following two balls to the boundary. He hit Steve Harmison for six and started walking down the pitch to Andy Caddick and smashing him over midwicket. I joined in by going after the off-spinner Richard Dawson, hitting him for five boundaries.

It was as if we were playing a Twenty20 game rather than the first day of an Ashes Test. Like everyone else, I was in awe of Haydos' power. I had often told him how I'd love to be able to hit straight sixes like he did, and he always responded that he'd love to hit it behind point like I could. That's how it was—we had confidence in each other.

We were similar types of people but very different players. When we walked out onto a ground it was like walking into a fight with a big mate. There was grit in what we did but there was also great joy, and that made the difference. There were serious times, of course, but that day at the MCG we were laughing and joking between overs. Sometimes we talked about fishing or what we would have for dinner; at other times we encouraged each other to 'wear them down'. That was our main theme when batting together—to work hard to wear down the opposition, and then pounce on them like a couple of hungry lions.

Haydos got his century but then got out. A couple of overs later I smashed Dawson for a boundary and then a six to bring up my own century. That moment was amazing. For the few seconds that it took for the ball to travel from my bat to clear the boundary, I was in a vacuum and felt untouchable. I *knew* the ball was going for six from the moment it left the bat, but none of the other 75,000 people watching its flight did. I was already standing in the middle of the ground, my arms raised in the air in triumph, when the noise erupted as the ball sailed over the fence. Imagine that feeling—a century against England in a Boxing Day Test! It just doesn't get any better than that.

In the afternoon session we scored 147 runs—it was the most exciting session of Test cricket I had ever played. I slowed down a bit later in the afternoon, although we kept scoring at around four runs an over. We had lost a couple of wickets but Steve Waugh came in and we steadied the ship. I had reached 140-odd close to stumps and was getting tired after a long but wonderful day. It was then that I had a moment of revelation.

My concentration was beginning to wane, so I was forcing myself to have breaks so I could get through to stumps. As I've discussed earlier, one of the secrets to batting for long periods is learning to switch on and off between deliveries. There are times when you have to block out the sound of the crowd in order to concentrate, but at other times you can let it wash over you to give your brain a breather. This was one of those times.

Most of my family had flown across from Western Australia for the match and I spotted them high in the stands above the Barmy

Army. I could see Sue and the girls and my parents alongside them, part of this massive crowd and yet so identifiable within it. As I watched, I had a sudden realisation: this moment was about as good as it could get for an Australian Test cricketer—140-odd not out against England in a Boxing Day Test—and yet it meant nothing compared to the love of my family and friends.

Having this isolated thought in the middle of the thumping noisy arena felt strange, but I knew it was important—and that one must keep perspective in life. I later learned that, around that time, one of the commentators at the match said, 'Langer looks so calm, it is almost as if he is meditating.' If only they had known about the cross on the crease.

The next day I turned my century into a double-century, again smacking Dawson for a boundary to reach the milestone. I was eventually out for 250—Dawson finally got me—and it would be my highest individual score. Looking back, I wouldn't rate it as my best innings, but it was very special, if only because it was made on such a big occasion and in front of my family and friends.

Sue and the kids always regarded the Melbourne trip as special, but for different reasons, as she explains.

● ● ●

I planned my whole year around the two weeks of the Boxing Day and New Year Tests. A lot of people think it must have been terrible to always be away from home at Christmas, but it was such a special time. The kids and I loved it; after all, we were in a nice hotel with all the festive trimmings, we were being pampered for a change, and we were surrounded by the friends we'd made through the game—our other family, if you like.

I suppose it was like other people going on a beach summer holiday where they stayed in the same place and saw the same people year after year. We were very lucky because we were in at a time when the team was pretty stable so the families present at the celebrations were usually the same each year. Believe it or not, my closest friend is Matthew Hayden's wife, Kelly. I know it sounds strange that I found friendship off the field with the wife of Justin's on-field partner, but that's the way it happened. In fact, Kelly and I had become friends long before our husbands had joined forces or had even established themselves in the Test side. We met in the summer of 1994–95 when Justin and Matthew were both in the Australia A side.

Our relationship isn't based on cricket, although we are probably bonded in some way because of our similar experiences. I like to think that it's because our personalities blend well. Kelly and I often ended up yakking on the phone while our husbands were batting—not discussing their performances but just chatting as friends. Over the years we've been on holidays together, at their place on Stradbroke Island or at ours in Mandurah. We were married within a month or so of one another and we've supported each other as our families have grown.

Mel Gilchrist is the other close friend I've had over the years, for pretty much the same reasons. Not only do we have similar personalities, but our life experience is similar—we both met our future husbands at school and built our relationships along with their careers.

Kelly, Mel and I would visit each other's rooms during the Christmas break in Melbourne and Sydney, bathe our kids and even cook meals together. When our kids were really young there would be a convoy of strollers along the Yarra as we made our way to the MCG each day. The kids loved it too—Christmas Day in a posh hotel with Santa Claus, face-painters, clowns and carollers. Jessie, who is now thirteen, had her first Christmas in Perth as a nine-month-old baby and then all the others in Melbourne until her dad retired.

The one exception was 2005, when Justin was injured and missed the Test. It was devastating. I had just given birth to our youngest, Grace, and everything had been carefully planned. Yet just a few days before Christmas everything changed. The whole family was quite glum at a time when we were usually so happy. Justin moped around like a lost soldier, unhappy that he'd been ruled out when he believed he could overcome the injury, and the rest of us missed out on our annual holiday. Thankfully, Justin was fit enough to play in the New Year's Test, so I jumped on a plane to Sydney with Grace. That gave me a chance to catch up with the crew and also to relax for a week.

On our last trip to Sydney in 2006–07, our brood of four children meant we qualified for a suite with three bedrooms. We got the penthouse on the 33rd floor at Quay West, overlooking the Harbour Bridge and the Opera House. Our view of the new year's fireworks was breathtaking, making Justin's last game all the more special.

● ● ●

Given that I mentioned the symbol of the cross during the Melbourne Test of 2002–03, this is a good place to explain the part Christianity, or spirituality, has played in my life.

I often talk about having a 'four-box theory' about being a successful cricketer. What I mean is that, in my view, there were four boxes I needed to tick off in order to be successful. The first three are obvious—mental, physical and technical—but the fourth is less so. It was my spiritual or emotional box, and it was much harder to identify, let alone to check off and maintain.

I have a strong spiritual side. I'm not exactly sure where it comes from, but over the years I have studied the philosophy of Buddhism, amongst others, to help with my concentration, meditation and physical well-being. I was raised in a Catholic household; my grand-parents, in particular, were very religious and my parents are regular church-goers. I went to a Catholic school, and I turned back to the church and its teachings several times during my life and career.

When I returned from the tour of Sri Lanka and Zimbabwe in October 1999 I was in a bad state of mind. My on-field form was ter-rible, which probably magnified the personal problems I was having off the field. In particular, I was finding it difficult to balance a career that had no guarantees with my obligations to my young family.

We began a home series against Pakistan in November, but I was still struggling. In the First Test, in Brisbane, I had scored just one run, but we won comfortably nevertheless. I returned to Perth to do some training at the WACA before the next Test in Hobart. One evening, on a whim, I decided to speak to Andrew Valance, our team pastor. I wasn't afraid to talk to sports psychologists when I had problems, so I didn't see it as a big deal to talk to Andrew.

'I can't work it out,' I began. 'I'm batting at number three for Australia, I've got a beautiful wife and two gorgeous kids, a great house and car, money, friends and my health. I should be happy— but something's missing.'

Andrew listened for a while and then asked, 'Have you read the Bible lately?'

The fact was I had never read the Bible, other than the minimum required of me at school. We talked about this for a while and parted company.

The next morning I was leaving early with the West Australian team for a one-day match against Queensland, before I would fly to Hobart for the Second Test. Pastor Valance was at the airport with his family and presented me with a leather-bound Bible.

I thanked him but didn't know what to do, given that my teammates were boarding the plane with copies of sports and men's mags. I probably hid the Bible behind something else, but then I started to read a few of the scriptures Andrew had marked for me, including one that read: 'I can do everything through God, who gives me strength.'

The scripture really resonated with me but I didn't think much about it until a week or so later in Hobart, when Gilly and I played our famous partnership to win the Second Test. I've looked back at the tapes of that day; the commentators kept talking about my concentration. Little did they know I was doing a form of meditation. In between mid-pitch chats with Gilly, I would think of what I had read on the aircraft: 'God gives me the strength to do anything.'

Another memorable example took place a couple of years later, in late 2001, just after I had begun to open the batting for Australia. Given my blazing start as an opener, I find it strange now that I felt so nervous before the First Test against South Africa that season. I think it must have been the occasion, because the series was being billed as a shootout between the two heavyweight cricketing nations. There couldn't have been any other reason—after all, Haydos and I had run rampant since being installed a few months before, and I had scored three centuries and a half-century in my last four Tests.

Still, the night before the match I was so nervous that I walked down to the Adelaide Oval late at night, convinced a security guard to let me in and sat by myself in the stands, contemplating the game.

I stayed for around an hour, taking in some of the atmosphere, then made my way back to the hotel. It didn't do me any good and I lay awake, tossing and turning.

The tennis great Margaret Court is a neighbour of mine in Perth. She's the head of her own church called the Victory Life Centre. We had become friendly over the years, talking in the street, quite often about spirituality and religion. She'd once written down a scripture reference for me to use if I needed to chill out. I thought of it as I lay in bed that night but couldn't find it as I scrabbled around in the dark.

It was still the middle of the evening back in Perth so I chanced it and gave her a call.

'Have you got a Bible by the bed?' she asked, and directed me to the verse.

It reads: 'For God did not give us a spirit of fear, but a spirit of power, of love and a sound mind.'

Margaret and I spoke for twenty minutes or so, after which I drifted off to sleep. The next morning everything had changed. The message to me from that verse was not to have fear but to be confident and have a go. So many people live their lives in fear of failure—and even in fear of success. Suddenly, the South Africans held no fear for me, and I batted that way, scoring my fourth century in six innings. I even hit a six to bring up the three figures.

During the last series I played in South Africa, in 2006, Archbishop Desmond Tutu was at a function we attended. He gave an amazing speech about apartheid. I was seated at his table and asked him to nominate his favourite scripture.

He looked up at me, scratching his chin as he thought, then said, 'My favourite scripture, Justin, is Romans, chapter five, and I suggest that you read it before you go to bed tonight.'

I went back to my room, found a Bible in the top drawer and looked for the chapter. It talks about how adversity forges strength and character. I'm sure Archbishop Tutu mentioned it because of the anti-apartheid movement in South Africa, but it resonated with me for my own battles.

That's what I find inspiring about religion and faith. I don't go to church every week but I do love going into churches. They are beautiful places and I love their musty smell and their silence. There is a lot of strength in silence, and sitting alone in a church has often helped me clear my mind and place things in perspective. I have always been someone who responds to messages and, I have to say, I have found a lot of powerful messages in the Bible.

21. Spits and fits

Of all the disappointments that I have experienced in professional sport, nothing compares to the day in April 2003 that I watched Glenn McGrath deal with the news that his beautiful wife, Jane, had suffered a cancer relapse. We had left Australia for the Caribbean the day before with expectations of victory and plans for a whitewash, but they faded into insignificance during a stopover at Gatwick Airport in London. I will never forget the look of utter devastation on Pigeon's face as he told us he had to go home and didn't know whether he would join us on tour. It was a sobering moment and put everything in perspective for the whole team.

Speaking of sobering, I had made one of the worst decisions of my sporting life a few weeks before we left for the West Indies when I had decided to give up alcohol for a while. That might not seem like a bad thing, particularly as I had given it up as part of the Easter tradition of Lent, but the impact it had on my state of mind is interesting to look back on.

Don't jump to conclusions about my dependency on alcohol, though. There are numerous stories in this book about raucous but harmless nights of mateship and celebration, but in reality they were few and far between. Most of the time I was training hard, watching my diet and honing my skills. Alcohol was an occasional and, usually, a moderate way to let off a bit of steam and celebrate a victory.

Even though I did well personally in the Caribbean, toning down the celebrations went against everything I believe in. My motto has always been to work as hard as you can and then celebrate your success, because if you can't celebrate success, then what is the point of all the hard work?

With more positive news about Jane, Pigeon had rejoined us in time for the Third Test, in Bridgetown, Barbados, but it was clear he was not settled and that Jane's health problems had rocked him. It didn't show in his performance as much as in his demeanour, which blew up in the Fourth Test, in Antigua, when he had an unfortunate altercation with West Indian batsman Ramnaresh Sarwan.

I was very close to the action at the time and heard what happened. Glenn started it, trying to unsettle Sarwan, who had been batting well to help the Windies chase down a big total and win the Test (which they did). The exchange has been well documented and I won't rehash it here, but in essence it was sparked by a misunderstanding. While I would never condone what happened, I will always defend Glenn because of the circumstances. He apologised later but that still wasn't good enough for the media, which tore him apart, ignoring the stress he was under.

This brings me to a real bugbear of mine—sledging.

It seems that every Australian summer, as the international

teams arrive, one of the first questions asked by the media is about sledging—can the visitors stand up to the on-field psychological attacks of the Australian team? Of course, the visiting captain insists his team can cope, but invariably this starts a wildfire of stories about sledging and the behaviour of the Australians.

This really steams me up because most of it is rubbish. There's always a bit of gamesmanship in Test match cricket, as teams pressure the opposition by reminding them of the tight situation or challenging their ability to face the bowling, but in all my years I only ever saw a couple of incidents that crossed the line. Test cricket is a physical, technical and psychological test that is not for the fainthearted, so a few words here and there is all a part of the contest. Frankly, I wouldn't want to see it any other way.

There is no doubt that the Australian team plays hard; after all, that's the way we are brought up. There is pressure out there, not only personally but as a team. You could call it the Anzac spirit because it means we fight all the way, and it would be a very sad day for Australian cricket if that spirit and killer instinct was drummed out of us.

I was certainly challenged on the field, mostly by players telling me I was an average player, but it only got my back up and helped me play better. As I've already related, in January 2000, when I scored a double-century against India at the SCG, Javagal Srinath kept calling me the worst Test batsman who ever played. The more he said it, the better I went.

In fact, the most effective psychological tactic against me was to ignore me, since I put more than enough psychological pressure on myself. That's how mates like Simon Katich and Matty Hayden treated me when we faced each other in domestic cricket. On one occasion in Sydney, Simon and I had dinner the night before a match but the next day he wouldn't even acknowledge me when I came out to bat—he wouldn't even make eye contact. Instead, he kept throwing the ball back to the wicket-keeper just over my head.

The point is that if I didn't take such pressure to heart when playing against my mates, then our opponents shouldn't either. If sledging or gamesmanship is too much to bear, then I'm afraid you have to harden up a bit or find something else to play. There's a line that shouldn't be crossed, of course—racial, sexual or personal vilification—but in reality, sledging is more of a media beat-up than anything else.

● ● ●

While on the subject of regrets and aggro, I'll say a few things about anger. I had a reputation for getting cranky about being dismissed, and at times it was justified. Looking back, I have a few regrets about my post-innings performances in the change rooms. I wasn't alone in needing a bit of space in the first ten minutes or so after getting out. Quite a few of my team-mates would acknowledge that it was best just to leave them alone when they first came off the ground.

Imagine the situation from my perspective. I'm involved in a fight out there. If a bowler makes a mistake he gets plenty of chances to come back and make amends, but for a batsman one mistake means you are gone. All of a sudden the fight is over and I have to walk off the ground, despondent and defeated. I was the sort of batsman who needed to get rid of emotion—I spat the dummy, had a few minutes by myself to think about it, then perhaps had a cup of coffee. It was my way of getting it out of my system rather than hanging on to it for too long. After that I was usually alright.

I made an arse of myself a few times, although thankfully

I mellowed as I got older. I remember chucking a bat across the change room in one of my early state games, then watching in horror as it bounced off my gear and hit Brendon Julian, who is one of the coolest and nicest guys around. Of course, that wasn't what I had meant to happen and I was very embarrassed.

I've punched a few lockers over the years and cracked a few bats, and every time it happened I regretted it immediately. One day I hit a locker so hard that it dented and I couldn't open it to get to my gear. On another occasion at Somerset I kicked a plastic bin several times and smashed it; I immediately felt terrible and rushed out to buy a big sturdy metal bin, on which I wrote 'JL's bin'.

A similar incident in 2009 confirmed my decision to retire. I was in India, captaining Somerset in the Champions League Twenty20 competition, and the team needed a big innings from me to have a chance of winning our way through to the semi-finals. I got a start but then got out. I came off the ground in a foul mood and stormed back into the change rooms, knowing I was going to have a spit. I slammed the rickety door hard, only to hear the glass falling out and shattering all over the floor. The funny thing was that the match referee was none other than Javagal Srinath, who kindly let the whole incident go. I paid for the door, of course.

Another one that comes to mind happened when I was a nineteen-year-old playing for Dover in England. Sue had come over to spend a few weeks with me and we had plans to go to Paris the next day. She was horrified when I had a change-room meltdown after getting out and walked off without her to the house where we were staying with our friends Mick and Irene Mart. I phoned her later to apologise and tried to get her to come to the pub, where I was having a drink with Mick and my team-mates, but she refused.

I tried to make up hours later when I got home after a few too many pints of Guinness but, unsurprisingly, Sue told me to get into my own bed—we were sleeping in two singles. The next thing I knew, she was shaking me awake in the middle of the night and calling me a disgrace. She was right. In my stupor I thought I was in the toilet, while actually I was relieving myself on the TV set sitting between our two beds.

Sue still wouldn't talk to me the next morning, and by the time we got on the ferry to go to France our hosts were starting to notice the tension. I eventually admitted what I had done, including the TV set, which they thought was the funniest thing they'd heard. But Sue wasn't convinced, and the next three days in the city of romance were icy, all because of my change-room dummy spit.

● ● ●

There's no doubt Justin was a fiery young bloke, probably because of his desire to do well. He took his planning and preparation very seriously, so when it all went wrong he got very down on himself.

I remember a couple of his change-room explosions very well, including the Dover incident, which happened pretty much as he tells it. The morning after, the others thought it was hilarious but I'd taken a stand. Even though I was laughing on the inside, I couldn't let Justin see any weakening—call it a woman's pride.

I also remember the rubbish bin incident at Somerset, but what Justin doesn't mention is that it was me—not him—who had to go out and buy the replacement. I was at home with the girls in our village just outside Taunton when I got a call on my mobile phone. I panicked, because the only time I ever got calls during a game was if Justin had been injured.

He told me what had happened and how embarrassed he was,

then asked if I could drop what I was doing, drive into town, buy a new bin and bring it to the ground. Not only did I have to carry it through town, but he also wanted me to walk through the car park at the cricket ground, past all the quizzical looks of the people who knew me, and deliver it to him in the change rooms.

Thankfully, Justin matured over the years and retirement has eased the stress even more, although life remains very busy. Nowadays, if Justin gets upset about something he usually goes very quiet and heads off to water the garden. I follow him out to ask if there's anything I can do, but it never really works. As he says, leaving him alone is the best solution, although on occasions I have tried to break the tension by suggesting he go and read his own book, *Seeing the Sunrise*, and take some of his own advice!

● ● ●

I consider that my poor averages against the Test minnows Zimbabwe and Bangladesh are the strangest statistics of my career. Playing them always appeared to be an opportunity to cash in and offset some of the hard yards against the best pace attacks, like those of the West Indies and Pakistan, but I managed to muck it up every time, averaging less than 30 in five matches against them.

Haydos and I were licking our lips in the summer of 2003–04 as we prepared to take on Zimbabwe at the WACA in the first of two Tests. The day before the match Haydos came over to my place to chill out for a few hours with a swim and a bite of lunch. I picked him up at the team hotel and then slowly cruised back to City Beach with the windows down, the sun shining through the windows and Jack Johnson's laidback song 'Wasting Time' on the stereo. The day was perfect as we strolled across the road to the beach, stopping at a cafe to order lunch.

'That'll do me,' Haydos said, pointing to the seafood platter.

'But, Mr Hayden, that's for two people,' said the attendant.

Haydos grinned. 'That's fine—I'm a bit peckish.'

We had a dip in the Indian Ocean while we waited, then demolished lunch. Later that night Haydos cooked dinner for my family—red emperor in Thai spices and nasi goreng. Life couldn't get much better.

By the next morning things had turned around. The beach, the sun and the music were forgotten as I stood with Haydos and the team for the national anthem at the WACA. I was nervous because of the weight of expectation. Not only were we playing a side against which I was expected to do well, but we were at my home ground.

John Buchanan tried to calm me down with a few encouraging words in the change rooms after we won the toss, but I was still nervous and it showed. When we went out to bat I was playing stand-and-deliver shots from the first over—I raced to 26 with five boundaries.

I walked down the pitch at the end of the fifth over, gazed around the ground, which was full and buzzing with expectation, and declared to Haydos, 'If I keep going like this I reckon I'm going to make 300 today.'

Cardinal sin.

The very next ball I blocked medium-pacer Sean Ervine into the ground, but the ball bounced over my head and hit my stumps. I wandered off dejectedly, having failed yet again, then I watched as Haydos played one of the great Test innings.

At every break he'd come into the change rooms and we'd put on 'Wasting Time' and sit around talking like a couple of surfers waiting for the next wave. The other blokes got sick and tired of the same song going over and over again, but we refused to change it, arguing that it was keeping Haydos in the rhythm for a triple-century. And that's what he made—380 off 437 balls with 38 fours and eleven sixes.

I can look at his innings two ways, I suppose—I can either be happy that the next best thing to making 300 is if my best mate does, or I can think that my big mate stole my innings. I'm still mulling it over.

Ian Healy, 4th Songmaster, 1996–99

JL: How did you come to be songmaster in the Australian team?

IH: I guess it was being a good drinker, and enjoying a party and the afterglow of a Test match, whether it was in commiseration or celebration. Boony, having retired, stood on the table for one last time and handed it over. It was quite a nerve-racking experience, wondering if it was going to be me and then trying to think what I was going to do with it.

JL: When would you sing it?

IH: It varied. It wasn't set in concrete and was at my discretion. I don't think I left it too long during the night, because I needed to capture the emotion and the relief of the victory.

JL: Did you always sing it in the rooms?

IH: I think we did. I liked it in the rooms because that was where the sweat and tears had gone in over a long period of time. Cricket is unique in that we compete for 30 hours and then you have to unwind, and that was the start of our unwinding.

JL: Can you remember any particularly special ones?

IH: I remember they complained about us in Barbados after one Test match and tried to kick us out. The one at Lord's on the pitch stands out, and another at Cape Town. Pakistan also stands out. They were all pretty loud.

JL: Can you remember handing it over?

IH: I thought I had one more game but I had been dropped, so I must have rung Punter or seen him at practice. I remember going into the Gabba during that First Test against Pakistan in 1999 and handing it over with the team in the circle. I felt quite sheepish going in to do it. I was in the ring with my arm around Warney and I bumped his beer bottle into his tooth. He wasn't good having the stubby go into his tooth. He was off.

JL: Why is it important?

IH: The importance of it is that it's tradition. We are continuing something that is not initiated by us, and to carry on someone else's idea is pretty special. I don't see too many opposition sides with something like that. It stands out as another symbol of our camaraderie—the love we have for each other when we are playing cricket for our country.

22. An Indian summer

Ajit Agarkar was a fast-medium bowler for India, but certainly not the most fearsome bowler I ever faced. His Test statistics support my view, and yet those same numbers also show that Ajit got me out on more occasions in Test cricket than any other bowler. I faced the sheer speed of Shoaib Akhtar, the guile of Wasim Akram and the bounce and accuracy of Curtly Ambrose and Courtney Walsh, yet it was Agarkar—nippy and fiery, at his best—who snared me six times.

He troubled me because of his late inswing, trapping me LBW three times. The perception that I was Agarkar's bunny even drifted down to grade cricket in Perth. Not long after I'd faced him in 2003–04, I played a few games of club cricket for Scarborough and in one innings this young bloke started taunting me with a call to his bowler that he should 'bowl like Agarkar'. It was a stupid move, however, because it just got me fired up, which made me impossible to dislodge.

The Test series against India that summer had been amazing, not because of Agarkar or me, but because of the folly of administrators and the magic of champions. I'll deal with the former first. I went on the record lauding India and its champions after the four-match series ended 1–1. Their batting was just extraordinary. 'There is a lot we can learn from them,' I said. 'They look so patient, as if they are in a meditative state. It's awesome the way they apply themselves. I can't remember being under pressure in this manner—the pressure to bowl against them, field against them, and to chase huge scores. I can't remember in my career playing a team like them.'

Without taking anything away from India's champion players, the series was hampered by the fact that the wickets were all very flat. There was a lot of discussion around at the time that this was a deliberate ploy to ensure that each Test would go the full five days. If that was true, then it was a misguided and very harmful policy as it created run feasts, which ultimately are not entertaining.

There were more than 1100 runs scored in Brisbane, both sides scored over 500 in their first innings in Adelaide, there were another 1200-plus runs in Melbourne, then India scored over 700 in its first innings in Sydney in a match which saw more than 1700 runs scored in five days. There were twelve centuries in the series—including four double-centuries—and the sides were bowled out in only ten of the sixteen innings played.

I shouldn't complain, really, because I made a couple of centuries myself, but it would be a great pity if the individual characteristics of each Australian venue are lost in the desire to standardise surfaces and prolong contests. Sydney used to be a spinners' wicket, the WACA was once the fastest and bounciest wicket in the world, the Gabba was fast but took spin on the last two days, Adelaide also started as a batsman's paradise but deteriorated by the last day, while the MCG was slower than Perth but had a strange, steepling, tennis-ball style bounce. It's much better to have an entertaining three-day match than a boring five-day contest. You don't need to change or trick up the game with pink balls or night Test matches. It's surviving perfectly well as it is, especially in Australia, and it would be a great pity if administrators tampered with cricket's traditional form.

Leaving aside my doubts about the pitches, the series allowed the champion batsmen on both sides to shine. Punter scored two double-centuries, Rahul Dravid and Sachin Tendulkar one each, while V.V.S. Laxman scored two big hundreds. They were all masterful and a joy to witness, even as an opponent.

Sachin Tendulkar was always a quiet bloke and I rarely saw him drink, but after India's win in Adelaide he came into the Australian change rooms with a bottle of champagne and stayed for a chat. I could never help being interested in champions and how they think. I monopolised his time a bit, grilling him about how he handles the hysteria in India, where he is godlike, and the pressure of the huge expectation about his performances.

He let his guard down after a while. 'I never read the papers or watch the TV reports,' he said. 'I don't need the media to tell me how I'm going. I know, and that's all that matters.'

I'd been given the same advice before by others, but somehow, coming from the best player in the world, his words made a big impression on me. If Tendulkar was subject to public pressures and had to devise strategies to ensure they did not affect him, then he was a shining example to someone like me—I definitely let the media's opinions affect me too much, especially early in my career.

● ● ●

The Fourth Test, at the SCG, had several highlights, including Tendulkar's unbeaten double-century and his 353-run stand with V.V.S. Laxman, who scored 178, but these were surpassed by the celebrations for Steve Waugh's last Test. We all wanted him to repeat the heroics of the previous summer against the old enemy, when he had reached a century from the last ball of the second day; he fell on 80, but still ensured we secured a draw to end the series.

Tugga's farewell that night was one of those events which you hope will never end. The disappointment of not winning the Test so we could sing the song with him one last time faded as we arrived at the home of his manager, Robert Joske. My head was in a spin because at the ground I'd been asked to give the testimonial speech for the skipper. I was honoured but completely overwhelmed. After all, how can you capture the essence of such an amazing career?

I decided to treat it like I would a wedding and not have a drink until I got the speech out of the way. It was a good decision, because I was nervous as hell speaking in front of the crowd of celebrities, sports legends and a few politicians, including Prime Minister John Howard.

The highlight, if I had to choose one, was the appearance of Jimmy Barnes and John Williamson, whose songs had been so much a part of our change-room spirit during Tugga's reign. At one point we all got up with Jimmy to sing 'Flame Trees' and 'Khe Sanh', swaying around the grand piano, lost in the words we'd belted out so many times around the world.

John Williamson then came up to sing 'True Blue'. Just as we linked arms, Haydos, who was next to me, looked behind him and noticed Mr Howard sitting at the bar nearby with a glass of beer in his hand. As only Haydos can do, he called out, 'Hey, Johnny, come and join us, mate.'

217

I have this vision of the PM, crushed between us, his glasses pushed askew and hanging off his ears, trying to sing along but not quite knowing every word like we did. He hummed and mimed the verses, but then waded in during the chorus with a loud and slightly off-key 'True Blue'. Imagine that—arm in arm, singing 'True Blue' with my mates and the prime minister of the day. I have to add here that John Howard always impressed me with his sincerity. He once met my grandfather in the change rooms during a Test match; when they were both in the rooms again several years later, he recalled my grandfather's name immediately, much to his delight.

I had tried to scribble some notes for the speech but in the end decided to speak pretty much from the heart. I've copped a bit of criticism over the years for my public admiration for Steve Waugh, but the fact is that he was an enormous influence not just on my cricket but also on my view of life, which is now so much broader thanks to his interest in other cultures and the side-trips he always arranged.

I spoke about Tugga's ability to make players believe in themselves and take pride in the game and its traditions. I also mentioned one of his best lines in the change rooms—'There's a lot of love in this room, boys.' That was indicative of the team spirit he engendered, and it was one of the main reasons the Australian team was and has continued to be so successful.

My speech over, I helped myself to some of the Moët that was going around the room. I'd never been a Champagne lover, but that night I realised how good it tasted on the right occasion.

● ● ●

Darren 'Boof' Lehmann was a great example of how different personalities could work so well within a team. Teamwork is about forging a united collection of individuals. Wouldn't it be boring if every member of the Australian side played the same way? I bet we wouldn't have been as successful.

Apart from both being left-handers and born in 1970, Boof and I were polar opposites in our batting and the way we went about the game. I planned everything and worked like a draughthorse to catch up to the geniuses I saw around me, while Boof was himself one of those batting geniuses.

He was unlucky to have played only 27 Tests, but finding a permanent place in the Australian middle order at the time was impossible when you were up against the likes of the Waugh brothers and Ricky Ponting. Still, his record was exceptional, with a Test average a tick under 45 and five centuries. He also played 117 one-day internationals and had an average of almost 39, not to mention his first-class average of over 57.

He was one of the best players of spin I ever saw. He was like a white Brian Lara with the way he whipped his bat and played into gaps no matter where and how you set the field. He was also one of the straightest shooters in the game—the sort of bloke who, if questioned by his missus, the captain or the coach about how many beers he'd had the night before, would admit to eight rather than pretend it was three, like a lot of blokes do.

Our tour of Sri Lanka in March 2004 was memorable for many reasons. We won a tough series under the leadership of our new captain, Ricky Ponting, I became songmaster in his stead and finally beat my demons against Murali in the Third Test at Colombo. (Having said that, if I had to face Murali today I still reckon I would struggle to find answers to his genius.) The pressure was off to some extent because we had won the series by the time we reached Colombo for the last Test. The Galle victory by 197 runs was tighter than it looked but the second test win by 27 runs in Kandy could have gone either way. I needed to back it up with a memorable team song so, as we drove toward Colombo in a bus, I arranged with local police to stop briefly midway across a bridge between the two provinces. I hurriedly led the guys off the bus, set up an esky in the middle of the road and stood on it while we belted out the song high above a raging river in the mountains of this amazing country.

I wasn't the only one to find form in the Third Test—Boof made 153 in the first innings to set up the victory. The different behaviour exhibited by Boof and me during the rest periods in that match reflected our different styles perfectly. Colombo is so hot and humid that you're wet from perspiration before you get to the middle. It feels like you have jumped into a lukewarm swimming pool. The only relief we got was to descend into the change rooms during the lunch and tea breaks, where the cool red concrete floor beneath the grandstand was a blessing. I would come in and strip off, take in as much fluid as possible, and maybe even have an ice bath to cool down or a bit of a massage. Before I went out I'd put on fresh socks and pants and a new shirt to make sure I was as comfortable and as dry as I could be.

Boof began as I did by stripping off completely, but then he'd carefully lay out his wet trousers, shirt, jockstrap, sweatbands and bike pants on the concrete floor. He'd then sit back with his back against his locker, stark-naked, light up a cigarette and order a large glass of Coke and ice, which he would slowly sip as he smoked his durry. He'd finish the Coke then light up a second cigarette, take a few puffs and get ready to go out again—not with fresh clothes but with the ones he'd laid so carefully on the floor. First the still sodden jockstrap would go on, then the socks, bike pants, trousers and shirt, and finally the sweatbands. He'd take a final puff, stub the butt out on the floor and head back out into the action. Different blokes, different strokes but the same result, and we loved and respected each other for it.

Murali had almost plunged me into depression during our tour in 1999. I'd had no idea where the ball was going, so I resorted—unsuccessfully—to trying to sweep almost everything. I was doing the same at the beginning of the 2004 tour and averaged just 15 over the first two Tests. The highs of the Indian tour seemed a long time ago as we headed to Colombo, where my first innings of 19 was more of the same.

Part of my problem, I realised, was that a spin bowler gave you so many options. Should I get down to the pitch of the ball and hit it over the top? Maybe I should sweep, or wait and cut off the back foot? There were always bat-pad fielders all around me. The options caused confusion, indecision and mistakes. I also knew that I tended to play Murali on his reputation rather than ball-by-ball.

In the second innings I decided to play the spinners as I would the speedsters, making sure I was sharp on my feet and getting my weight forward while watching the ball out of the hand and playing each one on its merits, Murali included. This completely changed my mental attitude and I found the confidence to play off my front foot.

It was a revelation, even though I was hampered by bad cramps that had begun after one of those ice baths—maybe I should have followed Boof's example instead. My calves went and then my hips, hamstrings and quads. I kept thinking about Dean Jones' famous double-century innings during the tied Test at Madras in 1986. He was batting with Allan Border but was so dehydrated that he was vomiting every few overs. He got to 170 and wanted to 'retire ill', but AB told him he was a weak Victorian and he wanted a tough

Australian like a Queenslander. Jones stayed and got his double-century. I was playing for Australia and so it never entered my mind to come off. Instead, Haydos came to my rescue and ran for me.

In my gym at home I have the words 'Hang in there—you never know what's around the corner. Sri Lanka 2004' hanging on the wall. That was the lesson I learned from playing in such tough conditions and against the toughest rivals. As long as you keep working hard and looking for ways to get better, the rewards will come. While I had to wait until the last time I ever played Murali to succeed against him, the reward was very sweet.

It would be a twelve-month period like no other—fifteen Test matches between October 2003 and October 2004—during which time we played two series against India, another two against Sri Lanka and one against Zimbabwe. It was a very intense period, expecting us to play Test cricket on 75 days in a year. In the period July 2004 to July 2005 we would play another nineteen Tests.

The two-match series against Sri Lanka in July 2004 was unique because we played both games in the tropical north. The First Test in Darwin was interesting mostly because of a controversial drop-in pitch which proved a bowler's paradise and a nightmare for the likes of me. We were bowled out for 207 and 201 but the Sri Lankans fared worse and managed just 97 and 162.

It would be the opposite in Cairns for the Second Test.

The night before the match we had a formal dinner at the ground. From where I was sitting, listening to Ian Chappell and Ian Healy giving speeches, I could see across the ground to the floodlit scoreboard. I kept visualising seeing my name up there—a tactic Steve Waugh had taught me and akin to Pat Farmer's suggestion that you should picture the finish line before you start the race. The figure I visualised was 160. I have no idea why I chose that number, but the next day Haydos and I put on our sixth double-century opening stand and I made 162. It is amazing how the human mind works. The series had been hard-fought but, to be honest, we had our eyes on another prize—beating India in India.

23. The Platinum Club

Touring is one of the privileges of international cricket; new countries, strange cities and exotic cultures. On the surface this all appears exciting, but—and this is no complaint—it can also be a grind physically and psychologically. Life on the road simply isn't as glamorous as it sounds, with long stints away from your family and most of your time spent in hotel rooms or at cricket grounds. The heavy schedules of modern cricket mean the days of golf, rest days and sightseeing are all but gone.

I once asked Steve Waugh how he handled the time on the road and the exhausting periods away from his wife, Lynette, and his children.

Without blinking, he looked at me and said, 'That's why I strive to be the best batsman in the world. If I'm going to make those sacrifices, then I want to make sure I'm making the most of my time away by being the best. Anything less and I'd feel like I was letting myself and my family down.'

Just as visiting teams have found touring Australia difficult over the years, we also faced challenges, particularly on the subcontinent, where the climate can be oppressive and the facilities vastly different from our own.

In my time in the Australian team, Mount Everest always had twin peaks. Obviously every series was important—especially against England and India and, more recently, South Africa—but there were two unconquered frontiers that stood apart.

The first was to beat the mighty West Indies in a series, one of the few things Allan Border didn't achieve in his amazing career. We did that in 1995. The second, and in many ways the most difficult, was to win a series in India for the first time in three decades. In 2001 the job looked all but accomplished, until V.V.S. Laxman and Rahul Dravid produced a miracle to deny us. Three years later we were back to try again.

We arrived optimistic, as we always were, although since we were without our injured skipper, Ricky Ponting, the job looked tough. Adam Gilchrist stepped up as captain and by the end of the Second Test we were 1–0 up. We had won the First Test, at Bangalore, in a canter, with Michael Clarke making an astonishing century on debut, then we'd been lucky to escape with a draw at Chennai when rain washed out the final day's play—India had needed just over 200 to win with all ten wickets in hand. The hot and humid conditions were extremely trying, so even though we came to Nagpur in a buoyant frame of mind we were all tired and on edge. But we knew a win in the Third Test would finish the job.

If you searched on a map of India for the country's central point, you would mark the city of Nagpur. It's a strange sort of place, even for India, in the sense that its population of over two million people is significant and yet it feels like a regional city the size of, say, Mandurah on the outskirts of Perth. Nagpurians—I love collective nouns sometimes; 'Nagpurians' sounds like something out of a Tolkien novel!—are particularly proud of the large, luscious oranges of their district, their contribution to the arts and literature, their famous hospitality, and their virtually crime-free streets, where people leave their doors unlocked and their bicycles leaning against a fence.

It would be fair to say, however, that Nagpur wasn't the ideal place for us to calm our edgy spirits in October 2004. We arrived late at night, probably around midnight, and the mid-30s temperature was stifling. There were crowds lining the road from the airport—thousands upon thousands of people—joyful and welcoming. We felt like the Beatles, but it was claustrophobic as we battled through the masses. When we staggered slowly off the team bus at the aptly named Pride Hotel, we were met by thousands more people, waving, chanting and snapping their cameras. As we entered the foyer, there were hundreds more cricket-loving fans wanting autographs and photographs. The whole thing was so surreal—it felt like we were entering the twilight zone of the Eagles' song 'Hotel California'.

We were tired and grumpy and most of us were bloody hungry. Always unsure of what to eat and drink in India, we were confidently ushered into the hotel's restaurant, which offered Chinese cuisine. A serve of fried rice, spring rolls and chicken with cashews seemed safe enough, but it quickly soured when a floundering cockroach was found in the soy sauce. We left, famished but unharmed, wondering what culinary delights lay in store for us over the rest of the week.

Thankfully, Matthew Hayden had planned better than most and had come with his very own kitchen in a bag. In fact, make that two bags. It's well known that Haydos loves to cook—he often visited hotel and restaurant kitchens while on tour and served meals for his mates and admirers, or for charity events. On this occasion, however, he hatched a master plan to cook for himself, Damien Martyn and me—the only members of the Australian cricket team's new 'Platinum Club'.

Most players have just one cricket bag on tour but Haydos turned up with three. Eyebrows were raised when he banged and clanged his way on and off the team bus, leaving staff totally confused about what he was bringing into their five-star hotel. But it wasn't until our first morning in Nagpur, though, that he opened his secret treasure chest.

I woke up to the smell of freshly made bread. I'd been kept awake most of the night by buzzing mosquitoes and the trains going past my open window. My head was thumping and it was already hot and sticky at six o'clock in the morning. I walked out into the hallway to follow the smell and realised it was coming from Haydos' room.

Apart from the aroma of the bakery in room 127, I could also hear a familiar gurgling sound as I banged on his door. Matty opened it with a grin and showed me in. The bouquet was coming from a breadmaker perched on a desk. Not only had he baked bread but he'd also managed to get hold of a Starbucks coffee machine and was brewing a pot of fresh coffee.

I rang Damien's room, woke him up and got him to come down before anyone else got a whiff of what was going on. And so the three of us sat there in Haydos' room, the day before one of the biggest Test matches of our careers, having fresh coffee with Vegemite and butter on warm fresh bread. I found it hard to stop laughing and joking with my two coffee buddies from the Platinum Club.

During breakfast Matty opened up one of his bags and started pulling out equipment—it was like Doctor Who's TARDIS! Apart from the coffee machine and breadmaker, he also had a gas-powered camp cooking stove, a toasted-sandwich maker, saucepans, a frying pan, plus plenty of tongs and utensils. Another bag was full of food, mostly from England, where he'd been playing in the Champion's Trophy before coming to India. He had pasta from Marks & Spencer, bags of Starbucks coffee, tins of vegetables and salmon and all sorts of herbs and spices—all brought and planned for that one week.

From breakfast on day one our week ran like clockwork. Each night after play, I'd go back to the hotel and have a session with a yoga instructor. Then I'd have a shower and call home to speak to Sue and the kids. By seven o'clock I'd be loose and feeling great, and I'd hear the coffee machine hissing and the frying pan sizzling in Haydos' room. I was in heaven.

You could smell the aroma down the hallway. Damien and I would head into his room, and the three of us would listen to music and chat while having a fabulous meal. One night Haydos made a salmon concoction, another night it was chicken and pasta or omelettes from eggs he'd scrounged from the hotel kitchen. Some nights we organised a few cold bottles of beer, or cans of Diet Coke, to help celebrate the day that had just been and to wash down the feast that we'd just enjoyed.

You can imagine the reaction of the other guys. Because they were battling the nuances of the hotel buffet, soon they were all banging on the door of room 127 and pleading to come in for a feed. Our only reply was to remind them of their lack of membership. Even though there were no concrete membership requirements for the Platinum Club, we made up some rules along the way, making it well nigh impossible for any of our team-mates to come in and join the feast.

Haydos' kitchen was our sanctuary in a place where there wasn't much to do but make our own fun. Punter was the other recognised member of the Platinum Club, but he wasn't on tour. Instead we took pity on Victorian Brad Hodge, one of the younger tourists. Although he wasn't allowed to feast each night, we gave him a Gold Club membership, which meant he could sit and chill out with us on some of those long Nagpurian nights. Having been in his shoes many times, I know how hard a tour is for the players not in the starting eleven, so the least we could do was look after the young fella with a few laughs and a cold beer or cup of freshly brewed coffee.

Even Glenn McGrath, who was playing his 100th Test in Nagpur, was turned away with a smile and swift kick up the backside. To this day he often chides Haydos and I about our 'stupid Platinum Club' and the fact that he was discriminated against because he was a bowler and therefore not allowed to enter the secret kitchen of Haydos's tiny, sparse room in the Pride Hotel.

We often laughed about the effect Haydos' ingenuity had on that memorable tour, and the result it seemed to have on the field as well. Marto, in particular, shone. He made 114 in the first innings of the Third Test and another 97 in the second, and he reckoned it was all due to Haydos' cooking. As the game progressed we even talked about the meal we'd had the night before, or what Haydos had in store for us that night. It was quite strange, really—in the hothouse environment and batting in front of 50,000 screaming, chanting Indian supporters, some of whom had the habit of lighting fires around the ground, here were Haydos, Marto and I chatting between deliveries about what we were having for dinner that night.

It says something about the relationship of the Platinum Club and the pleasure we took from being in each others' company. Such friendship was indicative of the camaraderie within the Australian cricket team, which I am sure was the catalyst behind us finally conquering that last frontier and beating India on their home soil. When the pressure was on, our friendships were the glue that kept us together.

Winning that series was definitely one of the high points of my career. Against all the odds, we set an Australian flag on one of the summits of our Mount Everest. We celebrated hard that night, but my most memorable moment was just sitting back with a freezing-cold beer.

Call me a simple bloke, but my experience in Nagpur had taught me that to be content in life, all you need is a couple of mates, some good music and a decent feed, no matter where you are in the world.

24. Old dog, new tricks

As much cricket as I played and as many hours as I spent practising in the nets, there were some aspects of batting that I could never get quite right in the latter half of my career. My batting coach Noddy Holder was always on at me in the nets to stand up taller and to be still at the crease so that I could swing my arms more freely, but no matter how much you train and practise, it's never the same as being out there in the field of play. As soon as I settled at the crease in a match, my natural instinct was to tap my bat repeatedly rather than stand like a statue—I found that it helped me find my rhythm and move my feet.

Two weeks after we'd won in India, we began the Australian leg of a five-match series against New Zealand. We were match-fit but probably a little weary, and I continued my run of failed good starts when I made 34 in Brisbane. I didn't get a second chance because the Kiwis capitulated for 76 in the second innings as

Warney and Pigeon took them apart.

By the time we got to Adelaide I was feeling a little jaded, and I played that way in the nets against Victorian paceman Brad Williams, who kept hitting me on the body. I was batting like a busted arse, as we say, and knew I had to change something, even if it was just a small adjustment. I thought of Noddy and stood taller and quieter at the crease, and it seemed to work.

That night I decided to take a risk and try the tactic in the match. It would be my 'cue'. The night before every Test, I went to bed thinking about a particular cue, so that I would have a clear directive in my mind as I went out to bat. I used to tell myself to get forward, or to move my feet, to stand tall, be sharp or watch the ball. I wanted to remind myself of what I had been working on in practice.

The next morning, it worked from the very first ball when I spanked Chris Martin for a boundary. With my mind refreshed and picturing what had happened the previous day, I followed it the next over with four boundaries from left-armer James Franklin—mainly cover drives, which were fast becoming my signature shot. I scored 30 from the first five overs while Haydos had only scored a couple of singles.

This time I wasn't going to make the mistake of wasting a fast start. Neither was I going to worry and ache about the nervous nineties. I hit a boundary off Daniel Vettori to reach my century, another off Jacob Oram for 150 and a six off Paul Wiseman to reach 200. 'I'm the aggressor', the headlines said the next day, as I teased Haydos about being in the one-day side while I had missed out (I've always been frustrated about my stunted 50-over career). Haydos reckons my double-century six was the highlight of my career—I stood there grinning, with my baggy green in my hand, offering it to the change rooms in celebration while the ball was still sailing over the boundary.

We had a two-week break after the Adelaide Test, and the Pakistan team arrived for the first series since our famous Hobart victory. As the First Test was to be played in Perth, I went home for a break. Instead of relaxing on the beach, though, I played in a couple of lead-up games, one for Western Australia and one for a Chairman's XI.

My diary entry on the eve of the match reveals another technique I used as a motivation tool—to imagine the media coverage of my heroics on the first day's play: 'Justin Langer today scored his 21st Test century . . . Justin Langer, 21 Test hundreds . . . Justin Langer, 21 Test tons . . .' and so I went on.

It had worked before, particularly during the 1991–92 Sheffield Shield final against New South Wales. The night before the match I scrawled in my diary dozens of times the figure '150', along with the words 'man of the match'. Not a bad prediction, given that I made 149 in the second innings and was indeed man of the match as we won the Shield.

Would it happen this time? Haydos went early but Punter and I had put on 50 for the second wicket and seemed to have got through the worst of a fiery opening spell from Shoaib Akhtar and Mohammad Sami. Then we lost four wickets in the space of eight overs and had slumped to 5 for 78. The Pakistanis were delighted until they saw Adam Gilchrist coming through the gate with the Perth crowd cheering like maniacs.

I couldn't help thinking about that famous Hobart Test against Pakistan as we put on 152 in the next 28 overs. But unlike Hobart, which had been a grafting rescue mission, this partnership was pure joy as we took the initiative away from the bowlers by refusing to go into our shells. The team's ability, individually and collectively, to keep attacking even when under pressure was another reason for our consistent success. Gilly made 69 in quick time and then Jason Gillespie gave me a lot of support as I made my 21st century.

I was moving towards a second double-century in succession but was the last man out for 191. It was unfortunate to miss out on the double-ton—and on the rare chance of batting through an innings—but I couldn't really be disappointed. One journo described the innings as 'coruscating', which is a pretty silly word to use in a match report but at least he was being nice. It means 'sparkling' or 'glittering'—a nice change from 'gritty' or 'scrappy'.

We knocked Pakistan over cheaply and I was back at the crease by the third day with a mission to score quickly. This time there was no collapse as Punter and I put on 163 for the second wicket. I was seeing the ball so well that I could have played with a stump rather than a bat. I moved into the 90s with a four and had my sights set on the cover boundary to reach another rare feat—a century in both innings of a match.

It seemed so easy—the sun was out, the match was safe and the home crowd was happy. I dispatched medium-pacer Abdul Razzaq for another boundary to get to 97, but the next ball he got one through my defence and bowled me. I could not believe it as I trudged off. Neither could my dad, who was sitting in the stands. He still won't let me forget it. Glenn McGrath took 8 for 24 in Pakistan's second innings—his best Test match figures—to dismiss them for 72. We had won by the ridiculous margin of 491 runs.

● ● ●

I was champing at the bit to play in the Boxing Day Test the following week, but in fact I would struggle to make the team. We played a sponsors match against the Essendon Football Club after arriving in Melbourne, then we trained the next day—23 December—at the MCG. I was running a warm-up lap with the boys and someone was kicking a footy around as we went. I bent over to pick it up and suddenly felt my back go.

I had never felt pain like it before or since—putting aside the self-inflicted pain of the tattoo on my arse—and by the time I'd hobbled from the far side of the ground to the change rooms, I couldn't even get myself onto the massage table. The medical staff carted me off for an MRI scan, which revealed I had a bulging disc. I was immediately declared unfit for the Test.

I was told I would need at least a month to get over my injury and that there was no way I could be fit in time for the match, which was in just three days, so Simon Katich was put on standby. Now, Simon was a close mate of mine, but there was no way I was going to give up my position in the team that easily. I'd played 41 consecutive Tests since my reinstatement as an opener, and I was intent on playing my 42nd if it was at all possible.

I managed to get back to the hotel, and for the next two days I lay on the floor or the massage table brought over by Errol Alcott and we worked through massages and icepacks for eight hours a day. I felt sorry for Sue and our three girls, who really looked forward to Christmas in Melbourne each year. Instead of Santa Claus, this year they had the Grinch lying on the floor moaning all day.

By Christmas Day I managed to stagger out to a Christmas function but soon realised I'd forgotten my anti-inflammatory drugs. I desperately staggered back to get them. I was moving again but very painfully, and I was starting to doubt my chances. Errol and I had a few pool sessions that afternoon, and by the evening I told him that I was starting to feel some relief. He was dubious but agreed to keep up the treatment that night and see how I was in the morning. Publicly I was being given no chance, and Simon was doing media interviews on how he had no fear of Shoaib Akhtar and was raring to go.

I woke up early on the morning of the match and lay still in bed, not quite sure if I wanted to move in case I felt a fresh twinge. It was only about five metres from the bed to the bathroom, and the previous two mornings I had shuffled across the gap like an old man. I didn't exactly bounce out of bed on Boxing Day but the change was remarkable. I stood under the shower and felt great relief, took another anti-inflammatory and decided to go to the ground.

No one quite believed it when I turned up that morning, but I insisted on being given a fitness test. I did a bit of running and stretching, hit a few balls in the nets and declared myself fit to play. Everyone thought I was mad, but because I was a senior player and in such good form, they had little choice. I ended up scoring a half-century and we won the Test match. Kat would have to wait a little longer for his chance which, I'm glad to say, he had grasped with both hands.

● ● ●

I love to read—self-help books and big novels, mainly—but, as I reflect on it now, there was something strange about the fact that I could read a book almost 1000 pages long during the last Test match of the return leg of the New Zealand series in March 2005. *Shantaram*, a rollicking adventure novel by a convicted Australian bank robber named Gregory David Roberts, was not essential reading, and neither was it so engrossing that I couldn't put it down. I think it was more an indication of my state of mind; perhaps it was the first inkling—although I did not know it—that I had entered the twilight of my career.

Gone was the desperation to overcome my serious injury and play in the Melbourne Test just three months before. Instead, I had put on a bit of weight, grown my hair and, at one stage, even had a few days' worth of stubble on my chin.

Even worse was my attitude. To put it simply, I was bored. As appalling as that sounds—and with no disrespect to the New Zealanders, who always put up a fight—I was in a good place personally and I felt secure in a side that I believed would win comfortably. It was as if the hunger, struggle and fears of youth had given way to the comfort and security of middle age.

The trip Haydos, Michael Kasprowicz, Jock Campbell and I made to Waiheke Island near Auckland during a day off before the First Test was indicative of what was occurring. Instead of training hard as I normally would at the beginning of a tour, or following Steve Waugh's example and perhaps spending the time exploring Maori culture, for example, we chose the path more travelled and sat in a vineyard and demolished a cheese platter, which was washed down with a pleasant Bordeaux.

What's wrong with that? you might ask. It was a day off, and unwinding during a tour isn't a bad thing. That's true, but being switched-on is far more important, particularly when the tour has only just started.

Signs of complacency were starting to sprout, and would flower in the Ashes series a few months later. The Australian team was hugely successful, senior and very settled. The coaching reins had been loosened just enough to let us go our own way as individuals rather than as a unit, and as a result our discipline had begun to fray.

Bad weather made it difficult to see on the field when we won the First and Third Tests by nine wickets, and we would have cantered to victory in the Second Test at Wellington if it hadn't been rained out. I had a decent series, finishing with an average of almost 69, but without making any big scores. Still, it was flat.

The one highlight was the performance of Ricky Ponting. Of all the great innings he played while we were team-mates, the cameo he played in the second innings to win the Third Test showed his true genius. He'd already scored a century at almost a run a ball in the first innings when he came out to join me in our chase for victory late on the fourth day. We needed the modest total of 164 but the skies were darkening and the weather was closing in. We batted steadily for a while and then it started to drizzle.

We only needed another 40 or so when Punter wandered down the pitch at the end of an over. 'Mate, should we go off for the bad light or have a crack at it tonight?' he asked.

I had no doubt. 'I wouldn't mind trying to knock them off tonight. I'd like to get home and see Sue and the girls a day early if we can.'

'Righto,' he said, walking back to his end of the pitch. 'Leave it to me.'

The next ball he hit Chris Martin back over his head for six, then for consecutive boundaries. It was a batting exhibition, not slogging but perfect cover drives, pulls and cuts that went like tracer bullets. Punter simply had the ability to take it up another gear when required. Four overs later we were home and racing off the ground, grinning like Cheshire cats.

But our joy was short-lived, and those grins would turn to grimaces in a matter of months.

● ● ●

There was one other unusual element of the New Zealand tour. I have said that only players and staff were in the rooms when we sang the team song but there was one occasion when I relaxed the rules (with the approval of Punter). Our victory in the First Test at Auckland was a special milestone for one of the team's most enthusiastic supporters, Luke 'Sparrow' Gillian. Luke had been running cricket tours over the years and was attending his 100th match. He'd been in the change rooms on many occasions but always had to leave when the song was sung. Not on this occasion. I'll let him take up the story.

My usual post-match lap of the dressing room soon became a 'lap of honour' as the boys expressed congratulations for 100 Tests, thanks and appreciation for my support shared with a collection of photos and autographs. As I downed my third beer, Ricky Ponting approached, asking if I would like to join the boys singing their coveted team song. I was stunned. After all, who was I? A spectator. This was sincere, as was my acceptance to enter the team's ultimate inner-sanctum . . . a very rare moment to treasure.

The boys, drinks in hand, moved into a corner of the room to form a circle around Justin Langer. With Ricky Ponting on my left and Jason 'Dizzy' Gillespie to my right, Justin addressed everyone: 'This is a brilliant team . . . we've played some awesome cricket, beaten the best that the rest has thrown us, and come out on top. It's not because of luck, or the result of a coin toss, but because we are the world's best cricketers and we prove that time and again. What I want is for each of you to tell us your highlight, your most treasured memory playing with this team.' Dizzy elbowed me and whispered, 'Bet you didn't think you'd ever be part of this, eh?'

Everyone's moments were stated. Justin stood on the table as we gathered, our arms wrapped around each other, and spoke: 'Once again, let me remind you that we are a brilliant team . . . you have earned the glories that no one can take from you. We wear the Baggy Green, we are Australian and so "Underneath the Southern Cross I stand . . ."' Three resounding verses of this fabled 'team only' song iced my 100th Test match cake. As the team broke away, I wiped my brow as my heart-rate slowed. I looked at Dizzy who extended his hand and pulled me in for a giant bear hug. 'What did you think of that, my friend? Pretty awesome isn't it!' I could barely whisper approval.

25. Premature salutation

I'll never forget walking out onto the hallowed grass of Lord's to open the batting with Haydos at the beginning of the 2005 Ashes series. I have always been a cricket history buff, so this was a special moment—entering the arena at the home of cricket for the first time in a Test match. I had played there a few weeks before in a one-day match for Somerset, but this was different. This was a Test match. This was the Ashes. This was Lord's.

I had a habit of listening to music before an innings to ease my nerves. On this morning, I'd been listening to Eminem's song 'Lose Yourself', which made a lot of sense to me.

Look, if you had one shot, or one opportunity
to seize everything you ever wanted—one moment
would you capture it or just let it slip?

I was standing at the top of the grand staircase and about to enter the famous Long Room when I heard the last line: '*You can do anything you set your mind to, man.*' It was the perfect motivation.

Lord's is like no other ground. The change rooms are above the Long Room, and you have to descend into the building and then thread your way through the most famous room in the game, past the oil paintings of bygone cricketers like W.G. Grace and Sir Donald Bradman, with the Lord's members crowded on either side of you, politely clapping but no doubt hoping you'll be back soon, before you reach the field of play. The one downside of Lord's is that if you get out cheaply or to a bad decision or poor shot, you can't show any emotion until you've walked all the way back through the Long Room, past the happy members and up a couple of flights of stairs to the privacy of your change room.

I was very nervous. Playing at Lord's is always a big moment in the career of a cricketer, and I was a bit on-edge and slightly nauseous. There are three smells I hate when I feel this way—coffee, bacon and tobacco—and guess what the Long Room smelled of. Talk about a triple whammy. They were feeding the members bacon sandwiches (butties or sarnies, as they call them) and fresh coffee, while cigar smoke positively oozed from the walls, having been infused in the stone and wood for over more than a century. I was lucky not to throw up on the members as I struggled through in front of Haydos, who gave no sign of any nerves.

Once we were out onto the ground it was different. Excitement supplanted nerves as I played my customary practice drives, kicked my legs and we were out there. The sky was low, grey and cloudy but it was the grass, the hallowed turf, that really got me. It was like carpet, so fine that I felt like I was floating out to the middle.

But that was where the fairytale stuff ended and reality set in.

Steve Harmison took the new ball and there was a roar of anticipation from the packed crowd. England hadn't beaten us at Lord's
since the 1930s, but we had begun the 2005 tour badly, losing a
few one-dayers and having some niggling problems in the team, and
there was a real sense among the English public that their team
could wrest the Ashes away from us for the first time since 1989.

Then a strange and quite unnerving thing happened. Normally
when a fast bowler charges in to open an innings, the noise increases
as he thunders in, reaching a crescendo at the moment he releases
the ball—after one match in Bangalore I couldn't get the ringing
out of my head for days. But on this most important morning, the
noise suddenly stopped as Harmison reached the crease. It was as if
someone had flicked a light switch. The sudden silence was, as they
say, deafening as Harmison's delivery flew past me and smacked into
the wicket-keeper Geraint Jones' gloves, still climbing.

I looked around and saw fielders were rushing towards me. They
were all moving in anticipation—it was like having a room closing
in on me.

I walked down to Haydos to have a chat and ease the tension a
bit. 'Mate, these guys mean business.'

He'd noticed it too. The pressure was almost claustrophobic, and
that showed in what happened over the next two hours. The next
ball Harmison charged in again and hit me on the point of the right
elbow. I dropped my bat and walked around a bit, grimacing. A massive lump quickly developed, which made it look as if I'd broken my
arm. Errol Alcott rushed out and gave me some treatment, which
made me look like a bit of a hero, but the truth was I didn't feel too
much pain—maybe it was the adrenaline.

I kept batting, and for the rest of the session everything seemed
to move in fast-motion. We scored quite quickly but, as I later

quipped, Harmison turned our change room into an emergency ward. After hitting me he smacked Haydos in the helmet, which I'd never seen happen before, and then hit Punter with another delivery that reared off a good length. It split the captain's cheek, a scar he still bears today.

None of the English players came to see if he was alright, which really riled me. I mouthed off to England's spinner Ashley Giles, who was fielding close by. 'What's going on here?' I said angrily. 'This isn't a war. At least show some respect and come and see if he's okay.'

Giles mumbled something back and some of them came in, but the message was clear—this really was a war. By lunch we were five down for less than 100 (including me for 40), then were bowled out for 190, but by stumps McGrath had reduced England to 7 for 92. It was an amazing start to an amazing series and showed, as we would later see, how the first minutes of a match can set the tone for an entire series. Having reflected, I can say that the first two hours at Lord's in July 2005 was the best session of cricket I was involved in during my entire career.

Despite Harmison's fantastic start, we went on to win the match, thanks to Pigeon's counter-attack and a much better batting effort in the second innings. Glenn and Warney took four wickets in England's second dig to roll them for 180 and hand us a big but surprising win.

We had a great night that night, smoking cigars up in the change rooms. My parents had travelled from Perth for the series, and I took them out to the middle of the ground. Imagine the thrill of doing that with your parents. The actor Hugh Jackman turned up and we invited him to join us in the rooms. Matty gave him one of his cricket bats and Hugh reacted as if he'd won the lottery.

Then I made a decision that would come back to hurt us. It is with some hesitancy—and a giant *mea culpa*—that I relate the following, but here goes.

It was nearing midnight and we were full of ink. We had been celebrating since the match finished in the middle of the afternoon, and I, as songmaster, decided to take the guys across to the empty English change rooms and sing the song in the camp of the enemy. It was fun at the time and was witnessed only by Pete, our faithful attendant, who wasn't really in a position to stop us.

There was a sense—false, as it turned out—of 'here we go again'. Even though England had flogged us in the first session of the match, we had still come back and beat them comfortably. Instead of waiting until we had won 3–0, which is what we expected would happen, our celebrations began in anticipation.

What I normally did before we sang the song was to stand on a bench or a chair in the middle of the mob and then, going from one to another, to talk about each of the boys, cheering their performance and maybe spraying a little beer over their heads. It made us all feel part of something special. McGrath copped plenty that night, not only because he'd taken his 500th Test wicket—I took the catch—but because a pair of gold cricket boots with the number 500 had then been brought out onto the ground. It was some publicity stunt but it made him look like a knob, I said with a laugh.

I finished going around the group and then noticed that name-tags for the English players were still on the lockers above the plush blue leather seats where they sat. That was when I took things one step further.

'Look, there's Michael Vaughan's seat. How do you reckon he's feeling tonight?' I called out, tipping beer over his seat. 'And what about Ian Bell—he let Warney go and was plumb LBW! Here's Andrew Flintoff's spot by the window . . .'

And so I went around the England players, having a laugh at their expense and spraying beer. We finished with a raucous rendition of the team song and then left. Call it arrogant, call it fun—nowadays, I just call it stupid. Forget Pigeon and his gold boots. I was the knob that night, and it came back to bite me and the side on the arse.

● ● ●

It didn't take long for fate to step in after my change-room indiscretion. I was standing only a few metres from Pigeon on the morning of the Second Test at Edgbaston while we were doing our warm-up. A few of us had been throwing around a football; I watched as Glenn stepped backwards to catch the footy and trod on a cricket ball.

It was like a slow-motion cartoon, me in horror, hands clasped to my cheeks and calling out 'No!', as he tumbled backwards and rolled on the grass in agony. My fears were mixed with a little cynicism, given Pigeon's delight in practical jokes, but it was immediately clear that he was in trouble.

I want to correct a myth here. Ricky's decision to bowl first if he won the toss was widely criticised. That's fine in hindsight, but it was always the plan, right or wrong, and nothing changed because Glenn was injured. The conditions were overcast, there was a bit of grass on the pitch and we expected there would be some moisture underneath. The idea was to demoralise England while we had the chance. There were reports in the media at the time of a stand-up blue between Punter and Warney over the decision to bowl but, having been there, I can say nothing like that happened. Adam

Gilchrist says the same thing in his autobiography, and he was the bloke who supposedly had to separate them.

The injury to Pigeon was significant—bloody huge, in fact—although we didn't realise it at the time. Losing him in the hour before play hurt us, although we still believed we had the depth to overcome his loss and beat England, whose players, we believed, were psychologically fragile after losing the First Test.

The flipside, though, was that the England team was buoyed by the news and thrilled that we had decided to bowl first. So too were four English lawyers who were at the ground early tucking into some cheese and red wine when they saw Glenn getting carted off the ground. Apparently, they put down their glasses and immediately retired to the betting shop, where they put a stack of money on McGrath *not* taking a wicket in the match. The odds must have been fantastic.

In the first session Marcus Trescothick and Andrew Strauss batted beautifully, and their century partnership set up a day in which they scored 407 runs at more than five runs an over. The next day we lost our way with the bat and fell 100 runs behind on the first innings. Thereafter we struggled, particularly when Flintoff imposed himself on the game, firstly by holding together England's second innings when Shane Warne and Brett Lee were threatening to destroy them, and then with the ball as he made some important initial breakthroughs, including my wicket, which wrecked our chase for the gettable target of 282. Somehow, though, now courtesy of the batting of Binga and Warney, we almost won the match. A famous last-wicket partnership between Brett and Michael Kasprowicz brought us to within a couple of runs. The pictures of Flintoff commiserating with a distraught Brett said so much, not only about the match but also about Freddy's sportsmanship, and the respect we had for each other.

As heroic as our tailenders' effort was, it would be difficult to justify anything other than an England victory, although we still felt the loss as a hammer blow. I later realised that I had been involved in the two closest victories in Test match history—England beating us by two runs at Edgbaston and, of course, my first Test back in 1993, when we were beaten by one run by the West Indies. There are a lot of similarities between the matches. Both began with Australia 1–0 ahead in the series, and both finished with unlikely partnerships by tailenders after our top order had failed taking us close to victory. What's worse, though, both times we went on to lose the series 2–1.

Looking back at my diaries, I can see that even then there were worrying signs. This was part of my entry on day two of the Edgbaston Test:

We've been pretty average. The feeling in the group is very slack. Big egos, small application. We're on the back foot and [it] will have to be a sensational effort to get a victory from here. Buck gave us a rocket tonight. Well deserved. I'll be interested to see how our egos respond.

26. Punch-drunk

My Test career almost came to a shuddering halt near the end of the Third Test at Old Trafford, although not because of my form but my state of mind. England had had us under pressure when Michael Vaughan scored a great first-innings century, then we fumbled our way to a meagre total to be 142 runs behind.

By the afternoon of day four, Andrew Strauss and Ian Bell were taking the game away from us and giving their side a great chance to win an important victory. I was in a foul mood fielding out on the boundary, not only because of the state of the match but also the behaviour of the crowd.

It was unrelenting. I won't go into details, but suffice it to say it wasn't very choice and descended to comments about my wife and even my mother, who was actually in the crowd, although thankfully on the other side of the ground. At one stage I looked over to a security guard and indicated clearly that I'd had enough and would he do something about it.

The train bombings in London had happened just one month earlier, so our safety was on our minds. We'd been assured by the security company at the ground that everything would be okay, but clearly this guy was not going to help. When I tried to engage with him he just looked at me and started laughing along with the crowd.

My mood didn't improve when England declared late in the day, which meant Haydos and I would have to bat for a few overs in the evening. As you would expect, it was tough going against Steve Harmison and Andrew Flintoff, but we managed to fend them off for several overs before the light started to go. Rather than go off, Michael Vaughan brought himself on to bowl off-spinners, which made me even more tentative and almost led to my downfall. I pushed forward to one delivery and it hit me on the pads. The England players went up in unison but thankfully I escaped.

Eventually, Haydos and I walked off unbeaten but I was still dirty when I walked back into the change rooms. 'That LBW appeal wasn't even close, was it?' I enquired loudly, expecting vocal support from my mates to make me feel better.

Instead, I got straight-up honesty from Gilly. 'I reckon you were a bit lucky, actually,' he said in his usual light and breezy manner.

I exploded in a series of expletives, the stress of the day's events overcoming me. Gilly, the umpires, the English team and their supporters, the security guards and anyone else who tried to placate me could all go and get fucked.

Gilly backed off, realising that something was amiss as I threw my bat across the room and kicked a bin. Punter tried to step in but I told him he could get fucked too.

The pressure of the Ashes had built to bursting point.

When we arrived back at the team hotel we were met by a pair of local drunks with Barmy Army shirts on, who decided to have a go at me by getting down on their knees and singing the Seven Dwarfs song. I walked past and into the foyer but then stopped. I'd finally had enough. I dropped my bag, turned around and stormed back to the idiots, raised my fist and slammed it towards the face of one of them. I wanted to vent my fury by splattering his nose across his face. In those seconds, which seemed like minutes, I could feel the sense of freedom it would bring.

Punter reckons he saw the incident in slow-motion, just as I had seen Pigeon's accident before the Second Test, and he tried desperately to stop me before I ruined my career—which it undoubtedly would have done. He wouldn't have made it but, thankfully, I halted my bunched fist a millimetre from the bloke's nose.

After settling down and having dinner with Mum and Dad I woke up the next morning determined to use my anger to my advantage and bat all day. I was on 14 not out and was ready for a fight, this time with my blade instead of my mouth and fists.

Instead, I lasted one ball, getting a huge nick through to the keeper off Matthew Hoggard. It was typical. If I was in a happy frame of mind I scored runs, and, likewise, if I was tense and tight I usually failed.

Punter rescued us that day with a fantastic century, while Pigeon—who probably shouldn't have played, although he took five wickets in the second innings—and Brett Lee held off England for a few tense overs at the end of the day to let us scramble a draw. We celebrated that night as though it had been a famous victory—a rare event, but we knew the draw had kept us in the series. One-all with two matches to play was good, considering everything that had gone wrong on the tour so far.

Our growing problems were bigger than Glenn's injury. We had a number of players struggling for form. Gilly was in a bind because of the bowling tactics of Flintoff, Haydos and Marto were out of touch, and Jason Gillespie was struggling with the ball.

For the first time, this great team had a number of players with form or confidence problems at the same time. In the past those who were struggling always had players around them who could pull them out of a hole, but this time it was much tougher. What made it worse was the pressure off the field. The media was all over us, as were the crowds and the public. Suddenly we were under the pump, not as individuals but as a team. And it showed.

● ● ●

The Fourth Test, at Trent Bridge, began the same way the Manchester Test had ended. The crowd seemed intent on making our lives a misery as England took the ascendancy with a 259-run lead on the first innings. Freddy Flintoff came good with the bat, scoring a great century, and our batting fell apart at the seams. As we prepared to follow on, however, I had a weapon—no, not my fists of fury, but a technique given to me by Reg Dickason, our security manager.

Reg is a former copper, and one night he took me aside and told me about his experiences of being abused by crowds while maintaining police lines, linked together arm-in-arm. He used what he called 'white noise' to combat the stress. He allowed the combined noise of the crowd to wash over him, almost as if it were the static of an untuned television. In my case, this would mean letting the noise of the game, the crowd and their taunts merge together into a sound that actually meant nothing.

Perhaps it was my training in meditation or the martial arts, but Reg seemed to be making sense, and from then on I found it quite easy to 'tune out'.

We made a better fist of things in the second innings and set England the modest total of 129 to take a 2–1 lead with one Test remaining. Warney helped reduce England to 4 for 57 before Kevin Pietersen and Freddy righted the ship and they won by three wickets.

The three of them were key figures in the last Test as well, but I want to discuss Haydos and myself before getting to that. Matty had been under enormous pressure in the lead-up to the game at the Oval and there were suggestions he might be dropped. I was safe and having a good series personally, but the notion that my partner was being questioned was almost as annoying as being targeted myself. I knew he would come good, as champions do, and he didn't let me down.

● ● ●

The team was struggling, but I was feeling good and was playing well without landing a big score. My form was partly due to a refreshed attitude after my slackness during the New Zealand tour, and partly to my diet. I had gone off red meat and was sticking to fish, and was also doing a lot of yoga. I felt fantastic, and when an offer to do a television commercial for Johnnie Walker was slipped under my hotel door one night, it was too good to refuse.

I worried a bit about advertising alcohol, but I decided to go ahead and was really happy with the result. It was filmed in a single day—a bloody long one, mind you—and I repeatedly had to walk along a central London street lined with Georgian mansions to depict the journey through the life of a cricketer striving for a century. They gave me a fabulous new black suit and shoes, which unfortunately gave me blisters a couple of days before the Fifth Test. No harm was done, though, as I scored a century.

The ads were shown in Australia the following summer when the West Indies and South Africa toured. And it seemed everyone knew the words I'd spoken as I was filmed walking past buildings with prominent numbers: 'They haunt me and define me. For some, it is always how many. For me, it is always just one more.' How true.

• • •

Warney took six wickets to help keep England to less than 400 in the first innings of the Fifth Test at the Oval, and give us a chance to win, so Haydos and I were determined to build a big stand. We had reached 112 just after tea on the second day before we decided to accept the umpires' offer of bad light. Our decision has since been criticised, given that we had to win the game, but even in hindsight the light was so bad that we had little choice, especially since England would have continued to use its frontline bowlers.

We continued the next day and eventually put on an opening stand of 185, of which I'd made 105 off 126 deliveries. Haydos went on to make 138, and with the team at 2 for 277 at the end of day three, we felt there was a great chance to push for a big lead and then roll England on the last two days. That's when Freddy Flintoff stood tall.

He came out on day four and bowled an amazing spell, wrecking our innings. Instead of a big lead we were six runs behind. Coupled with the continued bad weather, our failure that day meant we missed an opportunity to rescue the Ashes campaign.

We clung to hope on the last day as Pigeon, who removed Vaughan and Bell with consecutive balls, gave us an outside chance of victory. Then Kevin Pietersen imposed himself on the game. It might have been different if Warney had held a slips chance when Pietersen was on fifteen—that would have left England in big trouble at 4 for 89. As it was, we were still in the game when Warney took two wickets just before lunch, which left England at 5 for 127. Pietersen was still there but he was struggling.

The tension was amazing. Apparently, at lunch he had asked Michael Vaughan how he should play. Michael told Kevin to 'take them on, take the game away from them'. That's exactly what he did, hooking sixes and belting cover drives for fours. He eventually made 158, including fifteen fours and seven sixes. It was one of the best innings I have ever seen. The left-arm spinner Ashley Giles—who was an unsung hero, in many ways—then made 59. England had weathered the storm, drawn the match and won the bloody Ashes.

It was only looking back on the Ashes defeat that we realised what had gone wrong. John Buchanan and his Brains Trust had decided that because we had such a group of senior players, perhaps we could just do our own thing. Suddenly, instead of having a pack mentality at training, we all went our own ways. When the pressure was on, the loss of that cohesion started to tell.

A few weeks after getting back from England, we began preparations for a series against an ICC World XI. A group of us went to see Buck and told him we needed to have more structure in our training, and that it was in this that we had let ourselves down. Buck agreed, and I'll never forget the intensity of that first training session. It was electric. It showed me that even the best players need some structure and organisation in what they do. And that, in turn, will bring out their best.

I know Warney disagrees with this. I've heard him bag John

Buchanan dozens of times—which shits me, frankly, because he did great things for the side. One of the best things he did was to help bring us back together after that loss.

It might seem silly to say it, but losing the Ashes in 2005 was probably good for world cricket. We kept hearing that we were winning too easily and there wasn't enough competition. But it was also good for a team that never thought it would lose. We'd had our arses kicked, we were human and we could fail. It was a tough lesson but we learned it well.

The Ashes series had been close and fantastic but I was pleased when it was over. After the stress of such a tight run of matches, I was yearning to get home, and I arrived just in time for a new baby and a Father's Day surprise.

● ● ●

Justin had been on at me for years about getting an Australian flag for the front of our house. There are a couple of them in our neighbourhood, fluttering away in the afternoon sea breeze that we call the Fremantle Doctor, and there are a few companies around Perth that will come and install the giant flagpoles at the drop of a hat. I know Justin wears his national pride on his sleeve, but there was no way I was going to let him ruin our house and garden with his 'nuffie flag', as he called it.

Maybe it was the fact I was seven months pregnant with our fourth child, Grace, perhaps I was feeling sorry that the team might lose the Ashes or maybe I had just missed him—whatever the reason, I relented in the final weeks of the 2005 campaign and installed a flagpole in time for his return around Father's Day.

Justin said nothing when he got home, driving in straight past the thing and then walking into the house without a word. Eventually, I had to ask if he'd seen it. He just looked at me blankly. 'Seen what?' he replied. It was white, just like our house, and so tall that he hadn't looked up and seen it. So much for the surprise.

It's still there, although last Australia Day someone scaled our fence and stole the flag. Justin, who was away at the time, was livid. I tried to calm him down by suggesting that maybe the thief was so passionate about Australia that he just had to have it, but Justin was having none of that. If he ever catches the culprit . . . In the meantime, I'm thinking about hoisting my own flag—one with a champagne glass on it—to tell my own friends that I'm ready for a glass at the end of a hard day.

In November 2005 our fourth child, Grace, was born, which gave us a neat collection not only of daughters but also of birthdays. Ali-Rose was also born in November, while Jessica and Sophie were born in late March and early April respectively. Not everything has been so neat, of course, and there have been a lot of sacrifices along the way, one of them being the girls' birthdays, which Justin was never able to be home for.

He always tried to make up for it and, to be honest, it was probably something he missed more than they did. One year he sent pink helium balloons to Jess and another year he put a notice in the newspaper saying he was sorry he couldn't be there.

We had two big parties at home last year for Grace and Ali-Rose, and I think Justin probably found them more exciting (or scary) than the girls did. Ali-Rose wanted to have a dress-up relay and decided to do it in Dad's cricket gear. It was hilarious watching the girls putting on his pads, shoes, gloves and helmets.

I think Justin got a real kick out of the whole thing, as he did the day he got home and realised the kids had actually been playing backyard cricket. He could see a plastic rubbish bin which they'd turned upside-down for a wicket and a cricket bat leaning against it. Those little things make such a big difference.

The kids never really noticed anything different about their dad. We've always just got on with things, knowing that Justin would be away on tour seven months of the year. It happens to other families when the father is a businessman or consultant or maybe a pilot, so it wasn't so unusual—except that his job was to play cricket.

There have been times when the girls' schoolmates would point out that their dad was famous, to which they would screw up their noses and scoff, 'No he's not—he's Dad!' Their reaction was the same if they saw his picture in the paper, and although the TV was usually on if he was playing, it was more likely that they'd want to switch to a kids' program.

Their perspective is funny sometimes. Recently, I watched Gracie, who's four, talking to one of her little friends. She asked her friend where her father was, and her friend said he was at work. 'Oh, cricket or the gym?' Gracie replied.

As Jess has got a bit older she has shown some interest in her father's sport. She enjoys going to the cricket and has even attended some of the coaching camps Justin holds each summer.

I think Justin has only ever come to one school function with me—a quiz night—not because he didn't want to be involved but because he was never there. He always did the school runs when he was here, and he always tried to make up for his absences.

I've never thought of myself as a single mum. Even though I have a busy life with four kids, I wouldn't insult real single mothers by comparing myself to them, because they do it much tougher. There were many times when I was lonely, though, particularly at night after the kids had gone to bed, but I always knew Justin was at the other end of the phone, that I had his support and stability, and that we had money to pay bills and put food on the table. That's a lot more than many people have.

The interesting thing for us now is learning to compromise. For the past fifteen years everything was done my way out of necessity, but now there are two of us here most of the time. I still tend to do everything because it's easier that way—when he asks how to turn a heater on, for example. He has never had to do it up to now, because his life was, essentially, an eternal summer. Now that's changed, and so have we as a couple.

Ricky Ponting, 5th Songmaster, 1999–2004

JL: Why is the team song important?

RP: It's the one chance we have to really celebrate winning a Test match. I don't think people realise how hard it is to win a Test, and while we had an incredible run a few years ago, I am recognising that more now. When you win, the song symbolises our chance for a release and it also signifies closure for me; a celebration and then time to move on to the next challenge.

JL: Can you remember Heals handing over the song to you?

RP: I think Heals rang and asked me to take over the reins. I invited him back into the Brisbane change rooms so that he could officially hand over the song. That was a special moment in my life.

JL: Did you enjoy being the songmaster?

RP: Loved it, every minute of it. Still to this day it is one of the best things that ever happened to me in my career. While I was nervous about the job and had to think a bit about it every time so that it was memorable, it also marked a sign of respect for me. When Heals, as one of the 'old school' legends asked me to do it I felt like I had earned their respect and thought that they must have seen something in me. It was like they thought I had a 'future' in the game and that meant a lot to me.

JL: Do any of your songs stand out?

RP: Yes, the 1999 World Cup song was memorable. At the start of the campaign I wrote a poem. In it I talked about doing the hard yards so that we could sing the song when the World Cup was won. The night we did, I took the boys out onto the Lord's wicket. Tom Moody put me up on his shoulders. I re-read the poem and then belted out a great rendition of 'Underneath the Southern Cross'.

JL: Even after everything you have achieved, do you still enjoy the song?

RP: As much as ever. I loved leading the song but now as the captain and most senior player I just love watching the emotion on the young guys' faces. Being part of the history of the song and watching the young guys enjoying the tradition is very satisfying to me today. There is no doubt it is one of the best things about playing cricket for Australia.

27. Mates

I'm happy just to sit here round a table with old friends,
And see which one of us can tell the biggest lies

These are my favourite lines from any song (barring our team song, of course). The Cold Chisel classic 'Flame Trees' pretty much sums up the atmosphere in an Australian cricket team change room at the end of a Test match victory—a group of mates sitting around, sipping a few beers, having a laugh and telling a few tall stories.

Over the years, 'Flame Trees' and that legendary Aussie beer song 'Khe Sanh' must have been played hundreds of times in the Aussie change rooms as we celebrated victories. The only song played as much might have been John Williamson's 'True Blue'. There might be some who shake their heads at this and think it was all a bit cliched—in fact, that was the reaction of guys like Warney and Stuie MacGill, who would sigh and say 'Not again, fellas'—but it really epitomised the feeling in our sanctuary after a game, and particularly after a great win.

Somebody would choose the song on the CD player and suddenly we would be standing up, our arms around one another, belting out the words. That camaraderie really was the essence of why we played the game. I think it was ultimately what set us apart from other sides—we simply loved winning, and success is contagious.

However it looked from the outside, winning was never easy. I cannot remember an easy Test match, even during our two amazing periods of sixteen consecutive victories. We may have gone into matches or series as the favourite to win, and we certainly always expected victory of ourselves, but you must still have the true desire to win and a plan of how to do it.

There was never a moment on the field when any of us waited for victory. There was never a time when we thought that winning was simply a matter of turning up. We had to work hard, and when we got into trouble we had to hope there'd be one or two who'd get us out of the hole. We chased victory, grabbed victory and clutched onto victory for dear life. And that's why our celebrations in the change rooms afterwards were so important to our culture of winning.

There is so much going on during a Test match, and so many people everywhere wanting your time, that the change room becomes a sanctuary. My greatest memories will always be in those rooms, wherever we were in the world, sitting with my mates, talking shit, telling lies and listening to music.

The great paradox of the Australian cricket team is that there is enormous competition to get into the side, and then to stay there, but once you're in it becomes a brotherhood like no other, a special club that has only ever had 400-odd members in its history. It feeds into the idea that the team is everything, more important than the eleven individuals who make it up.

Winning is addictive and you just want to be part of it. When we were close to victory out on the field, the boys often geed each other up by talking about the night ahead and the song that would be its finale. It wasn't that we were celebrating too early, but quite the opposite—we were reminding ourselves of how good victory would feel and how much we wanted it.

Some people say that all there is to winning is bowling a good line and length and playing a great cover drive, but I disagree. The glue that keeps everything together under pressure is character, and it is the character of the group and its individuals that sets teams apart. I speak about team spirit quite often at public events because I believe passionately in its power. It's something that has to be nurtured—you cannot simply manufacture mateship. It has to grow naturally amidst a group of blokes who want to be there for each other.

I fed off the leadership of Steve Waugh, Adam Gilchrist and Ricky Ponting, the optimism of Glenn McGrath, the worldliness of Matthew Hayden and the loyalty and honesty of players like Jason Gillespie, Darren Lehmann and Jo Angel. I had a role, too, mostly as the guy who'd battled to be in the side and therefore knew what it was like to be struggling. There were times when I sensed that even champions like Tugga, Gilly and Pigeon needed a friendly ear or an encouraging word to let them know that I understood what they were going through.

I saw this kind of spirit in very few of the England sides we played against, and I am certain that the reason teams like Pakistan are so inconsistent is that they lack this 'glue', not the talent. It was something that I know players from other teams talked about, and I believe it was a key ingredient in our success. Without it, we would not have set many of the records we did as a team, no matter how good our batsmen and bowlers were.

I feel privileged to have made some terrific mates through the game of cricket, and I'll put a few of my thoughts about them on the record now.

MATTHEW HAYDEN

What can I say about Haydos? Let's begin with the obvious. He was a gladiator for Australia. It felt like I had one of the Greek or Roman warriors like Spartacus or Maximus beside me every time we strode onto the cricket ground. He was the size of a warrior, walked like a warrior and batted like a warrior and yet there is so much more to the man than belting fours and sixes off the world's fastest bowlers.

The first time we met summed up the complexities of the man. It was 1995 and I was in the Test wilderness. Rod Marsh had encouraged me to come back to the Academy in Adelaide as an associate coach, but I also worked on my own batting and tried to rekindle the international career I had begun in 1993. One weekend there was a specialist batting camp with promising young players from around the country, and Matty was invited down from Queensland. We had played against each other before, but I don't think we'd really met. He was also struggling, having forced his way into the national side and then been dropped.

We held a panel one night to discuss various aspects of batting. Many questions were about technique, but invariably they drifted into the personal sphere. Then someone asked Matty what it was like to be out of form. The question, innocent as it was, was directed squarely at him because of his run of outs, and I was interested to see how he would react. Would he get angry?

Instead, Haydos leaned back in his chair and rubbed his chin thoughtfully. It wasn't an act, as I would later come to know just how deep a thinker he was. Haydos thought for a minute, then looked at the guy and said slowly, 'Yeah, I can tell you what it's like. When you're out of form, you go out to bat and it feels like you've got someone else's dick in your hand. You know what I mean—your bat just doesn't feel right in your hands.'

I could have fallen over laughing. From that moment I sensed we would become great mates. After the event finished, a lot of the others were heading out for dinner and a drink but I wasn't really in the mood, mainly because I was training really hard at the time. Matty felt the same, so we went back to my place, had a coffee and listened to some music. We ended up sitting out on my balcony over-looking the North Adelaide Golf Course and just talking about life. It got pretty deep, from what I remember, which would be the norm for countless similar nights we'd have over the next decade.

We had been through similar difficulties, struggling to stay in the Test team and over-analysing ourselves instead of trusting our abil-ity. That night laid the foundation for what was to come between us. We wouldn't cement our friendship for several years because we weren't in the team together, but I am certain the mateship we developed when we did come together was the base of our opening partnership together from 2001 in England.

RICKY PONTING

If Matthew Hayden was my soul mate then Ricky Ponting was my little brother. Our friendship began when we were both young tourists of the West Indies in 1995, and it would blossom into a rela-tionship in which we swapped clothes and equipment like brothers. We even argued and wrestled like brothers, with gritted teeth and a determination to beat each other, but at all times with a respect as well.

On that 1995 tour I felt responsible for Punter because he was the new boy. He was a budding prodigy, but still a young bloke who needed some guidance. He was a bit wild back then and we were away from home.

We are likeminded, both being a bit stubborn. What I like best about him, however, is that he is just a tough, honest and generous bloke. We usually had a red-hot wrestle after a Test match. I remember one night in Nottingham after we'd won a Test match and it was obvious he'd had enough to drink and should retire. I volunteered to get him upstairs to his room and tried to sling him over my shoulder, but he wasn't going anywhere. We fought and wrestled and laughed our way up the stairs over the next half an hour.

It was typical of our relationship. There must have been a dozen Test match victories after which we wrestled like kids in a schoolyard, tearing each other's shirts, kidney-punching and pinching the other's triceps muscles until they bled. It was very much a bloke thing and never once was there any anger or malice. I'd never want to fight him for real, though, because you could put him down but Punter would always get up and come back. He's the sort of bloke you'd want standing next to you in a fight because he would never go missing.

STEVE WAUGH

When I meet mates like Haydos, Punter or Gilly I usually give them a hug to say hello, but with Steve Waugh it's always a firm handshake. It's not that he is any less of a mate—quite the opposite, actually, because there is no one among my former team-mates who has had a greater influence on my career or, in many ways, my development as a person. Our relationship is just different.

We first played on the same team back in 1993, but I was in awe of the man. I think my sense of respect and eagerness was very obvious to him and was perhaps the reason he took me under his wing, at least initially. I realised it had become a friendship when I was having dinner one night with Tugga and his wife, Lynette, who was talking about meeting the great motorcycle champion Mick Doohan, who had impressed her as being a nice person.

'He reminds me of you, Justin,' she said simply.

I was a bit taken aback and realised they both must like me as a friend. Until then I had seen our relationship as one of 'master and apprentice'.

Tugga never said much but showed great leadership, using his toughness to get his message to the team. I've already written about when he faced up to Curtly Ambrose even before he became captain, but there were other times as well, like the Boxing Day Test during the Ashes series of 2002–03.

Steve was under pressure to retire. The media was questioning his individual record—which is just impossible to believe, when you look at the stats—and I guess Steve decided to stare down his critics. I was on the way to my highest Test innings when he came out to join me in the middle. He was agitated and prowled around the crease. You wouldn't have known it from the TV coverage but he was angry—not at anyone else but at himself. The expletives were flying from under the helmet. I'm not sure he knew I could hear him, but he was admonishing himself between shots.

'Idiot! Why didn't I listen to myself?'

Bang! A four.

'Bloody hell. Should have been doing this for six months.'

Smack! Another four, one bounce over point.

Tugga made 77 in that innings and stalked off still fuming.

A week later, at the New Year's Test in Sydney, he almost flew out to the middle of the SCG when I was dismissed and went on to score one of the great centuries by an Australian captain. The other members of the Australian team were glued to our seats in the change rooms, just like everyone else, including the huge television audience, as he stormed towards three figures late in the day. As the shadows lengthened across the ground and he used his ragged red towel to wipe his brow, Tugga prepared for a finale we all knew must happen.

The last over came and the English captain Nasser Hussain chose to go with his off-spinner, Richard Dawson. The tension was incredible as Tugga managed to get to 98 with one ball to face. Hussain, like the rest of us, believed Tugga would probably try to slog-sweep Dawson—he'd been doing it all session and it was his signature shot. He brought in the fieldsman at midwicket and Dawson bowled fuller, hoping to draw an errant shot. Instead, Tugga stepped inside the ball and smashed it through point to the boundary.

There were tears in the change rooms that night and we celebrated as if we'd won the match, which was probably why we ended up losing it. No one really cared at that point—we were celebrating our captain's magnificence. He'd seen off his detractors and the fickle media and had shown, once again, that you can never write off a champion. Lynette came in and shed a few tears, while the rest of us were high-fiving and hugging each other because we had just been part of a magical moment. In the midst of it all, the Ice Man just sat there quietly with a satisfied smile on his face.

It was his answer, just as he always delivered his opinion to others. His advice came rarely and always in few words—he'd simply tell me to sharpen up in the nets, to ignore the media or not to mess with my form. It was always said as a personal challenge; his presence was a constant reminder that the pursuit of excellence required a single-minded approach.

But there was another side to Tugga, a softer side, which prompted all those side-trips we made while on tour. The message he was giving us was that being well-rounded people who considered the world around us was just as important as practising our batting in the nets. Tugga shines as a champion of the people with his extraordinary efforts in charity through the Steve Waugh Foundation.

We had dinner together during my last Test and, as usual, he wasn't full of plaudits but advised me that in order to make the most of my retirement, I would have to work very hard. That wasn't all, of course. He gave me the orange worry ball he had tossed from hand to hand and scrunched in anxiety during our 1999 Hobart Test against Pakistan. It's one of my prized possessions.

ADAM GILCHRIST

When I first met Gilly, I thought he was too good to be true, and felt it wouldn't be long before he let down his guard. The greatest compliment I can pay my friend is that he hasn't changed in the twenty years I have known him.

He is a champion in every sense of the word. Gilly was the consummate entertainer. From the moment he entered international cricket he had an impact; when he retired he walked away as one of the all-time great players. Clouting 100 sixes in Tests pretty well sums him all up. Everyone loves watching the ball sail over the boundary, whether it's in the backyard, on the village green or at Lord's. He revolutionised the role of the wicket-keeper. Not only do they have to be mistake-free behind the stumps, but able to open the batting in one-day cricket and average in the forties with the bat in the traditional form of the game.

I never saw a player who could hit the first ball they faced as cleanly as Gilly. His ability was freakish. Having him at No. 7 was psychological murder for any opposition. After working hard to dismiss Australia's top five, they always knew more was still to come in the form of one of the most consistently destructive players of all time.

Apart from his genius on the field, Adam Gilchrist was a great leader. His rare talent was to combine being one of the boys, while still playing his role as the team's vice captain or captain. Usually the leader has to be a little removed from the group but through sheer respect and a charismatic character he could be both. Great leaders perform under pressure and that was especially evident in 2004 when he captained Australia in India and we won the series for the first time in decades. A lot of that success was due to Gilly's ability to formulate and then execute a plan.

Gilly and I have had one dust-up over the years, an incident in 2005 I wrote about in an earlier chapter. That night he wrote me a note which he slipped under my door. It said: 'Can't believe I could possibly let these pricks and our situation ever slightly interfere with our trust and friendship. I love you mate and regret whatever took place. Thanks for always being alongside me through thick and thin.' It might seem like a simple thing but it was huge in the context of what was happening, and shows his desire to tackle problems head-on and find solutions. I really admire that quality.

DAMIEN MARTYN

I have a special bond with Marto that is as complex as his character. We may look alike and even both come from the northern suburbs of Perth, but in most respects we are polar opposites. Our careers were linked in so many ways, yet we had a rivalry that went back to our junior days in Perth.

I heard about a teenager who was scoring hundreds in the juniors on a Saturday morning and then crunching more in the afternoon playing A-grade cricket. When I first went on a junior cricket tour with him he was the long-haired bad boy with earrings and I was the crew-cut good boy. He was the dashing stroke-maker and I was the grafting blocker.

To think that we both went through the journey together is quite extraordinary. I remember boarding the plane with him to go to the Cricket Academy in 1989. Marto said to me, 'I wonder if we're going to be doing this together for the rest of our careers.' As it turned out, we did just that.

Our links go further. He captained Western Australia and I was his vice captain. I got a place in the Australian side in 1993 because of an injury he had sustained, and he replaced me when I got dumped in 2001. We never really talked about it but we were both keenly aware of the competition between us.

We were an odd couple, in a way, because Marto had extraordinary talent whereas I had some natural ability but made up for it with hard work. I was envious of his ability and I think he envied my work ethic. To this day, he is still the most naturally gifted player I've ever seen, and that includes players like Sachin Tendulkar, Brian Lara and Ricky Ponting. He could hit shots that I only dreamed about.

I admired his determination, too. I recall a match when he was at rock bottom and was one game away from being dropped from the West Australian side. I batted with him and he got 200. There's an old saying that if nothing changes, then nothing changes; Marto took responsibility for his life and turned it around, and I have enormous admiration for what he achieved. He was the first bloke I remember who went on a low-carb, high-protein diet, and he dropped a huge amount of weight during an off-season and became one of the fittest guys in the side.

I even understand the motive behind his sudden disappearance from the Australian side. Even though he loved living the high life, Marto was always a guy who shunned the limelight. When he decided he'd had enough, he melted away and didn't make a fuss. On reflection, perhaps he should have retired after scoring a brilliant century against South Africa in what was my 100th Test. It was as though he had returned to the side after being dropped just to prove that he could do it. But really, he had nothing to prove to himself or anyone else.

GLENN McGRATH

I always describe Pigeon as positivity personified. Above all his other characteristics, which included being a serial pest, it was his catch-cry of 'Never better, mate' that struck me as being his calling card.

'How you going, mate?' I'd ask him, just to hear his reply. Almost always it would come back the same, no matter what had occurred on the field, how many overs he'd bowled or what was happening in his personal life. 'Never better, mate.'

Even when his wife Jane was diagnosed with cancer he remained positive. They were both extraordinary. Jane was the sort of person whose laugh would light up a room. They used to banter with each other, which showed the delight of their relationship. Towards the end, I would ask how things were going and his reply, although not 'never better', was always one of hope: 'Yeah, it's going good, mate.' That was a great lesson to us all.

I met Pigeon in 1991 when I captained a Cricket Academy team on a tour of Sri Lanka. This string bean from Narromine was amaz-ing. If I asked him for a few overs of outswing, he'd do it. If I asked for a few overs of fast and full deliveries, he'd do it, and it was the same with inswing, bouncers, whatever suited the occasion. I came back from the tour and told anyone who'd listen that this guy would be playing Test cricket within six months, and I was right.

But Glenn was also the guy who'd throw grapes around the room at dinner—once even at the Prime Minister. His stock joke with me was to reach those long arms around and tap on my right shoulder and then walk off to the left. He'd get me every time and laugh with a dopey grin on his face. He was a man of simple pleasures and routines—a swim in the morning to loosen up, and chocolate at night to calm down.

Even though I had been the senior player when we met, he became the superstar as our careers progressed and, although a team-mate, to me he was the great Glenn McGrath.

In June 2004 we both played for a Northern Territory XI against Sri Lanka in the lead-up to the Test series. He was really flat on the first day, bowling well below his best. That night he came to see me, worried. 'Mate, I'm going to retire,' he said. 'I don't have it in me anymore. It's time to go.'

I was shocked, firstly because he was coming to ask my advice, but more so because he was actually considering giving the game away. It was far too early. I told him to think about it a while longer before making up his mind, and I gave him a copy of my favourite book, *Zen in the Martial Arts* by Joe Hyams, which discusses motivation and overcoming setbacks.

Glenn came back to me the next day a changed man, having read the book overnight. A week later he snared five wickets in the first innings of the Test match. From then on, he carried the book with him whenever he travelled; he swore that when he turned to it, he'd always take another five wickets.

SHANE WARNE

The first time I met Shane Keith Warne was the day I moved into the Alberton Hotel in Port Adelaide. It was 1990 and I was nineteen years old. I was excited as hell, having been selected—along with some other promising schoolboy cricketers, including my mate Damien Martyn—to join the Australian Cricket Academy.

It was an evening in late summer when Damien and I arrived, our suitcases carefully packed by our mothers, to find this bloke calmly sitting in the dining room by himself. He was steadily making his way through a family-size pizza and had a can of VB by his side. He was older and bigger than us, cheerful and brazen, and was sporting a big blond mullet. He'd driven across from Melbourne in his white Cortina, which was straight out of Chapel Street with mag wheels and a sunroof.

Warney was the schoolboy bully, the top dog, and he knew it. It's not that he threw his weight around, but even then he had an aura about him; he was in another league. Nor was it arrogance, because he was—and remains—a very likeable bloke.

The Alberton was owned by the Brien family, with whom I still keep in contact, and it became a central part of our lives. I loved my room at the top of the creaky stairs, probably because it was my first home away from my family. We all shared a bathroom along the narrow corridor and ate together each day in the dining room. The front bar was also a hangout, mainly for the pool table, which probably still dominates the room.

Warney was king of the table. He was always a bit of a gambler, and he and I would spend a bit of time playing, mainly on Sundays when the bar wasn't too full and we could have the run of the place. Warney was a shark when it came to pool and I was his perfect victim. He'd challenge me, knowing two things—firstly, that I rarely beat him, and secondly, that I was pigheaded enough to come back for more punishment. He fleeced me almost every week during that marvellous year and, truth be told, I still owe him money from my ridiculous double-or-nothing attempts.

I reckon it was on that pool table that Warney began developing his array of deliveries—in particular, his famous flipper. If he wasn't beating me, I was watching, transfixed, as he stood at one end and spun pool balls into the pockets by flicking his wrist and his big, thick fingers. He would impart leg-spin to make the ball go into the left pocket, then send a wrong'un into the right pocket, and he could even bowl a flipper to make the ball suck back to him along the green felt.

Warney and I spent a lot of time together that year and afterwards, and although we have never been as close as I am with Punter or Haydos, for example, we have always got along well. I can't say how he feels about me, but I've always liked and admired him. We're simply different types of people. For example, I was always one for training hard physically, running and pushing weights in the gym, whereas Warney was never that keen. He would join in and play his part, but reluctantly.

That doesn't mean he didn't commit and train hard. Warney was a man of his art, a spin genius, but his success was as much due to his hard work as to his natural talent. He was the naughty kid and I was the teacher's pet. He was the genius and I was the worker. He was Hollywood and I was Perth. We may have been different, and we probably pissed each other off on occasion, but there was always a level of respect that made us mates.

● ● ●

Jo Angel: He only played four Tests for Australia but I would pick him in my team any day. Western Australia's best bowler in my time, he was as wholehearted a player as I ever played with.

Michael Clarke: Pup's 'bling, bling' and cocky personality made him a rough diamond needing polishing early in his career. Underneath the polish is a fierce determination to succeed. It feels like he's my little brother.

Damien Fleming: Although we didn't play a lot together, Flem was a special character whose humour and good spirit was important to the Australian cricket team. Because he had the ability to swing the ball, he was a very good bowler who added value on and off the field.

Jason Gillespie: When I first set eyes on Jason 'Dizzy' Gillespie, he had a ponytail, a run-up as long as Shoaib Akhtar and was really quick. He was always professional and one of the great characters of my time in the game as well as being loyal to a fault.

Brad Hogg: Pure work ethic and desire made Hoggy one of the players who I really wanted to see succeed. The boy from the bush who played in two World Cups for Australia and who was a laugh a minute with his antics.

Michael Hussey: The best compliment I could pay Huss was that I handed the responsibility of leading the team song over to him when I retired. Through sheer hard work and perseverance he has developed into an outstanding international cricketer whose statistics at the highest level are magnificent. You would go a long way to meet a nicer bloke.

Michael Kasprowicz and **Andy Bichel:** In terms of great team men these two best mates are incomparable—big-hearted Queenslanders who were competitive with hearts of gold. If I had to stand in the trenches these two would be there every time.

Simon Katich: I would never like to fight Kato. He is tough as nails, with a steely resolve and stubborn demeanour on the cricket field. He is a natural leader and a person I like and respect enormously.

Brett Lee: Fielding at bat-pad was always fun when Binga bowled because you could see raw intimidation in the eyes of the batsmen. The game is worse off without Brett Lee, the smiling assassin with his flowing blond locks, white sweat bands and sheer pace. One of the nicest blokes you'd meet.

Michael Slater: Whether he had a guitar or cricket bat in his hand, Slats' enthusiasm and passion for life made him an infectious character. He was always a hard act to follow out in the middle because he cut, pulled and drove from the first ball he faced. Although I replaced him as an opener at the end of the 2001 Ashes series, we had a lot of fun together and still enjoy each other's company.

Andrew Symonds: Simmo and I are poles apart in terms of personality but we get along brilliantly. He is one of the players I would always love in my team and one I wouldn't like to fight. His raw strength and toughness can be intimidating and his competitive spirit is inspiring on the field. He roamed the covers like a lion protecting its territory. He was one of the most destructive and talented players of my time and one of the most honest characters with whom I have shared a change room.

Shane Watson: I always like to see a person with a great work ethic succeed. Not only is he a very nice person, but he has shown enormous character to fight back from adversity to become a superstar on the world stage.

Mark Waugh: The Rolls-Royce was a joy to watch and play with. His honesty, in this politically correct world, was refreshing and provided plenty of humour for his mates.

28. Lucky bastard

Perception, as I discovered many times in my career, is a dangerous beast. If you always believe what others tell you without making your own judgement, you can develop a warped view. I had to live with skewed perceptions about my batting, which made me very cautious of making presumptions about others. Meeting Kerry Packer is a great case in point.

Even though he was not a player of any substance, Packer was a man whose influence over the game of cricket was probably greater than that of anyone but Sir Don Bradman. He was always a mythical figure and fabulously rich, and by reputation he was fearsome. But, as I found out one night in 2005, this was a far too simplistic view of him.

It was mid-October and we had settled back in Australia after the disappointment of the Ashes. The team got together again in Sydney for a match against an ICC World XI, which was supposed to be the first of a series every four years. As it turned out, our dominance in both the 'Test match' and the one-day matches was so complete that any notion of a future series was crushed.

Haydos and I had got to know the radio personality Alan Jones, and asked him if we could meet Kerry Packer sometime. It never seemed likely to eventuate until the night before this match at the SCG. Packer invited Haydos and I to meet him at home, along with Brett Lee and Shane Watson. Surprisingly, Tugga had not met Packer—he was also invited but said he would meet us there because he was having a book launch. Alan Jones would also be there.

Haydos and I didn't know what to wear and eventually decided that our formal Australian team suits would be the best idea. Watto, the young bloke that he was, turned up in jeans and a white shirt unbuttoned almost to his waist.

My heart was thumping as we pulled into the driveway of a huge mansion in Bellevue Hill. The whole experience was daunting. I expected an ogre, such was Packer's reputation, but when he answered the door the only ogrish thing about him was the sheer size of his hand as he shook mine.

'I'm very pleased to meet you,' he said simply. 'Welcome to my home. Please come in.'

We followed him inside, past this massive statue of Buddha. The place seemed the size of Buckingham Palace. We were ushered into a sitting room and two waiters came out and offered us drinks. It was the night before the Test match so we all requested soft drinks.

Packer sat down with us. Apparently he had two nurses with him, but I had no real idea of just how sick he was until he died two months later. I can't remember if he had a drink but he did smoke. One of the waiters brought him a freshly opened pack on a silver tray. In this day and age you would expect a smoker would go outside or ask the others in the room if they minded. Not Kerry Packer, and certainly not in his own home. He leaned back and drew on his cigarette luxuriously, as if to say, 'I'm king here and I don't need to ask permission from anyone.' Not that I was going to challenge him.

We talked for a while about the Ashes campaign before we were called into an amazing dining room for dinner, complete with silver-service cutlery and a buffet of seafood and vegetables. He was really laying it on and was a generous host. It was quite unsettling to be offered a spoonful of peas and carrots by Kerry Packer.

The conversation was the thing that really got me. Here we were, sitting around the table with Australia's richest man and one of our most influential radio broadcasters, talking about anything from sport to politics to business. Packer and Jones were mates and talked to each other so frankly and easily. They didn't hold back in front of us, either. My jaw was on the table most of the time.

Then we got back to the Ashes. Instead of being harsh, as he might have been, Packer said, 'Well, sometimes in life you need a bit of luck, and maybe you boys were just out of luck.'

He launched into a tale about his grandfather, who had apparently found ten shillings at the races in Hobart, bet on a horse that won, and with his winnings bought a ticket to Sydney. 'If it wasn't for a bit of luck, we wouldn't be sitting here now,' he concluded.

Then he spoke about his father, Sir Frank Packer, who he reckoned was the luckiest bloke in the world because of a printing press deal that had made the family fortune.

'Let me tell you about my luck,' he said.

I was expecting a story about his gambling or a famous business deal, but Packer stopped and looked at me. 'You've had a bit of luck yourself, haven't you, young fella?' he said.

'Yes, Mr Packer,' I stammered, agreeing I was the luckiest bastard in the world.

'Yeah, you have,' he continued. Drawing on his cigarette, he finished, 'Lucky they invented helmets or you'd be fuckin' dead!'

He looked across the table to Jones and burst out laughing. He couldn't contain himself and neither could anyone else. Haydos was crying so much he fell off the back of his chair.

The night continued like that. Packer held court and we all listened and gawked. He was polite and generous but you could sense the sheer power of his personality. The thing that got me was his blunt honesty. He gave us one last piece of advice I'll never forget.

Towards the end of the night he asked Alan, 'Hey, AJ, should I give them our special advice?'

Alan nodded his head.

'Okay, boys. Remember this. As long as you know who you are and your mates know who you are, then the rest of 'em can go and get fucked.'

As we left he shook our hands again and thanked us for taking the time to come to his home. We felt it should be the other way around. Haydos and I talked about it on our way back to the hotel. Apart from the laughs, the thing that impressed us was the honesty of the evening. The conversation may not have been politically correct, but Packer's directness and straight-shooting just highlighted the bullshit that goes on around us a lot of the time.

Alan Jones is another bloke who cops his fair share of criticism, but whatever the public perceptions, the man is one of the most generous and smart people I've ever met.

I first got to know him when we exchanged a few letters. From memory, I wrote to him, thanking him for addressing the players before we left for the 2001 Ashes tour. It had been the best speech I'd ever heard. He wrote back after I was dropped from the team and was inspiring, telling me to hang in there because things would turn around. When I was selected for the Fifth Test, he interviewed me on his radio show and we have stayed in touch ever since.

I attended an event that he hosted during the tour of New York's Mayor Rudolph Giuliani. I was sitting at the top table as the guest auctioneer for a number of items being sold for charity, one of which was a bat signed by the 1938 Australian side that toured England. The bidding went up $1000 at a time—five grand, then six, seven and eight, and the final bid was $8500.

'Sold!' I said, and called for a round of applause for the winner.

When I sat down, Alan leaned over. 'I just bought you a present,' he said.

'What do you mean?'

'The bat. I know you're into the history of the game and I thought you'd really like it. Pick it up as you leave.'

I couldn't believe it. Jones' generosity is much broader than gifts, however. My father set up a Make a Difference Foundation in Perth, which has done some great stuff over the years. For example, they built a house for a young man named Guy Wallace, who was training to be an Olympic equestrian competitor when he fell off his horse and was left profoundly disabled.

When he was setting it up, Dad wrote to some of his business associates and mates to ask for donations. He asked me if he could write to Alan Jones. I was a bit reluctant because I didn't want to pressure our friendship. In the end, Dad wrote to Alan just to let him know about what was happening. A few weeks later, as I was playing in a club match for Scarborough, Dad came rushing up to tell me he'd just got a letter from Alan. Inside was a personal cheque for $20,000.

• • •

One of the perks of being a recognised sportsman is the chance to meet other successful people from various walks of life. Last summer I was invited to play in the golf pro-am in the lead-up to the Johnnie Walker Classic tournament in Perth. Even better, the organisers had slotted me in to play with Greg Norman and jockey Damien Oliver. As you can imagine, I was pretty excited about the opportunity, even though I only play golf a few times a year.

I was back playing grade cricket at the time, and four days before the tournament I tore my calf muscle. It was really sore but I was determined to play, no matter what, so on the morning of the pro-am I went to the physio, who strapped my leg from ankle to thigh to make sure I could put some weight on it as I swung the club.

Not satisfied with my temporary ability to walk, I decided to get in some practice on the way. I headed to the Wembley Golf Course driving range, where I hit not one but three buckets of balls. I had about a dozen balls left when one of the club pros walked past.

'Hey, JL,' he called, 'I hear you're playing with Greg Norman this arvo.'

Word got around fast in golf circles.

'Yeah, I'm pumped but I'm bloody nervous,' I replied. 'Got any tips?'

What a dumb thing to say. Of course, he suggested that I change my grip. I tried what he said and it felt awful, yet I managed to hit a few down the middle. With that, I jumped in my car and headed to the course.

A few hours later I met the Shark on the first tee. A good crowd had gathered to watch as we were introduced before hitting off. 'First on the tee, Mr Greg Norman,' called the announcer, and Greg promptly creamed one down the middle. 'Next on the tee, Mr Damien Oliver.' Damien also smacked a respectable one down the fairway.

'Next, Mr Justin Langer.' It was my turn. I had a gammy leg taped up under my trousers, Greg Norman was watching, I was holding the club with a new grip and playing in front of spectators who made the crowds of 100,000 in India seem like a walk in the park. I swung and hoped for the best, then breathed a sigh of relief as the ball hooked into the trees. At least I'd got it off the ground, and we were playing Ambrose, a team event.

The next hole I sliced it, narrowly missing the gallery. The Shark quietly told me to try to rotate a bit more rather than sway. Now I was thinking about my leg, my grip, my nerves and my shoulders. You can guess the result.

I played terribly, but in the end I didn't care—I was playing golf with Greg Norman! He later left a message on my answering machine: 'Hey, Justin, Greg Norman here. It was great playing golf with you yesterday.' I was going to make it my ringtone to show off to my friends but I lost my bloody phone.

Occasionally, however, the world of celebrity has encroached on my private life, as Sue explains.

● ● ●

Perth might be a city but it feels like a small place at times, and it's inevitable that Justin gets recognised. Early in his career, I was surprised when a group of kids turned up at our house and asked if Justin lived there. I didn't know if I should tell them, but I did and they seemed satisfied and simply walked away.

There have been occasions when we're on the beach and people walk past and say 'Hi, Justin' as though they know him. 'Who was that?' I whisper to him, to which he just shrugs his shoulders. I guess recognition comes with the territory.

The funniest situation happened not long ago when our area got a new post-office deliveryman. He came to the door one day and seemed to be hanging around after he gave me our parcel.

'Is there something else?' I asked.

He pointed to the name on the delivery schedule. 'Langer—just like the famous one. Is it him?'

'Justin? Yes, he lives here,' I relented.

The man danced around joyously. 'I knew it, I knew it!' he laughed as he went off.

After that he always loitered around the door, looking past me and obviously trying to sneak a look to see if Justin was around. He never was, though, and the poor bloke always left disappointed.

Then one day Justin happened to be home, so I asked him to go out and sign for the parcel because it would give the postie the thrill of his life. Justin obliged and ended up signing a book for him and giving him a few other souvenirs, including a shirt.

The postie, who like all Indians was a cricket tragic, was so happy he invited us around to his place for dinner, where he promised to make black dhal, one of Justin's favourite dishes. He's still asking when we're coming over, and in the meantime we now get the best service you could ever hope for!

29. Ton up

The number 100 is significant for cricketers and particularly for a batsman. Scoring a century is always the goal, and even in training I had techniques that focused on scoring a ton. Right up until the day before my last competitive innings—in India for the Champions League Twenty20 series in October 2009—I went through the routine I call 'running a hundred'. Much to the chagrin of my Somerset, West Australian, Middlesex and even Scarborough team-mates over the years, the call of 'let's run a hundred' came out often, and it was always met with expressions of dread.

The idea was that I run 100 shuttle-runs between two plastic markers, or stumps, on the centre wicket or the outfield of the ground we were about to play on. First I would scamper a single, then a two, then three, then four and five runs, and back down through four, three, two and one. That made 25 runs. I'd do that four times to make the century. Sometimes I did a few sit-ups and push-ups between sets, and when I'd made 50 I would raise my bat as if I were acknowledging the crowd. I'd do the same at 100.

People watching me from the sideline probably thought I was a bit of a clown, but that didn't worry me. I found it a really good routine to keep me physically fit and mentally focused. The exercise also gave me a sense of being at the wicket, so it helped me get a feel for the ground and the conditions we'd be playing in.

I've run a hundred on cricket grounds all around the world, usually the day before the match and always striving for the magical three figures. Sometimes I would even run more and enjoy the make-believe elation of reaching 150 or 200, but I would never settle for anything less than the landmark figure of 100. I always felt I would be judged by the number of centuries I scored, and towards the end of my career I dreamed of reaching the elite figure of 100 first-class centuries. Although I didn't make it—I scored 86, including 23 in Tests—the ambition of reaching the milestone kept me hungry for batting success, allowing me to play good cricket right up until my last game for Somerset.

Similarly, playing 100 Tests became a positive ambition. Only a handful of cricketers have ever played 100 Test matches for Australia, so as the opportunity approached in 2006 I naturally became excited at the prospect. We toured South Africa in March after whipping the Proteas 2–0 during the Australian summer as we built towards taking revenge against England in 2006–07, which was something I reminded my team-mates of every time we celebrated a win.

Those two victories—in Melbourne and Sydney—were the beginning of what would become our second set of sixteen consecutive Test victories. I had played in the drawn First Test in Perth but had withdrawn from the Second Test in Melbourne because of a hamstring injury. Phil Jaques made his Test debut in my place, but I was back in the team in Sydney for our big win there.

We left Australia a month later, confident but wary of the South Africans in their own country. The First Test at Durban would be my 98th, the Second Test at Cape Town my 99th and the last Test, at the Wanderers in Johannesburg, would be the magical 100th. I was anxious as the goal came closer, firstly about keeping my place in the side, and secondly because my parents and closest friends were planning to make the trip to South Africa. We had two good wins in the first Tests but I was becoming more and more apprehensive; I was overawed by the number of letters and phone calls coming from all over the world, which only emphasised what a big deal it was to have reached this milestone.

My diary, as usual, suggests I was battling my demons. Looking back on my entries from that time, I can see I was attempting to give myself a stern talking-to rather than to record an account of what was actually happening.

In a lot of ways the 100th Test has become more of a distraction than anything else. I've been living a long way into the future . . . rather than the zen philosophy of living in the moment. As Haydos says, the more you chase the butterfly, the more elusive it becomes.

Mum and Dad did make the trip, and they gave me a beautiful pendant of a cricket bat with a diamond cricket ball embedded in it. Nigel Wray and his daughter Lucy also flew over from London.

Ricky Ponting cornered me as I was walking back to my hotel room after dinner the night before the Third Test and asked me how I was feeling. He thought I might be nervous, but by then I was feeling excited. In a way, I was also a bit relieved that the day was finally about to arrive. There had been so much fanfare that I was just looking forward to getting out there and into the action.

As it turned out, we bowled first, and Punter asked me to lead the team onto the field. Having never captained Australia in a Test match, it was with incredible pride that I did so. It was an even first day and we were batting by the second morning after dismissing South Africa for 303.

Like most cricketers, I was a creature of habit and superstitions played a part in my preparation. I always placed two pieces of P.K chewing gum on the peak of my helmet next to me, with my gloves and bat nearby. I would strap on my right pad before my left, then have a drink of water and pop the chewie in my mouth before leaving the change room. Just before stepping across the boundary, I would tap my bat a couple of times and play a few practice straight drives. I'd step onto the field, kick my legs up behind my knees to loosen up, and walk to the wicket.

My preparation that day was normal—besides a bit of extra dreaming about scoring a century in my 100th Test—and I remember feeling pretty good as I crossed the white line with Haydos. The Proteas' fast bowler Makhaya Ntini was opening the innings. I always found him difficult to handle, mainly because, like Courtney Walsh, he tended to bowl from wide on the crease and angle the ball across me. He also tended to be either a bit full or a bit short, making driving and pulling huge temptations, but the awkward angle of his bowling made these shots low-percentage options.

On that morning he employed a strange and very attacking field, particularly since it was the first over of the innings. There was a bat-pad, a deep forward square leg, a fine leg and even a leg slip. It was an interesting strategy, and I assumed Ntini was planning to bowl straight at my body. There was a fair bit in the wicket, so

Haydos and I were prepared to be watchful for a while to get used to the conditions.

I recited my usual mantra of 'head forward, watch the ball' as Ntini ran in and bowled the first ball from over the wicket. It was short, pitched outside leg stump and seaming back in to me, almost like a bodyline delivery. I didn't want to play a pull shot or even guide it down because of the legside field they'd set, so I decided to go under it and let the ball pass over my head.

You would think that after 100 Tests I would have known better, but instead of watching the ball as it went through to the keeper, I ducked and turned my head. The ball kept a bit low and hit me flush on the back of the helmet. Normally, the ball glances off the helmet at an angle, maybe to the wicket-keeper or slips, but this one hit me so square-on that it bounced straight back up the pitch to Ntini, who picked it up in his follow-through.

I'd been hit many times but I knew I was in trouble. The effect of being hit in the head by a brand-new cricket ball travelling at 150 kilometres per hour was a bit like pulling a TV's power cord out of the socket. My mind went blank in a millisecond. The ball split the back of my helmet and cut my head open. I had a massive brain shudder and went down on one knee.

Haydos came down to see if I was okay and our physio, Alex Kountouris, ran out. The South Africans were playing it hard and didn't come over at first, but when it became apparent that I was in trouble the slip cordon soon gathered around me. As groggy as I was, I remember Haydos putting his arm around me and reminding me that there were no heroes in Test cricket.

Although I managed a grin for my big mate, I was in gaga-land and there was no way I could go on. Despite everything, I had no choice but to retire hurt. The only thing I could manage was to walk off, holding a towel at the back of my head to stop the blood dribbling down my back.

I realised later that I'd been knocked down by the second ball in my first Test match and then by the first ball in my 100th. Some might say I hadn't learned much in those thirteen years.

As it happens, there was a funny side to all this; well, it's funny in hindsight, I suppose. I was in the medical room lying face-down on the table while they examined me. My mum, who'd watched the incident from the stands, came rushing in to see if I was alright and was holding my hand as the doctor had a look at me.

Outside in the middle Haydos had lost his wicket, caught in the gully off Ntini, and we were suddenly in a bit of trouble. Andrew Symonds, who had to pad up in a hurry, came rushing into the medical room looking for some tape to bind his wrists, which he always did before going out to bat. He happened to enter just as the doctor was about to put an injection in the back of my cruet. I don't like needles at any time, and this one was particularly sensitive. Just as the doctor was inserting the needle, Roy walked past the table and accidentally kicked its leg, causing the needle to be jabbed deeper into my head than intended. I don't even think he noticed. If he hadn't had to go and save the day, Mum might have given him a right hook for hurting her little boy. How sweet.

I was taken to hospital to have some precautionary brain scans. I was feeling really awful by this stage, so Dad stayed with me while they did the tests. It was late in the day when the hospital staff said I could go back to our hotel. They took me downstairs, where these young guys were standing around a Corolla sedan which they called an ambulance. Another two blokes were standing by them with guns on their hips. They were the police escort I was getting through the city. If I'd known what was going to happen next, we would have taken a taxi.

Dad got in the front and I tried to get comfortable in the back. I don't know where they trained these ambulance drivers, but they must have been driving at 140 kilometres per hour through the city streets in this tiny car. It felt like we were in a Formula One race. Dad was scared out of his wits and I was feeling like a dog being thrown around in the back. Somehow we got back unscathed, and I spent the next three days in bed at the hotel, feeling sorry for myself as the Test progressed. I still can't believe how sick a blow to the head and the subsequent concussion can make you feel.

It was also awful for Sue. It is one thing to put yourself in the firing line but, as she points out, it is quite another to watch someone you love being in danger a lot of the time.

● ● ●

It was always hard to see Justin get hurt. I was at the ground for his first Test when he was hit by Ian Bishop, and I was watching on TV in the middle of the night when he was hit by a bouncer when he opened the batting for the first time during the 2001 Ashes at the Oval. He didn't move for a couple of minutes, and in our dark lounge room on the other side of the world I was worried sick.

The worst, though, was the 100th Test when he was hit by Ntini. I hadn't flown over because Grace was just a few months old and I didn't want to leave the other kids, so I already felt bad about missing such a big occasion. Hearing about it only made things worse. I was in a car park in the late afternoon, loading shopping into the car and struggling with the kids, when I took a phone call—not from Justin but from a doctor, assuring me that my husband was okay. You can imagine my alarm.

Several more phone calls followed, including one from Colin, so by the next day when Justin called I had calmed down. He promptly asked me if he should bat in the second innings. The wife and mother in me wanted to tell him, 'Don't be ridiculous! Put the bat down and come home!' But knowing him the way I did, I couldn't do it. I just hoped he wouldn't be needed.

● ● ●

With one day to go, the match was in the balance. South Africa had taken a 33-run lead after the first innings, but we'd struck back and bowled them out for 258 in their second knock so we needed 292 for a great victory. It wasn't an easy task, but Mike Hussey (89) and Damien Martyn (93 not out) had got us to within 44 runs of victory by the end of the fourth day.

I'd been keeping in touch from the hotel and was in a lather about what to do. The doctor was telling me that under no circumstances could I bat, and yet we were so close to both victory and defeat. Without me, we were effectively seven wickets down. What if Marto was left stranded with a few runs to get? It was a moment for heroics, but even Dad was saying I would be a fool to play—although he'd probably have batted with two broken legs.

I felt I had to talk to Marto that night. I found him during dinner, explained that I wouldn't be able to bat, then went to bed feeling like a coward.

I tossed and turned all night, wrestling with what I should do. I knew I'd never be able to forgive myself if I didn't go out there if the team needed me. I kept thinking about players in the past who'd soldiered on in adversity, like Rick McCosker, who went out to bat in the 1977 Centenary Test against England with a broken jaw wired shut to help Australia to victory. Images of Allan Border batting with a gashed eye and Dean Jones battling chronic dehydration in India were invading my conscience, and I couldn't help but ask myself how my situation compared.

The doctor confirmed the worst the next morning. My mind agreed with him but my heart was saying the opposite. Dad came in and told me again I couldn't play because I'd be putting my future and my family at risk. I decided I had to go to the ground, even though I was still feeling really sick.

By the time we got there I felt a little better, and I went to see Steve 'Brute' Bernard, our team manager, to tell him that I was ready to play if needed. He refused and repeated that under no circumstances would I be allowed onto the field. They had a duty of care, he explained, and he was not prepared to risk my health. He even threatened to put security guards on the change-room door to stop me from going out there.

Resigned, I went down to the nets behind the main stand to tell my team-mates that I couldn't play. It was a really emotional moment, because we always talked about standing together and being there for one another, no matter what. Yet here I was, doing the opposite—at least, it felt that way. I looked around the faces and saw that most had accepted my decision.

But there were two blokes—Matty Hayden and Andrew Symonds—who I could tell weren't convinced. I had told Haydos the bad news the night before, and his reaction had been that I should do what I thought best. The look in his eyes that morning, however, said something different—he believed I should have a crack if I was needed. Roy was the same, and I walked away still feeling very conflicted.

I sat and watched with the others and cheered up a bit when Marto got his century with a back-foot drive off Shaun Pollock, but five balls later he was out and we were seven down—effectively eight, without me. We still had 34 to get. Stuart Clark went in to join Brett Lee. Like most of the others, I thought we were gone—to have any chance, we needed Marto in at the end.

I snuck out the back and was putting on my whites when Brute came in and caught me. I felt like a schoolboy doing something wrong and started to make up excuses, saying I'd only go out there if we needed one run and I could stand at the non-striker's end.

But he wouldn't have a bar of it. I stood on a bench and looked through a small window above the lockers to see what was going on outside. I felt like I was in prison—even the windows were barred. Brett and Stuart were poking and prodding the ball around, somehow surviving and moving the score closer and closer. We needed 25 to win when Stuart banged two fours—through cover and extra-cover—and suddenly we needed just seventeen.

The next ball he tried to pull Ntini to the square-leg fence but got a top edge and skied the ball to the wicket-keeper, Mark Boucher, who took the catch. We were eight down now, effectively nine, and our number eleven batsman, Michael Kasprowicz, went in.

By now I had psyched myself up to bat and no one was going to stop me. Punter came inside and turned white as a sheet when he saw me. I had my pads on and was jumping up and down to loosen up.

'You're not going out there,' he told me. 'I'll declare before I let you.'

I was angry now and shouted back at him: 'If you declare, then that's the end of our friendship.'

Punter persisted. 'I'll bring in security if I need to. I don't care if we lose this match—you're not going out there.'

I wasn't thinking about the amazing sacrifice that he, as captain, was making for my benefit—that he'd risk the match before one of his players. I persisted. 'My mind's made up, Punter. There is no way in the world that I'm not going to bat if I have the chance to win us the Test match.'

The security guys assigned to protect us on the tour were now inside the change room, having been told to protect me from myself, if necessary. It was going to be an interesting confrontation.

As the argument escalated, with Brute prowling around and getting angry with me—out of concern, I realise—the boys in the middle were edging closer and closer. Kasper paddled one to deep square leg and they scampered two, then they got another three on leg byes to fine leg before Brett pounded a boundary through the covers.

Now we needed just eight runs. The argument continued inside the change room and we all kept watch through the windows. The next over Kasper played and missed three times before hitting a boundary of his own, and suddenly we needed four.

I was nervous as hell, wondering what on earth I was doing— what if they bowled another bouncer and it hit me? Yet I was thrilled by the excitement and the chance to do what most of us dream about—being a hero in a Test match. My head was still telling me to stop but my heart had won out. I was pumped and ready.

Punter had gone quiet and was watching the game on one of the television sets in the room. He wanted to be outside with his team but he had a duty to keep me behind the locked doors of the change room. Brett got a single off the first ball of the next over, and then Kasper got another. Two to win, and the South Africans brought their field in close to force Brett to hit over the top.

I'd stopped bouncing now. I'd forgotten about my head and was caught between hoping that Brett would hammer a boundary and that he would get out trying so I could go out there and hit the winning runs.

Pollock bowled a short ball outside the off stump and Brett cut it over the fielders for four runs. We had won an amazing match, but no one knew what had been going on inside the change room, although Dad, who was sitting outside, apparently had a good idea and correctly reckoned that I was making a stand. Even though he had warned me against going out there, he knew how I felt and would have backed me if a wicket had fallen.

I made a point of going out on the ground in my pads to show the South Africans that they would still have had to get through me if another wicket had fallen. The important thing to me, though, was that I'd followed my heart and my team-mates knew I would've gone out there if needed. The doubt I had seen in the eyes of Haydos and Simmo that morning was replaced by respect. They didn't have to say anything—I just knew.

Even thinking back to the day now, I feel the same way. Punter and Steve were right to try to protect me, but my decision was the right one as well. This was not 'just a game'. This was my livelihood, and my reputation was on the line—that meant a lot to me. As a Test opening batsman I took a major risk every time I walked out to bat. I've been hit many times but the battle was what you strive for. That's what the day at the Wanderers represented. My head will always tell me I was being stupid but my heart will always say my belligerence was right.

The celebrations that night were among the best I remember. We had won the series 3–0, and we'd taken the last five Tests against the Proteas on the trot, but this had been such a close match with so many unknowns, including whether I would play. I led the team song that afternoon, which was very emotional, particularly because my parents were there. Afterwards, we sat out on the grass banks, playing music and reminiscing. The evening was warm and the beer was flowing, although I couldn't drink because of the concussion. I hadn't realised what a huge impact the blow was having on me.

There was a bitter end to the night, though. The team was leaving the next morning for Bangladesh to play two Tests, and Merv Hughes, a great mate since our early skirmishes in New Zealand and who was also the duty selector on the tour, had to tell me that I wasn't going. They couldn't take a risk, so I was heading home.

It was a critical moment for me. At 36 years old, I knew I was at the crossroads. I was too old to be certain of being in the side and unable to enjoy a couple of easy Tests against a minnow Test nation and boost my average. Not for the first time in my career, I wondered whether I would ever get to play for Australia again. And I was desperate for revenge against the Poms.

30. Peter Perfect and the spiders

Aussies aside, who was the fastest bowler I ever faced? Who gave me the most trouble, who made me fear for my safety, who was the cleverest, the tightest and, above all, who was the best bowler I faced in Test cricket? The answers are not simple.

Let me first knock on the head any suggestion that I or any other opening batsman actually looked forward to doing battle with the speed demons. It's rubbish. Frankly, there is little fun in facing fast bowling. For years I had to say I loved facing the fastest of them, but that was more to do with bravado and strategy than the truth.

As brave as we appear, every opening batsman has a natural fear as we walk out to face the first over of an innings. There wouldn't be one around who could honestly say that, in the back of his mind, there isn't a nagging concern about getting hurt. Fast bowlers are like bullies in a school playground, and if you don't show intent then you will be bombarded.

One of the main reasons I took up boxing and martial arts was to get used to fighting, because when you face fast bowlers that is basically what you're doing. Martial arts improved my fitness, reflexes and footwork, but it also prepared me psychologically for the battle. There is nowhere to hide in the boxing ring—body language is critical and aggression is the best form of defence. I took those principles out into the middle of the cricket ground. If I showed weakness, a defensive frame of mind or hesitancy in my actions, then I was in trouble and could get hurt or—worse—get out.

Alternatively, if my head was forward and I was on the front foot and looking to score runs, then my defence would be better and my positive body language would show my aggression. Against the guys I'm going to discuss, this was important, because my frame of mind and my ability to adopt a 'fuck-you attitude' was paramount to the success I had as a batsman. The best fast bowlers could smell fear, and unless I was willing to stand up and fight, then my tenure would always be short-lived.

Let's start with the fastest. There are three bowlers, leaving aside Brett Lee, who were blinding. The best known was Shoaib Akhtar. He was consistently the fastest by a clear margin. They called him 'the Rawalpindi Express', and a stream train wasn't a bad analogy. It was bad enough watching him from the striker's end as he kicked off from the pickets, his hair and arms streaming as he flew straight at you, but what a lot of people wouldn't know is that Shoaib was often just as intimidating for the non-striker as well. You could actually hear the loco firing up as he approached, grunting and heaving, going faster and faster. It was as though he was using every ounce of energy as he tore in, before his arm went back at the last second and he released his missile with a roar.

People sometimes ask if I could actually *see* the ball at Shoaib's speed, which was close to 160 kilometres per hour. The simple answer is yes, of course I did, although the key was watching the ball being released from his hand. If I saw it out of the fingers, my body went into an automatic response, almost like a machine, and I would move into line behind the angle of the delivery. If I detected that the ball was short I looked for it off the wicket, but, frankly, the bouncer was not the ball I was most worried about. A bouncer may knock you out or cause physical injury, but it's the delivery that's full and swinging that will cause you the most trouble.

I've also been asked if there was a big difference between facing a bowler at 145 kilometres per hour, which is really quick, and a bowler of Shoaib's pace. The answer is definitely yes. Mohammad Sami was one of the new fast-bowling hopefuls for Pakistan when champions such as Wasim Akram and Waqar Younis retired. While Sami was pretty nippy, he felt like a medium-pacer when I was facing Shoaib from the other end. By himself he was quick, but when partnered with Shoaib his sting was diminished.

A bowler like Shoaib is raw pace, and there is a price to pay for all that speed. It is simply not possible for him to place the ball on the right spot consistently. This means he can tear through the tailenders and intimidate the top order, but I always felt that I could score off him if I was brave enough to remain still, get in behind the line and shorten my backlift. That was where my boxing training came in. There is a degree of physical courage required to stay still when facing this type of aggression. Not only must your head stay as still as possible, to ensure perfect balance, but you must also keep your mind still, to eliminate the inevitable fears of physical intimidation.

Shoaib and I had some classic battles over the years, including in the famous Hobart Test in 1999 when he hit me in the face-guard and then on the hand with a beam ball. I thought he had done some serious damage and didn't even want to take off my glove, which felt like it was full of blood and bone. I walked towards square leg, had a peek and realised it was okay, so I walked back and smiled at Shoaib to let him know he would have to throw more at me than that. This set him off, and rather than returning a polite smile he became more incensed and ran in harder and harder. As soon as he did that I knew I had him, because the angrier Shoaib got, the looser he bowled, which meant more opportunities for me to score runs.

In my time there were two other bowlers who, although a step behind Shoaib, fit in roughly the same speed category. Waqar Younis, also from Pakistan, had not only pure speed but also the ability to move the ball both ways—and he was the first bowler to perfect reverse-swing. This was a lethal combination and produced a different form of intimidation. Waqar's run-up was just as long as Shoaib's but didn't have the same raw, guttural energy; his approach was a flash of white armbands pumping as he charged in like an Olympic sprinter. He also bowled a lot fuller and straighter than most others, which was probably what earned him such a good strike rate.

The other lightning-quick bowler was a West Indian, but not one of the frontline legends. Jermaine Lawson, from Jamaica, is the only bowler I have faced to have come close to Shoaib's speed and—in one innings, in particular—to probably have matched him. At Barbados in 2003, during the Third Test, I became the third victim of an unusual hat-trick taken by Lawson. He had taken the wickets of Brett Lee and Stuart MacGill to finish our first innings, then he trapped me LBW for a golden duck in the second. It was particularly annoying because we only needed eight runs to win the Test.

But it was during the Fourth Test, at Antigua a week later, that Lawson bowled an unforgettable spell. I honestly thought he was going to kill me, so much so that I had a fit of the nervous giggles. I appeared to be cool, smiling and laughing at him—which confused Haydos, who reckoned I was crazy—but the truth was I simply couldn't help it. Somehow I made 42 before Lawson got me, the second of the seven wickets he took in one of the best displays of raw fast bowling I've ever seen.

On that day he was hostility at its best, and I was happy to have lived to tell the tale. Sadly for him and the game, Lawson was reported for 'chucking' after that innings and his career never really recovered, losing his raw pace when he had to alter his bowling action. The game is weaker without his presence, as the fastest bowlers are a rare breed and contribute greatly to the entertainment of Test match cricket. Shaun Tait deserves a mention here, if only because of the way he forced his way into the Test side during the 2005 Ashes at my physical expense. Fast bowlers are much quicker in the nets because they constantly overstep the crease. In the lead-up to the Third Test at Trent Bridge, Taity bowled an over at me trying to impress selector Trevor Hohns. Boy, did he!

The first ball, an inswing yorker, cleaned up my off stump and the second ripped out my middle stump. The third hit me in the nuts and split my box. He followed it up with a shorter ball that smashed into my elbow. Hohns had seen enough: Shaun would make his Test debut. And me? My confidence had been shattered, my elbow bruised and my voice was a little higher than usual.

If the super-quicks were the runaway trains, the next bracket of bowlers were more like the scary spiders. West Indians Curtly Ambrose and Courtney Walsh were a nightmare pair—long-limbed menaces who not only scared the hell out of you with their pace and bounce, but also had the ability to tie you up and stop you from scoring. It was like being caught in a web from which there was no escape. I would add Bishop to this group, the guy who hit me in the head in my first Test.

Courtney was probably the bowler I found hardest to score from. He came from wide on the crease, all arms and angles, and his fingers were so big that you couldn't see the ball until very late. He bowled short of a length and gave you almost no room to cut or drive; and if you tried, you always worried that the ball would do something crazy and you'd get an edge. He would hit the seam at will, making the ball rip back in or away from you. Whatever he did with it, he always caused me trouble.

I want to mention Carl Rackemann, who, in my opinion, should have played more Test cricket than he did—he played only twelve matches. Carl was a big, strong Queensland bushman and the toughest bowler I ever faced in Shield cricket. He was like Courtney Walsh, running in and bowling from wide on the crease, in a tangle of arms and legs and at a good pace and ugly length. It was like he was chopping down trees on his bush block in a flannel shirt, R.M. Williams boots and with a bloody great chainsaw.

If Rackemann used a chainsaw, then Curtly Ambrose wielded a scythe. I drove him for three runs to get off the mark in Test cricket back in 1993, but I don't think I ever played a front-foot shot off him again. Curtly came from a great height and his action was majestic, but he seemed to be able to put the ball on a twenty-cent piece at will. The best I could do against him was occasionally to glide one down to third man or play a little tug-pull through the onside. In some respects, though, Curtly's consistency was a blessing, because I always felt as if I could rely on him to bowl like that all day. At times it felt like you were dancing with him, repeating patterns and footwork over and over simply because of his ruthless rhythm and accuracy.

Pakistani left-armer Wasim Akram was like a snake-charmer and a spitting cobra rolled into one. He almost had the pace of Shoaib but delivered his poison off fifteen metres rather than 50. He also began his run-up from behind the umpire, like he was playing a scary game of hide and seek. He would appear suddenly from behind the umpire and sling a whipping, snaking delivery that could pitch and move either way. He could bowl inswingers and outswingers, leg-cutters and off-cutters, bumpers and yorkers, and sometimes even reverse-swinging thunderbolts.

His favourite delivery to left-handed batsmen was delivered over the wicket, moving it towards the slips, but if you started creeping across the wicket to get behind the ball he'd produce a faster inswinger to trap you LBW. Wasim was an incredible artist with a cricket ball in his hand, and had the movie-star looks to match.

The left-arm fast bowlers seemed to cause me more trouble than most other bowlers, probably because of the angles they created. Chaminda Vaas from Sri Lanka was another mollydooker I rated highly. He was significantly slower than the lightning pace of some, but made up for it by planning his attack intelligently and strategically. He was a swing aficionado with a great action and perfect wrist, and this made him lethal with either the new ball or the reverse-swinging old ball. Facing him was like playing a game of chess.

There is another clutch of bowlers I'd put in the warrior class. Englishman Darren Gough wore his patriotism like a knight of the round table, the red cross of England stamped on his chest and a flag draped over his shoulders. Goughie was a big Yorkshire bull whose best asset was his never-say-die attitude. This trait alone was something I admired in him greatly. Danny Morrison from New Zealand was much the same. Neither man had great height or express speed, but they made up for it with their big-hearted performances.

South Africans Allan Donald and Nantie Hayward were warriors of a different ilk, combining lightning speed and a fierce attitude. Donald was like Peter Perfect, a character from a cartoon called *Wacky Races* that I used to watch as a kid. He was always immaculately groomed in white, had wavy blond hair and had such a technically perfect action. He had the fluency of Ambrose but without his height to get the awkward bounce. He also gave you a very clear view of the ball, which made life easier, in a sense, but his attitude was fiery and challenging, particularly at the end of his follow-through.

There was nothing perfect about his team-mate Nantie Hayward, who was perhaps more akin to the *Wacky Races* cavemen. He would tear in with his African beads bouncing around his throat, his wild bleached-blond hair bobbing, and would hurl down the cricket ball like it was a Zulu spear. Often he ended up at my end of the pitch. He was almost as quick as Shoaib—and, like others who bowled with raw pace, he was entertaining and terrific for the game—but I always felt I had a chance to score from him, which tended to take the pressure off.

Less confronting but more effective, Shaun Pollock was a greater threat than his team-mates. He wasn't as quick as the others and didn't have the height to be as intimidating physically, but his accuracy meant that he strangled you. His consistency was like that of Glenn McGrath or Sir Richard Hadlee, and, like Walsh and Ambrose, he was almost impossible to score from. I used to take a different approach when facing him. Rather than deliberately wind him up, as I tried to do with Shoaib, I did the opposite with Pollock. The South Africans tended to take themselves very seriously, and I found that if I smiled back at him after a good delivery—Ambrose in reverse, if you like—he got confused and a bit rattled.

The other South African I want to mention is Makhaya Ntini. He didn't have the pace of the quicker men but he could be dangerous—as I can attest to, having been smacked in the head by him in my 100th Test—and, on his day, he was as tight and controlled as Pollock. He was also in a fitness category all of his own. If Hayward was like a spear-throwing wild man, Ntini was like a Kenyan marathon runner. I didn't have time to smile at him between deliveries because he would already have run back to his mark and be ready to steam in and bowl the next ball. It was like when a boxer stands in his corner between rounds, as if to say, 'Look at me—I'm not even puffing.' Ntini would bowl 30 overs in a day's play and then run ten kilometres on a treadmill. You simply could not wear the guy down. Sometimes it was exhausting just watching him.

I didn't mix socially with many opposition fast bowlers, other than perhaps Andrew Flintoff and Steve Harmison. They were jovial and easy-going Englishmen but also among the fiercest competitors and best bowlers I faced. In the same category as Walsh and Ambrose, they were tall and gangly and had the priceless ability to get steepling bounce, which always made life difficult for opening batsmen.

I would have liked having Harmy in my team because of his skill, but I can understand why he had such a chequered career for England. At the end of the day, the greatest bowlers have consistency and longevity, and while Harmy was brilliant at times, his leaner patches counted against him. Either way, we had some great contests and I don't think there's a bowler who hit me in the helmet more times than he did.

If Darren Gough was a knight of the round table, then Freddy Flintoff was Sir Lancelot. He was an enigma in many ways, since he was so fierce on the field and yet acted like a jolly Santa Claus as soon as he reached the dressing room. He was horrible to face—big, strong and fast. He always bowled what we called a 'heavy' ball—there was no change of pace, but he was fast and banged it into the pitch time after time with no let-up.

In between balls, Flintoff just smiled quietly—like Ambrose, he was a smiling assassin. The difference was that Curtly smiled because he knew he had the upper hand, whereas Freddy's was the carefree grin of a bloke who simply didn't really care, which could be just as intimidating. He was also one of those rare players—like Gilchrist, Warne, Sobers and Lillee—whose personality and momentum could carry both his team and the crowd, so you were always fighting more than simply him as a bowler.

My favourite memory of Flintoff was the fourth morning of the last Ashes Test in 2005. We needed to win the Test to tie the series and retain the Ashes, and at 2 for 277 in our first innings and just 100 runs behind, we felt as if we were getting on top and could push for victory. We were playing at the Oval in London, which has a strange configuration. The visitors have to walk through the players' dining room and past the English change rooms to get to their own. As we walked by England's area, we saw Flintoff. He was sitting back in a chair in his boxer shorts and a singlet, smoking a cigarette and nursing a pint of Coke. He didn't have a worry in the world.

'Alright, lads? Good to see ya,' he smiled, as we trooped past.

We shook our heads in amazement at this English icon, who had his country's hopes resting on his tattooed shoulders and yet was sitting around in his underwear. An hour or so later, although heavily caffeined and smelling like an ashtray, he was dressed in pristine white and bowled all morning, taking five wickets to all but ruin our chances of retaining the Ashes.

There were also some bowlers I didn't really get on with. As I related earlier, Javagal Srinath of India was one of them. He had a bit of pace about him and I always found him difficult to face because of his height and accuracy. Like many fast bowlers, Srinath's bark was far worse than his bite, and as hard as he played on the field, he was an equally nice person off it. He was a gentleman without a ball in his hand, and he now works as an international referee.

Andy Caddick of England was another Jekyll and Hyde character. He was a fast bowler with whom I had a strange, but ultimately close, relationship. A beautiful seam bowler on his day, he was very difficult to score from because of his accuracy and steep bounce. Unfortunately, our relationship didn't start out too well. In 1998 I was recruited by the Middlesex County Cricket Club, which has the privilege of having Lord's as its home ground. We played Somerset in my first home game. I got out cheaply in the first innings but hit my straps in the second.

Caddick was bowling short at me and I kept pulling him. The more I pulled him, the angrier he got, snatching his hat from the umpire and storming down to fine leg, calling me the worst overseas signing in the history of county cricket. At first I was a little bewildered and couldn't believe his behaviour, but after about the 50th sledge I got the shits and started having a go back at him.

He was still mouthing off when I went past 100, then 150 and 200. 'I don't care how many you've got—you're still the worst signing in the history of county cricket,' he ranted.

Caddick was the most annoying opponent I'd ever played against, a typical bully-boy fast bowler. A decade and many battles later, I arrived at Somerset, where I was made captain, and I promptly changed my opinion. I found Caddick to be a big-hearted performer on the field and a good bloke off it, though without doubt he was one of the most ineffectual sledgers in the history of the game.

The South African Andre Nel was always a bit of a lunatic on the field. He'd stare at you down the pitch and bang his chest like Tarzan and then bowl at about 130 kilometres per hour. Harbhajan Singh was a very good bowler in Indian conditions, but outside the subcontinent his effectiveness fell away. He also had a reputation as a trouble-maker. I wouldn't have minded if Harbhajan's antics were intended to needle his opponents as a part of the game, but he went over the top on occasions. He was a bit like the third kid in a family—always looking for a bit of attention. It is a shame he was like that, because he was a very good player.

As for the spinners, Murali Muralitharan gave me more headaches and nightmares than any other bowler. Most times I had no idea where the ball was going to go. He was super-accurate and super-competitive, and I tended to get caught up in what he might do rather than just watching the ball.

The other spinners I faced, while world-class, rank a ways behind him, but I'd say that Anil Kumble was one of the best. He was a gentleman off the field but a fierce warrior once he was on the ground. A tall man, it seemed he had a fast bowler's attitude. In general, the finger-spinners didn't have much to hurt you with other than a change of pace and accuracy. The exception was New Zealander Daniel Vettori who was a class act, smart and with great guile.

Of all the finger-spinners I played against, Phil Tufnell of England had the best shape to his deliveries. The tragedy is that if he'd had more confidence in himself, he could have been a great Test cricketer, but I never played with someone who doubted himself as much as 'the Cat' did. When I was captaining Middlesex, he'd sometimes ring me two or three times a night, worrying about his performance. In fact, he was impossible to captain anyway. I remember one day at Lord's when Phil simply walked off the ground to have a smoke. He didn't say a word, just disappeared and left us with ten men on the ground.

When he finally wandered back, I asked him what had gone on.

'Aw, the stress, skipper, the stress,' he replied.

So who, after all that, were the *best* fast bowlers I faced? I rank Wasim Akram as the best, followed by Curtly Ambrose, Andrew Flintoff and Courtney Walsh. Shaun Pollock and Waqar Younis would probably be equal fifth. Shoaib Akhtar would be close behind because of his explosive pace.

31. Redemption

I always had an uneasy working relationship with the media, and it was made worse when journalists came to press conferences unprepared. The beginning of the 2006–07 Ashes campaign was a case in point. We were in Brisbane preparing for the First Test, and I was copping plenty about potentially being replaced by the New South Welshman Phil Jaques. The question had first been raised a few weeks before.

I played a game for Western Australia when I got back from England but was dismissed cheaply while Phil was busy scoring a century for New South Wales. At the press conference after the game I was asked whether I felt under pressure.

'What can I say?' I replied. 'I've played 100 Test matches and I've done pretty well. One first-class game ago I got 342 [for Somerset]. I missed out this game . . . but that's cricket. But thanks for asking.'

Obviously, I wasn't too happy, and it got worse over the next few days when the story took off and everyone seemed to be calling for my head. It was typical of these types of stories, when a single opinion spreads around like a case of chickenpox. In the past I'd accepted a lot of the criticism, partly because I struggled so much within myself about being good enough to be in a great Australian side. But this time it really stung. Even Dennis Lillee wrote an article in which he called us 'Dad's Army' and said we had no chance of winning the series. According to him, we were too old and past our best, and would be sitting ducks for England's fast bowling brigade. Surely I still didn't have to prove myself to the media after all this time.

My frustration came to a head at a media day on the eve of the Test. The event was set up with the media in a line; one by one, we had to move along the conveyor belt and answer the questions of all the print, radio and television journalists. The further I got along the line, the angrier I became because of the constant stream of questions related to Phil Jaques. Then I came to a reporter from SBS, who was reading questions from a sheet of paper. From her body language I could tell she didn't really understand a word of what she was saying.

'Do you feel under pressure from Phil Jaques?' she asked without even looking up.

I stayed calm and gave my standard answer, thinking she would be satisfied and move on, but she wouldn't. She kept banging on and on with the same line of questioning.

Bugger this, I thought. I stopped her and said, 'Okay, if you were a selector, what would you do?'

She looked embarrassed and stammered, 'Oh, uh, sorry, I was just told to ask these questions.'

That was it for me. The interview was over. It really annoyed me that I was being asked to justify myself to someone who didn't even know what we were talking about, let alone my record as a player. While experience had taught me that the media spotlight was just another distraction, I was at a stage of my career where I just wanted to get on with the cricket.

I had good reason to be pissed off. It had taken me just a fortnight to recover physically after being struck by Ntini in Johannesburg eight months before, but recovering mentally was much tougher. When I was ready to resume training, I called my batting coach, Noddy Holder, and fitness coach, Steve Smith—both close mates— and organised a lunch to discuss my future. Noddy told me it was time to retire.

His worries about my health had taken me by surprise, especially as he had played such an integral part of my development as a cricketer. Yet I couldn't simply dismiss his concerns so I had agreed to consider what he'd said. I knew his intentions were good but, as I told him a short time later, I couldn't let go until we had won back the Ashes.

That had become the theme of our eleven victory celebrations since the series loss in 2005. Our wins against the World XI, the West Indies, South Africa and Bangladesh had been great, but the only thing that really counted for us was winning back the Ashes. Every time I got up on the table to sing our team song I would remind the boys that we would be judged on the Ashes, not these matches.

Noddy and I had both known that for me to make a worthwhile contribution in the upcoming Ashes series, I would have to regain my confidence against short-pitched bowling. So I'd spent hours with him facing short balls from the bowling machine. I'd hated every minute of it because it had been so uncomfortable, physically and mentally, but I knew that unless I put myself through such a stringent test, I might as well retire because I would be batting like a punch-drunk boxer and of little value to anyone.

● ● ●

Media stress aside, the lead-up to a Test series in Australia is something I always relished. It fitted with my love of preparation and hard work, and the pampering we used to get as Australian cricketers was pretty addictive too. From the moment we checked into the team hotel we felt like kings. Anything we needed was at hand, all designed to ensure we were prepared mentally and physically. There were massages, ice baths and stretching. The bowlers worked on their rhythm, we all practised catching to sharpen our reflexes, and, most importantly for me, we hit hundreds of cricket balls in the nets. There are always plenty of net bowlers, nothing was too hard for the support staff and we felt special because of the fuss. Our preparation was rarely hurried; everything was patient and careful. We weren't really honing our craft at that stage, but rather ensuring, as best we could, that everything was polished.

The day before any match, Haydos and I used to walk onto the ground to get a sense of the arena and the conditions, the pitch and the alignment to the boundaries. We would take our shoes off and walk with bare feet to feel the grass—we'd scrunch it up between our toes and make ourselves part of the ground. Was this overkill? Definitely not! One of the things I loved about playing Test cricket was soaking up the atmosphere and intricacies of every new ground. Batting was more than just a technical skill; it was a psychological experience in which you used the atmosphere to your advantage—either enjoying the warm embrace of a home crowd or steeling yourself to silence the hostility of the opposition's supporters.

The night before the First Test I was sitting in my room and chilling out. It was fantastic to be lounging about in a T-shirt and pair of training skins; I felt super-fit and mentally prepared. I was comfortable with myself, for a change. I had played my 100th Test and had nothing to prove to anyone. Even the nagging stuff about Phil Jaques had disappeared. That afternoon I had watched a DVD by the champion surfer Kelly Slater which was all about letting go and trusting yourself. By the early evening I was lying back, listening to music and daydreaming about being a star the next day. I couldn't wait for the match to start. I had never felt so powerful or relaxed before a series. Then disaster struck.

I reached into a fruit basket sent by Sue and grabbed a cherry, popped it into my mouth and promptly bit down on the pip. In that instant I heard a crack. I had broken the back off one of my teeth, and my whole world started to spin out of control. All I could think of was that I had done all this preparation for nothing. What if I couldn't play because I had nerves hanging out of my tooth? I rushed downstairs in a panic and had it checked out by the team doctor, who, thankfully, reckoned it would be okay. Emergency dentistry ruined my perfect preparation, but at least I would be facing the first ball of the 2007 Ashes.

We won the toss and batted on a picture-perfect morning. This was it—the beginning of our revenge—and Haydos and I were leading from the front. Here is how the commentary on the website Cricinfo described the scene. It makes great reading because it sums up the atmosphere at the ground in the lead-up to the famous—or infamous, for the Englishmen—first ball of the series.

Good morning to everyone, wherever you might be. At last, we're nearly there and the Gabba—or Gabattoir as some call it and, judging by the cacophonous noise out there, it's damn close to a fortress-like atmosphere—is slowly filling up. Ricky Ponting had no hesitation in choosing to bat and both teams have gone with the tried and tested. The pitch is dry and, although there's a hint of grass, the cracks are visible and it could turn a country mile come the fourth day.

We're moments away—the ground looks a picture, under a morning sun which is already scorching hot . . .

Here come England to rapturous applause and cheers of 'Ingerland, Ingerland, Ingerland' from the hordes of England fans. Justin Langer and Matthew Hayden are on the boundary edge and they are seriously pumped up; swinging their bats wildly, sparring with them like boxers before a bout.

Now then, it'll be Steve Harmison bowling to Justin Langer for the first ball of the Ashes. The roar goes up—it is unbelievably loud out there.

Langer's wearing a sweater! 'He's obviously in it for the long haul,' says Andrew Miller.

0.1 Harmison to Langer, 1 wide, and it's wild and woolly, a massive wide taken by first slip. Welcome back to Australia, Steve.

From that commentary two things stand out. Firstly, I was wearing a sweater, which I now find a bit embarrassing. My ribcage was black and blue from the intense training against the short ball, and I had decided, quite sensibly, to wear a guard. What wasn't sensible—in fact, it was quite stupid—was my embarrassment at wearing the protective gear, so I had tried to hide it under a sweater. Paul Collingwood noticed it straight away and told me that Steve Waugh would turn in his grave if he saw me, not to mention that it was a hot and humid Brisbane morning.

And, of course, that first ball of the match flew to second slip, where it was scooped up by the team's captain, Freddy Flintoff. As innocent as it seemed, the delivery by Steve Harmison was a very significant moment. Just as I had noticed the steel in England's behaviour on the first morning of the 2005 tour, this time it was the opposite—they were all looking at their feet. Flintoff looked embarrassed, wearing a silly grin as he tossed the ball back to Harmison, who was giggling like a schoolboy. He later admitted that nerves had got to him and blamed the delivery on sweaty palms.

The rot had set in early for England and Haydos and I wanted to cash in then and there. I scored 82 off not many more deliveries that morning, and at the press conference afterwards wondered aloud whether Harmison's first ball would be a critical factor in the series.

My first innings was a great way to answer my doubters, although a century would have been even better. That came in the second innings, and we blasted a 277-run win and made our psychological mark on the series. At that stage it was just another win, of course, albeit a very important one. Having scored a few runs and with us sitting 1–0 up in the series, I felt so happy that I wanted to continue playing cricket forever.

The celebrations at the Gabba that night were rather subdued, though, because the Second Test, in Adelaide, was to start just four days later. Back-to-back Tests are really tough, so we were keen to keep our minds on the job and wait to celebrate properly when we won back the Ashes.

That said, we still had a great laugh that night. There's a photo—probably my favourite, actually—of five of us having a beer after the game. Haydos has an ice pack on each leg and I've got one on my shoulder. Punter, Pigeon and Warney are there with us, all in our baggy green caps and shorts. Someone must have told a joke because we're all laughing our heads off. That photo sums it up for me. We'd just won a hard-fought game, we were wearing our battle scars, sitting down with our mates and sharing a beer and a laugh. You can't get much more Australian than that.

● ● ●

The Adelaide Test started terribly for the team and for me. England made 551, thanks to a double-century by Paul Collingwood and 158 by Kevin Pietersen, who together put on 310 for the fourth wicket on a lifeless pitch. McGrath (0 for 107) and Warne (1 for 167) returned their worst career figures, and the Pommy media—not to mention our own—was having a field day, gleefully calling the champions past their prime and England on the way up.

To make matters worse, I got out cheaply in the nightmare period before stumps. It brought back memories from my first Test on the same pitch fourteen years before. That time I survived, but not this time. At stumps we were 1 for 28 and in trouble. Were the tables turning, just as they had in 2005?

On the morning of day three the mood at breakfast was flat as a tack. John Buchanan had declared in the Sunday papers that morning that we could still win the match.

'I am a bit of an optimist and I still think there's a win on offer,' he'd reckoned. 'There's three days to go. But we are not in the position to dictate at the moment. Our job is to go out there tomorrow and negotiate the new ball, get through that and build our partnerships: make 700 and bowl them out for less than 150 on the last day.'

He also backed his two champion bowlers with this gem: 'If you can bat against two of the greats of the game successfully, then sure, you take some confidence from that, but the ultimate confidence is whether you can keep doing that over a period of time and through a series.'

We all thought, like everyone else, that Buck was just being outrageous, but he kept on at us, and me in particular, when he came into the room.

'C'mon, guys,' he said. 'What's wrong here? Get a bit of life into you. We can still win this.'

I was always going on about there being love in the room when I wanted to gee things up, so he started poking me and using my line against me. By the time we left for the ground, though, we still thought a battled draw was the best we could hope for.

Then things changed and we saw Ricky Ponting at his best. We were at the nets warming up when he called the team together. Eyeballing each of us, one at a time, he said, looking around at our flat expressions. 'There's not one person in the world who thinks we can win this thing. Let's just see about that.'

And with that Punter went out and scored 142. Like a true captain, he led the way and the others followed. Mike Hussey was unlucky to get out on 91, Michael Clarke came of age with 124, and Gilly and Warney chimed in with 64 and 43 respectively. We didn't get the 700 Buck was after, but we made 513 and, at just 38 runs behind, we were back in the game.

By stumps on day four England had battled through to be 1 for 59 and so held a lead of 97. A draw was still likely, but Buck was bouncing around the place telling us we could win. We were beginning to believe it might just happen. After all, it was a deteriorating fifth-day pitch and we had Shane Warne.

It might seem trite to say it, but there are so many variables in cricket that almost anything can happen. Early on the last day Andrew Strauss got a bad decision, then Clarkey ran out Ian Bell. England was now three down, but the danger man Pietersen was to come. All he needed to do was score a quickfire half-century and the game would be safe. Instead, Warney bowled him around his legs for 2, and then Flintoff came and went for the same score.

England had slumped to 5 for 89 at lunch and the game had swung. It took some time to remove the last five batsmen but, amazingly, we had the gettable target of 168 from 36 overs, although now we had to negotiate the difficult pitch.

Haydos and I started the chase like it was a Twenty20 match. I walked down the track to the second ball of the innings from Matthew Hoggard and smacked it over midwicket for a boundary. Haydos started the same way, and although I got out soon after we were on our way, Punter and Huss carried on where we left off. We ended up scoring at five runs an over and winning comfortably. The team poured out onto the ground in jubilation. Unlike Brisbane, when we'd known there was a job to finish, we celebrated this victory because of the miracle that it was and the joy we took from achieving something others thought was impossible.

It was at that moment when we realised that if we could win from that position, we could win from anywhere. Perhaps more important, though, was the reaction of England. You could sense they realised the opposite—that if they could lose from that position, they couldn't beat us.

I have to restate here my utter support for John Buchanan. He copped a fair amount of criticism, most of which was entirely unfair, but he showed utter faith in us that game. He was the one who said we could win every game we played, and we won sixteen straight.

Belief and faith is paramount to success, and Buck's role in our team cannot be underestimated.

That night we had a huge celebration, staying in the change rooms until midnight. The strange thing was that Flintoff, Harmison and James Anderson were in there with us until the end. Usually opposition players might come into our rooms on the last night of a series, so this was strange. At the end of the night it was time to go home—but not before singing the team song. However, the three Englishmen were still there, and Freddy was insistent that we should let him stay.

'We've heard about it but we want to see it,' he protested.

I had to explain that singing the song was sacred and that there was definitely no room for our rivals, especially on a night like this. 'You've got to go, Fred. This is for us.'

So the England captain, as good a bloke as he was, got booted out. I'd have Flintoff in my side every time, but he was a gladiator, not necessarily a general. After they left we sang the song. It was raucous, and it was also the last time my great mate Damien Martyn would sing it with the team.

The next morning he was missing as we boarded the plane. At first I thought he had slept in and missed his alarm—which wouldn't have surprised me, considering the previous night's celebration—but by the time we reached Perth the news had broken that Damien had retired via a media release. To say it was a shock is an understatement, as he'd given us no indication that retirement was on his mind.

At the time I thought he had made a terrible mistake but, looking back, it was typical of Marto's very private style. His decision, although strange, took his own brand of courage. He trusted his gut feeling and didn't want his mind to be clouded by mates trying to talk him out of his decision.

Mike Hussey, 7th Songmaster, 2007–

JL: What are your recollections of me asking you to do the song?

MH: We had just defeated England in the Fifth Test at the SCG in 2007. I remember going home to see our families at the hotel and finding a letter [in which] you told me that one of your duties at your retirement was to hand over the song. You said you couldn't think of anyone better to sing the song and I was obviously pretty blown away by that.

JL: How did it feel to be the songmaster?

MH: I couldn't believe it actually. It was like the journey where I made my debut for Australia . . . making my first Test hundred, and then to be able to make runs consistently to finally feel a part of the team. I thought I could die a happy man [but then] to be passed the team song, I thought—how can life get any better than this?

JL: Why is the team song important?

MH: It helps uphold the traditions of Australian cricket. I also think it's really important knowing how hard it is to play one Test, how bloody hard it is to play well in a Test and how bloody hard it is to win a Test. Those times in the dressing room are what you treasure the most, so, as the songmaster, I want to make those times as enjoyable as I can for everyone. And I also want to pass that legacy onto the next generation as well.

JL: What will you be looking for in the next songmaster?

MH: I will be looking for someone who has an appreciation for the history of the game and the baggy green, also someone who plays the game because they love it and who are willing to do things for their mates.

JL: What's the best song you have sung?

MH: In Durban in 2009 when we beat South Africa. The togetherness was unbelievable and was a catalyst behind our series victory. The other one was in Johannesburg. We went out onto the pitch. Some media were still typing their stories up and some of the South Africans were still in the viewing area of their change room. We wanted to show everyone how close we were and how important that fight-back Test had been to us, so we roared the song so the media and the South Africans understood how close we were and how much it meant to us to win.

32. A perfect farewell

There's nothing better than knowing you're going to win. You sense that it might take a little time but victory is inevitable. It was like that in the Third Test against England in Perth. The match seemed all but over on the third day after England had been crushed, firstly by Mike Hussey and Michael Clarke, who both scored second-innings centuries, and then by an incredible innings from Gilly, who smashed 102 not out off just 59 balls. It was an amazing sight in so many ways. For a start, he was under a lot of pressure at the time for his batting, particularly when facing Flintoff, who came on to bowl as soon as Gilly arrived at the crease.

The ball-by-ball commentary of the Cricinfo website sums up what can happen in these situations. The commentary begins with the last ball of the 94th over; Monty Panesar had just taken his third wicket.

Three men round the bat for Gilchrist, who is on a pair.

93.6: Panesar to Gilchrist, no run, and Monty's arms come over in a greater flurry than usual, a quicker and flatter ball which is defended to leg.

94.1: Flintoff to Clarke, 1 run, too straight and whipped down to Panesar at fine leg.

And Flintoff is immediately going around the wicket to Gilchrist.

94.2: Flintoff to Gilchrist, no run, good ball angling into the left-handed Gilchrist, who shoulders arms.

Five in a line catching for Gilchrist, as Fred comes round the wicket. He also has a conventional cover, a mid-off, a mid-on and a deep backward square.

94.3: Flintoff to Gilchrist, FOUR, oof that was close, outside off—that nagging length which Flintoff seems to produce only to Gilchrist—and the batsman pushed at it, streakily so, and it flew past gully.

Ah, there goes the Barmy bugler. Parp.

94.4: Flintoff to Gilchrist, no run, pushed out into the covers.

94.5: Flintoff to Gilchrist, no run, and he goes for an expansive pull but is rapped high on the pad. Flintoff appeals, but that's going miles over the top.

94.6: Flintoff to Gilchrist, FOUR, cracking shot! Beautifully timed off the back foot, elegant even—just threaded the gap through the covers.

The sequence matches Gilly's recollection in his book *True Colours*, in which he writes: 'Then I hit a back-foot drive for four. It just felt perfect. That got me up. Some things trigger you.'

On the balcony none of us could believe what was happening. I was sitting with Haydos, gobsmacked as Gilly kept smacking them over the boundary, further and further each time. The commentary uses the term 'carnage'. Haydos always reckoned that batting with Gilly was like playing in a highlights package, and that's exactly what we were watching.

We were already on top in the match but what Gilly did meant we could declare earlier than expected, with a lead of 557, and then bowl at England late in the day. Sure enough, Brett Lee came out and took the wicket of Andrew Strauss.

The next morning there were a couple of partnerships that might have made English supporters hopeful, but the feeling on the field was that we were about to reclaim the Ashes. It was a matter of when, not if. It felt so special, almost magical, because we could soak in the atmosphere and be aware of what was going on, rather than becoming so caught up in the intensity of it all.

Panesar came in as last man just before lunch, with England still over 200 runs short of what would have been a world-record victory. It seemed strange to have a break at this stage but the umpires called time. When we walked back onto the field, Punter called the Australians together in the middle of the ground. It was unusual for him to call a team huddle but we came together:

'Look, boys. We're going to win here. We're going to win back the Ashes. But I want you to be humble in victory because the job isn't done yet. We set out to win this series 5–0 and that's what we're going to do. So enjoy this win but be humble.'

With that we walked off. I was thinking to myself, 'Gee, where the hell did this profound stuff come from? The boy from Launceston has turned into Winston Churchill.'

If Warney had said it then we'd all have had a laugh, but this was coming from Ricky Ponting, one of the most modest blokes you'd want to meet, so it really meant something. We had a massive celebration that night. We feasted on some fantastic West Australian crayfish, which a mate of mine—Ryan the seafood man—always used to bring in for the Perth Test match. We felt like kings.

But amongst it all, and even after leading the song, I felt a niggle in my mind for the first time. I wasn't really sure what I was feeling, but my first-ball duck in the second innings had made an impact. As I had walked off, bowled off my pads by Matthew Hoggard, the thought had crossed my mind that perhaps it was time to move on.

● ● ●

It would be foolish of me to suggest that retirement hadn't been on my mind since Noddy Holder had told me my time was up. Although I politely disagreed with him, the seed had been sown. It was easy to ignore at first because I was focused on redemption—regaining the Ashes. Now that had been achieved, it was inevitable that the R-word would return to my thoughts.

The first time I actually voiced my thoughts was in the evening after the first day's play in the Fourth Test at Melbourne. I had made 27 and been dismissed, annoyingly, late in the day after we had rolled England for 159. I sat talking with David Boon, the legend with whom I batted in my first Test and who was now a selector.

It was just a general conversation until I hesitantly said, 'So, what about retirement? How did you handle that?'

Boony looked at me. 'So you're thinking about it, are you?'

His response shook me a bit. 'Well, it's been on my mind a bit lately,' I admitted.

He suddenly got deadly serious. 'A piece of advice, then, mate. If you're thinking about retirement, at all, then you're a lot closer to it than you'd like to think.'

After the game a couple of things happened that cemented my decision. The first was simply sitting with Haydos in the change room. We'd just won the Fourth Test and he had a fire in his eyes, not because of what we had just achieved but because of what he still wanted to achieve. He was desperate to get back into the one-day side and prove to the selectors that they'd been wrong to drop him in the first place—something he would end up doing.

But where was I going? I had spent everything preparing for the Ashes, to win back what we as a team had lost in 2005, and I had achieved my goal. We now had a chance to beat them 5–0, but beyond that there didn't seem much for me to aim at. We had already beaten India in India and it would be another ten months until our next series. If I was already copping flak about Phil Jaques, imagine how much I'd have to endure during the lull. And I'd long given up on the one-day team, even though it still disappoints me that I was always overlooked.

But there was something more significant. I would be leading the team song that night and I realised that I just wasn't that pumped about it. Maybe it was the passion of Adelaide or winning the Ashes in Perth, but the notion of rousing the boys because we were 4–0 up and had won easily just didn't get me. Suddenly, I knew that the thing that had motivated me for so long—the team song—had gone. I'd had a couple of beers and a few laughs with my team-mates, and the thought of going out celebrating just didn't appeal. That's when I knew—it was time to go home.

Dad was in Melbourne for the Test and we'd arranged to have breakfast the next morning. When we made our plans I had expected I'd have a sore head after a night out celebrating our win. Instead, I woke up at about eight o'clock with a clear head and a clear conscience. I found a text message on my mobile from Dad: *How about a coffee?*

He'd sent the message at 5.30 am, which meant he'd been up thinking about something, unable to sleep. I went down to meet him and we sat down in a cafe at Southbank. I knew telling Dad was going to be the hardest of all. Every decision I'd made for the past twenty years had been about playing Test cricket for Australia—what I ate, where I went, when I went on holidays, what I said. Everything. Retiring was a huge decision that would affect not only me but also my family.

There was no easy way to say it so I just blurted it out: 'Dad, I think it's time for me to retire.' I looked at him for some sort of reaction.

What he said floored me: 'You know what? That's what I wanted to tell you this morning. I think it's time.'

It was amazing. I hadn't mentioned anything to him. In fact, I'd been dreading the moment when I'd have to tell Dad about my decision. I thought it would rock him, so it was remarkable to find that he was thinking the same thing.

Everything felt right. I told Sue and the rest of my family and the weight of the decision just lifted. I was actually relaxed and happy that I'd just made and announced what would probably be the hardest decision of my life, and everything was okay. Life would move on.

Then the embarrassment set in. I started to think about my timing. I would be retiring in the same match—the New Year's Test in Sydney—as Shane Warne and Glenn McGrath, who had both already announced their exits. It wasn't that I was worried about the limelight—quite the opposite. I was shy about putting myself on the same stage as those two legends of the game.

I didn't really know what to do. I couldn't start asking people around the change rooms. In the end I called Alan Jones. I told him about my concerns and he asked me if I was sure about my decision. I said yes.

'Then give yourself some respect,' he answered. 'Retiring with those guys is a great thing. And if you're going to retire, then do it well. Call a media conference.'

He was right but I was still worried about my timing. We flew to Sydney for the match and I still hadn't told anyone but my family and Jones. I had to take the next step, so I spoke to Punter. It was just as hard as telling Dad. Ricky kept asking me if I was sure, and I told him I was.

Haydos was downstairs having a massage. I interrupted and said bluntly that I needed to talk to him. When I told him, he was quite emotional and hugged me—after all, my departure would have a big impact on him as well, because it would split up our partnership. As I'd discovered, the relationship between opening batsmen is essential to its success. We were individuals but we batted as a team.

Somehow the media had got wind of what was happening, and I pleaded with them to give me some space. The situation was really frustrating. I understood that they had jobs to do, and that included breaking news before others did. But this was my decision, and I had the right to do it my way. From memory, they compromised and wrote that I was 'likely to retire'.

Before I held my media conference I needed to square things with Warney and Pigeon, since I still felt as if I was somehow raining on their parade. They were both fantastic about it. I'd known Glenn from the Cricket Academy and he was insistent that it was great the three of us could leave at the same time. Warney and I had known each other even longer, but our relationship was different. I'd say we're mates but I didn't have the same type of friendship with him as I did with guys like Haydos and Punter. We're very different people. He has always been the slightly naughty boy who pushed the boundaries and didn't like authority, whereas I am the opposite; I respect authority and like the order of things. I guess it fitted with our respective positions in the game—he was the genius and I was the hard worker. But we earned each other's respect because of those differences. One of the absolute privileges of my career was to have played with Shane Warne. One of his favourite sayings was that good things happen to good people, and I know that's how he regarded me and why he was happy for us to go out together.

In many ways, my decision to retire had bigger ramifications for Sue. At least I was in control of my career, but she bore the brunt of its consequences to the same degree, if not more greatly. She remembers that time in Melbourne as surreal.

● ● ●

I couldn't believe that Justin's 105 Test matches had gone so quickly and that the journey was almost over. Although he retired from Test cricket for the right reasons, wanting to spend more time at home with our family, I knew that he still loved playing the game and was giving up something he loved doing.

The day he told me his decision in Melbourne was very emotional for us. There had been some mutterings in the media, and we'd even spoken briefly about the possibility, but Justin really hadn't made up his mind. The day after the Boxing Day Test finished, we went for a walk along the banks of the Yarra River, got the kids ice-cream and he told me that Sydney would be his last game.

His words were typically straightforward: 'I think I'm going to retire.'

I looked at him, half-expecting the words but still surprised. I think I said something like, 'Are you sure?'

He nodded.

'Okay,' I said, 'if that's what you want, then let's do it.'

We had both been stoic up to that point but then it got emotional, watching the kids with their ice-creams and thinking how much our lives had changed in that moment. I had all sorts of emotions running through me. I was happy because we would have Justin back, sad because it was the end of something special, and fearful of the unknown and of losing something we'd had for so long.

The next week in Sydney was amazing and, strangely, one of the best times I can remember. The weight of the decision disappeared, and although I was terribly nervous during the match, wanting Justin to go out well, the spirit of the team and the players' wives and girlfriends was amazing. I'd made a lot of friends, so this was a time of celebration and reminiscence rather than sadness.

● ● ●

By match day I was feeling much more comfortable about the whole thing. We fielded first, and as we walked onto the SCG for the first session, I drank in the atmosphere and the excitement of being there on the day Warne and McGrath played their last Test. I had to remind myself that it was my last game too.

The match went our way, although I wasn't happy about my dismissal in the first innings. I was scoring at a run a ball and feeling pretty good when, for the first time in my career, I was caught down the legside.

We rolled England cheaply in their second innings, which left us with only 46 for victory. It was a great way to finish but I started to feel the emotion as I prepared to go out to bat for the last time. Even though it was a small target, I wanted to treat it as seriously as any other innings, so I was sitting at the back of the SCG change rooms in my customary place when Gilly came up to talk to me. He put his arm around me and said some pretty nice things. He even had a few tears; I was thinking, 'Give me a break, Gilly! I've got to go out and bat.'

When I stood up to go out the others gathered around me and started shaking my hand and slapping me on the back. Some of them were a bit emotional as well. I needed to get out there and do my job. The same thing happened on the balcony, where I always started limbering up before running onto the ground. I looked down and saw Dad in the crowd, and he was teary too. It was getting ridiculous—I still had to bat.

As we stepped onto the ground, Haydos grabbed me and gave me a big bear hug. I looked up at him and the big fella was pretty emotional. Enough, already. Then the England team gave me a guard of honour as I walked to the pitch. They weren't crying; instead they were kidney-punching me and kicking me in the shins as I went through. I jokingly asked Freddy Flintoff if he'd give me a few half-volleys but he laughed and told me the guard of honour was the only luxury I'd be getting.

That brought me back to the realities of the situation, which was lucky because Steve Harmison then bowled one of his best spells of the series. I was hit everywhere, cracking my ribcage and bruising my hand. It was like I was back in my first Test. I just wanted to be not out at the end.

Haydos and I grafted our way towards the total. When we were seven runs away, he came down to have a chat and ask me how I wanted to get the last few runs. He was asking if I wanted to score them myself. I was getting a bit emotional about everything by then, because the atmosphere was incredible.

I looked at him and grinned. 'The perfect scenario would be if you went back, hit a six to knock off the runs and we'll walk off as heroes.'

'Righto,' he replied. 'Leave it to me.'

He turned and swaggered back to the crease to face the fast-medium bowler Sajid Mahmood. The next ball he took an almighty swing but missed the ball, which shaved past his off stump.

I walked down the pitch and told Haydos not to worry and to take it easy. I wanted him to be not out at the end with me.

'Don't worry, little fella,' he laughed. 'Leave it to me.'

Mahmood delivered his next ball and Haydos planted one foot down the pitch and cracked it 25 rows back into the crowd over wide mid-on. Six. Scores were level.

He walked down the pitch and grinned. 'How about that! Do you want to score the last one?'

The crowd and the commentators probably wanted me to hit the winning runs, but I just wanted the match over. The whole thing was getting to me.

'Nah,' I said. 'You hit it and we'll go off together.'

Haydos walked back and carved the next one through covers. We ran the single and then headed off in celebration, hugging each other. Punter came sprinting out from nowhere and jumped into us. It was an amazing scene, just the perfect ending—we'd won the Test, won the series and won the Ashes. I'd been not out at the end and I was there with my mate Haydos. It just couldn't have been better.

● ● ●

Amid those exhilarating scenes, I realised something very important. I'd had a career that had been full of doubt and questions, but at this final moment I knew, looking around, that I had finally earned the respect I had wanted for so long. I had the respect of my team-mates, the crowd, even the opposition and, hopefully, at last from the media. I'd had a lot of ups and down in my career, always feeling that I had to justify my place in the side, but I never gave up. I think people who love the game respected that. I played in a team with some of the greatest cricketers ever to play the game. Sometimes I felt like the drummer in a band—but every band needs a drummer.

That night we celebrated on a boat anchored beneath the Sydney Harbour Bridge. I gave a speech and passed on the honour and responsibility of being songmaster to Mike Hussey. It was an emotional moment for me, particularly as we had included the wives and girlfriends in the song for the first time. I should let Sue have the last word:

● ● ●

As Justin would say, it was the best night ever. We saw firsthand what all the fuss had been about over the years and could appreciate our partners' enthusiasm and passion for their team-mates. I had always understood that the song was important, although there had been times when I rang Justin late at night after a victory and he'd still be in the change rooms. If I asked when he was coming home, the reply would always be the same: 'Oh, we haven't sung the song yet.'

On this night they sang—or shouted—the song five times, once for every victory in the series. It was louder and quicker each time. You couldn't help but be carried along by the moment, crushed by these big strong men in a tight circle, bellowing into the blackness of Sydney Harbour—underneath the Southern Cross.